My Life on Joseph Creek

By
Julie Davis Kooch

Illustration page 90 used by permission

I hope you enjoy the book!
Julie

©*Julie Kooch 2005*
Enterprise, Oregon 97828

ISBN 0-9773934-0-2

Dedication

I dedicate this book to the memory of my friend and companion, Lee Scott. The many adventures we shared while on the Monument Ranch revitalized my childhood memories and inspired me to write this book.

Lee was the most generous and unselfish human being I have ever known. If he had a quarter in his pocket, he was figuring what he could buy for someone else, rather than himself.

Lee, by the world's standards, would have been considered a "poor man," but by God's standards he was rich. I had the honor and priviledge of helping him realize how much God loved him. He made a commitment to God within a few months after we became friends. He was a man with many rough edges—he had "done it all"—but God worked at smoothing those edges, one by one, and was still "smoothing" 'til the time of his death!

So, "thanks for the memories, and until we ride together again, here's to you, my friend!"

Lee, with his girls, Melanie, Laurie and Staci

Contents

Dedication iii
Acknowledgements vi
Maps vii
Introduction xi
Dad and Mom 1
Getting Started 4
Preschool Years With Dad 12
Winters 19
The B & H Ranch 24
Lewis School and Grade School Years . . . 34
Farm Animals and Pets 48
Company 53
Grandma Berthe 56
Moving to the Valley 69
Slipping Away—Can It Be? 75
The Monument Ranch 95
Back on the Ranch 112
That First Fall 119
On the Feed Grounds and Calving Lots . . 128
Spring Turnout 138
Summer Range 155
Fall Gather and Cleanup Riding 177
Cow Camps 185
Hunters, Hunting, and Wildlife 209
Volunteer Help and Visitors 241
The Mountain Trip 248
The Next Summer 259
Wrecks 264
The Last Round-Up and Goodbyes 289
Conclusion 295
Genealogy 296
About the Author 299

Acknowledgements

Shirley Frye for her expertise in typesetting and the many, many hours in putting this whole thing together.

The gals at the county courthouse who were so helpful when I was searching for names and dates pertaining to the homesteading in the Joseph Canyon.

Bud and Zuah Birkmaier for the retelling of stories and furnishing many pictures.

Lucinda Davis Jensen for information on the Davis "Family Tree" and family stories.

MaryAnn McCrae Burrows for information on the McCrae "Family Tree" and family stories.

Gail Hillock for her time spent in proofreading.

Betsy Oliver also for her time spent proofreading.

Nancy Carlsen and the gals at the Wallowa Valley Visitor Center for providing information about the Eagle Cap Wilderness area.

Ken Witty for wilderness lake information.

AND—Thanks to my Heavenly Father Who allowed me to be born and raised in such a wonderful place—Whose hand of protection was upon me continually—Whose loving arms were always wrapped around me—Who was constantly there to comfort and heal during the hard times!

"...Never will I leave you, never will I forsake you."

Hebrews 13:5

WALLOWA COUNTY
(SEE BELOW)
OREGON

Joseph Creek
Snake River
Coyote Campground
Flora
Troy
Grande Ronde Rv
Mon Ranch
Chico
Promise
Chesnimnus
Creek
Hwy 82
Hwy 3
Crow Ck
Imnaha
Wallowa
Lostine
Enterprise
Joseph
N
W
E
S
Wallowa Mtns and High Lakes
Wallowa Lake
Imnaha River
Seven Devils Mtns
Paved Hwy
Gravel Rd
River/Creek

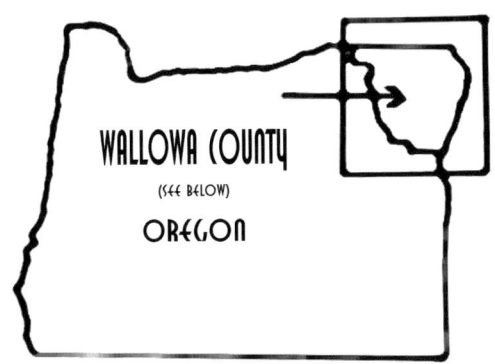

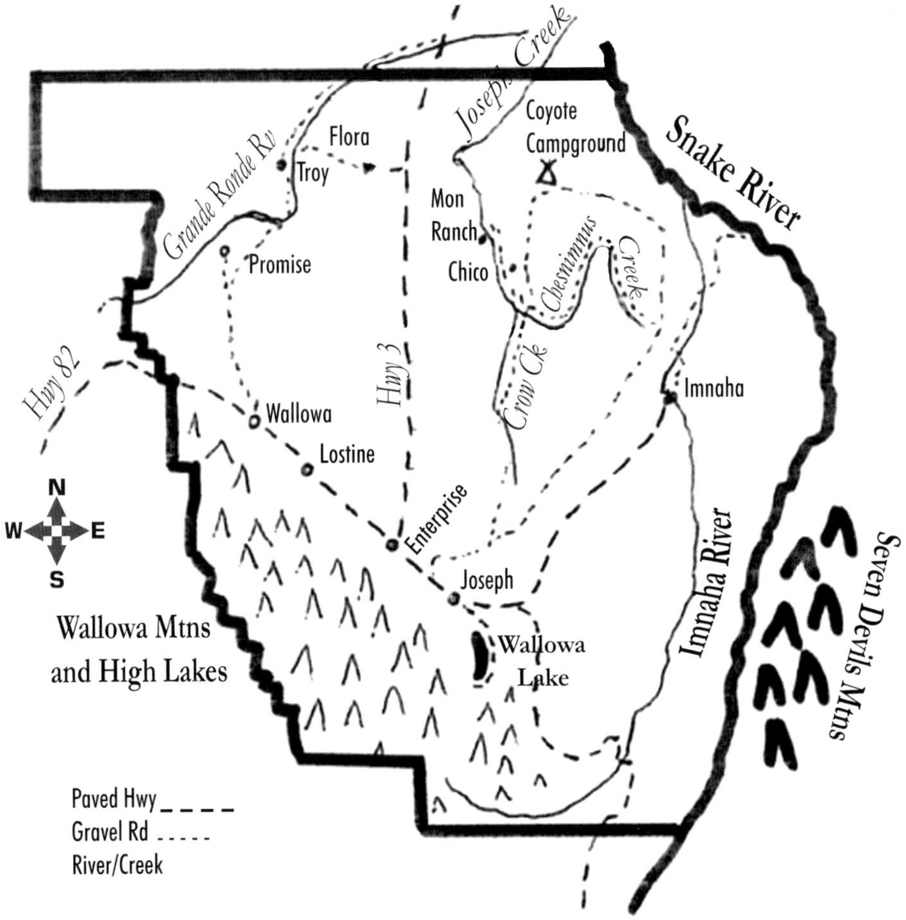

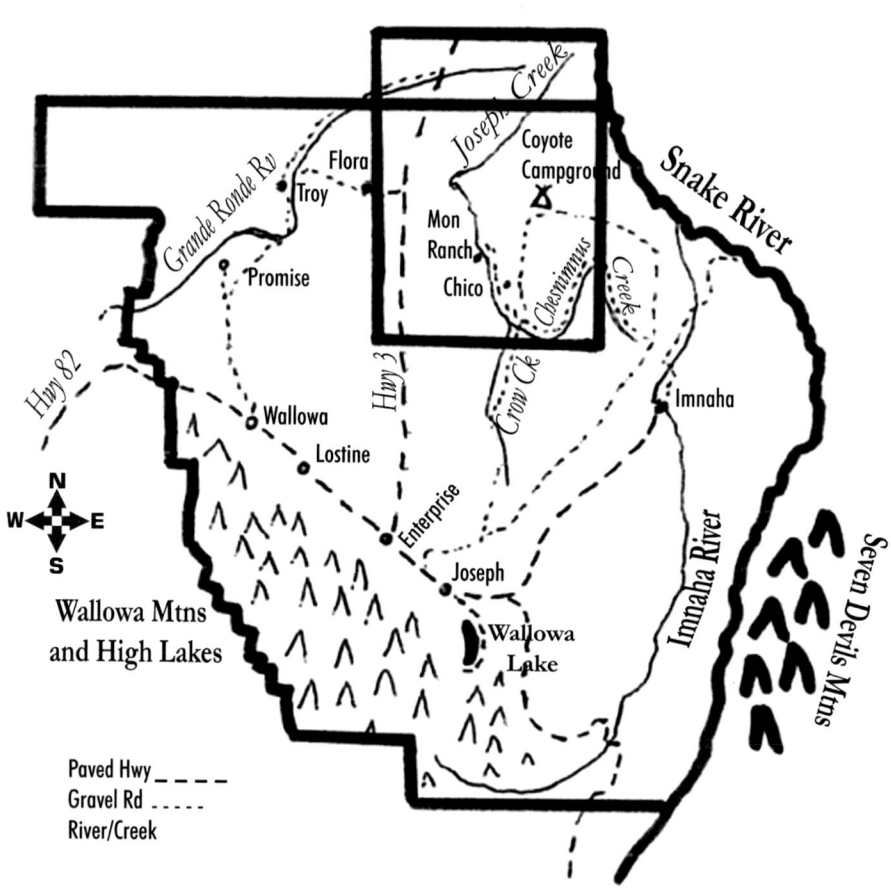

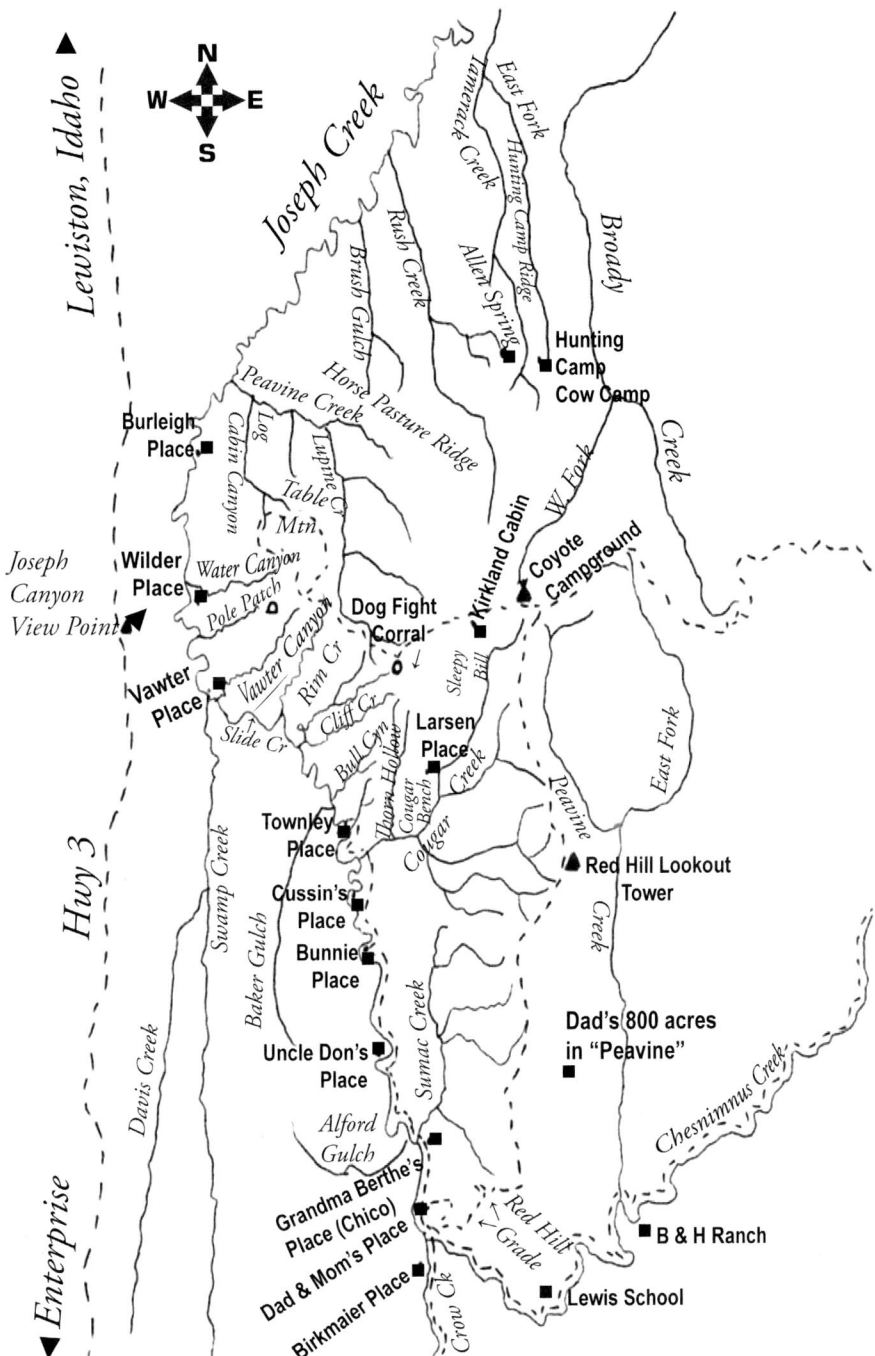

Wallowa Mountains

Introduction

Out west in the very northeastern corner of the state of Oregon, is Wallowa County. It is so sparsely populated that less than 7,000 people call it home!

The county displays rugged snowcapped mountains with peaks rising to almost 10,000 feet, which act as a natural boundary on its southern, and southwestern sides. Nestled at the base of these mountains is Wallowa Lake, a five mile long, glacier formed, lake. High in the mountains are numerous, beautiful, snowfed lakes.

On the northwest, north and northeast are deep, rugged canyons. Two of the most rugged of these canyons are the Grand Ronde River Canyon and the Joseph Creek Canyon. *Pictures on following page.*

Wallowa Lake, frozen over—Elevation 4,372—Depth 283 feet

Ice Lake—Elevation 7,900—Depth 193 feet

Horseshoe Bend of the Grande Ronde River Canyon as seen from a point out on Spencer Bacon's Place on Lost Prairie

Looking west into the Joseph Creek Canyon from cliffs, on the north edge of Table Mountain, which drop off into Peavine. The Paradise country is seen on the skyline.

Looking into the Imnaha River Canyon from the road to Hat Point

Looking down into the Snake River from Hat Point

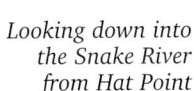

To the east is the Imnaha River Canyon, then beyond it is the Snake River and Hell's Canyon. Across the Snake River, in Idaho, are the Seven Devil's Mountains which rise to an elevation of 9,393 feet, making them visible from much of Wallowa County.

Looking down Hell's Canyon from just below the Hell's Canyon Dam

Looking east across the lush Wallowa Valley, and the grassy hills, to the Seven Devil's Mountains in Idaho

Me on one of our mountain ridges, Sheep Ridge, looking north beyond the Wallowa Valley to the rolling grassy hills which extend to the timbered area. Beyond the timber (not distinguisible) is the deep, rugged canyon country.

Within the perimeter of these mountains and rugged canyons, at the base of the mountains is a lush valley, which gives way to gently rolling hills and prairies, covered with native prairie grasses. Farther from the valley these hills become more rugged with timbered north slopes, and open, grassy south slopes, before crumpling into the rugged canyon country.

The county's variation of geological formations provide just as varied weather, vegetation and animal life, as well as life styles.

In the high mountains, the peaks rise above timberline—nothing grows there! The deep canyons drop to a few hundred feet above sea level, and produce, amongst other things, snakes and prickly pear cactus! The valley and rolling hills act as a buffer zone between these two extremes.

I was raised on a ranch where Chesnimnus Creek and Crow Creek come together to form Joseph Creek. My Grandma, Berthe Mink, had the next place down Joseph Creek. She lived in a log house, which at one time had also been the Chico Post Office.

Across the road was the Chico School where my dad had attended when he lived with an older brother, Don, and his wife Mary.

Bordering Grandma's place, on down the creek, was Uncle Don Davis's place. It extended on down Joseph Creek to what now is the upper end of the Monument Ranch.

When I was a child, a trip down Joseph Creek was a rare and relished treat. Even the folks who lived down the canyon didn't make the trip out just for the pure pleasure of it, but only when need demanded!

I suppose it is because I spent my entire childhood in the Joseph Creek Canyon, that the canyon has an unexplainable magnetism that keeps drawing me back!

Later in life, circumstances were such that I spent some wonderful years in the heart of the Joseph Canyon, on the Monument Ranch.

My goal in writing this book is twofold. First I hope that the reader will experience, at least to some degree, the joys, excitement, and peace that I have experienced during my life in rural, remote, America. Secondly, I have strived to give a very accurate account of the homesteading, and the events that accompanied it, in the Joseph Canyon and its neighboring areas. Names and dates have been acquired directly from documents in the clerk's office in the Wallowa County Court House. Some of the names, dates, and sequence of events were a surprise even to me!

To retain the atmosphere of the canyon country, in places I have written in the "language" of rural America, thus you will find grammatical errors. For instance, the people would never have said, "With whom are you going?" Instead you would have heard, "Who ya goin' with?" So, relax and enjoy!

Dad and Mom

Honeymoon—October 1942

They were newlyweds! She was young, a town girl, a schoolteacher, and very green to the ways of a canyon farmer and the hard life involved. She had never ridden a horse or done any of the manual labor required of a farmer's wife.

He was the youngest of seven siblings; his father died when he was but seven. His mother had managed to keep the family together and the children fed and clothed by milking a few cows, selling the cream and raising a few pigs and bucket calves. There was nothing unusual about their life style—it was the way many people lived at that time! He hired out to thrashing crews before he ever saw his teenage years, as did many boys back then. As his older brothers got married and went off to start a life of their own, more and more responsibility to take care of his widowed mother fell upon his shoulders. His mom repeatedly said, "Melvin will never marry and leave me."

When they were introduced by a local creamery owner, little did they know how quickly and completely their lives would change! They were married a short six weeks later!

He gathered up his small herd of cows and they moved to a cabin down Joseph Creek, and thus my roots were planted before I was ever conceived!

What remained of the cabin in the '60's

Their first winter was spent in the middle room of a three-room log cabin. There was no yard or fence and the cattle were fed in the flat around the cabin. Curiosity driven cows often poked their noses against the cabin windows.

He jokingly accused her of not being able to boil water without scorching it, but she was a willing pupil and soon learned to cook.

While riding to the cabin when the snow was on, and it was slick, he had coached her to kick her feet out of the stirrups if she felt the horse slip. Well, she did! In fact she kicked them out with such a force that she went off backwards over the rump of the horse!

She was musical—she played the piano, the trumpet and the accordion. She missed her instruments. He wanted to please her so he packed the trumpet and accordion in on horseback. The trumpet was no challenge but the accordion was! Being a full sized accordion, it was too large to fit in the pack boxes so he balanced it on the saddle horn. This poked a hole in the case. She praised him for his effort and taped up the hole.

She stepped outside the cabin, took a deep breath of the crisp winter air, then blew a few notes on the trumpet. The canyon walls echoed back each note. She was thrilled but the horses were terrified, having never heard such a noise. He had to gather the horses after they jumped a fence and headed down country! Thus her trumpeting was restricted thereafter to the confines of the cabin walls!

Winter passed, spring came! They bought a place of their own at the head of Joseph Creek, where Chesnimnus Creek and Crow Creek merge to form Joseph Creek.

This ranch was made up of three homesteads and some adjoining public lands. One piece was homesteaded by U.E. and Estella L. Endicott of Nez Perce, Idaho. Subsequent owners were Harvey Purdy, C.B. and Louisa Horner, then David and Anna Hearing. This was the location of our buildings.

Another piece, which we called "the bench," was homesteaded by J.R. Edgemand. He later sold it to David and Anna Hearing, so Hearings owned both of these pieces when Dad bought them.

The third piece of the land was the location of the Chico school and post office. This piece had been homesteaded by Thomas K. Edgeman, who was a single man. He later married a gal by the name of Melissa and they sold the land to William D. Fine. Later William D. and Minnie Fine sold it to Frank and Jessie Green. (When Dad was a boy and went to the Chico school, Minnie Fine was the teacher.) Dad bought this place from Greens and later sold it to Grandma Berthe, then bought it back when Grandma became unable to do the ranch work.

He feverishly set to work getting the small ranch into production. She toiled at making the small, unpainted house into a home!

They were my dad and mom! Melvin U. and Maxene J. Mink Davis.

Mom with her trumpet

Dad shearing sheep

Getting Started

Times were hard but treated everyone equally so no one felt poorer than his neighbor. Dad and Mom had what was needed to start farming their small canyon ranch—a minimal amount of equipment, and a team which was purchased from the money acquired when Mom sold her little Model T. A team was much more necessary than a car! They had a few milk cows. Grandma Berthe, Mom's mom, had given them a few blankets, pots and pans, and dishes.

Mom busied herself, with Grandma's help, in making curtains for the windows and throw rugs for the floor. She worked with a pride and passion that comes only from owning your own house—your very first home! Their little "mansion" actually had four usable rooms! A small kitchen was on one end, a living room in the middle, and a bedroom in which we all slept, on the other end. Well, almost on the end—there was a small storage room on the very end. The rooms were papered and had linoleum on the floors. There was no foundation so the floors were uneven, sloping in various directions. The outside was board and batten which had never felt the stroke of a paint brush, thus allowing it

Tim and Tom

Anna Hearing and ? on the front porch. Note: no storage room on right end of house at this date.

to weather to a combination of grays, rich browns, and rusts. If insulation had been invented back then, that little house knew nothing of it!

There also was a bunkhouse on the brink of the little hill above the swamp. Under the backside of the bunkhouse was the entry to the root cellar, which was dug into the hill under the bunkhouse. Mom canned as much fruit and vegetables as possible so as to have a varied diet during the long winters. It was stored in the cellar where it wouldn't freeze.

An icehouse with thick walls, filled with sawdust, kept ice into the summer months. That being the age of ice boxes rather than refrigerators, ice was a very cherished thing.

On January 31, 1944 a bundle of joy, in the form of a baby boy, my brother Ron, came into their lives only to be followed ten and one half months later by my birth, on December 18 of that same year. The family was complete and my life in the canyon burst into being!

There was no milking barn but there was a long row of stanchions along one side of the corral. Dad and Mom milked the cows, rain or shine, out in the open. Dad fixed a box type contraption on the top rail of the corral where they put us kids when we were just babies and toddlers, so they could keep an eye on us and keep us out from underfoot while they milked. If it was stormy, they fixed a "tent" of blankets over this to keep us as warm and dry as possible.

Coaly with Ron in stroller and back of house with storage room on far end

Me—Mom—Ron

Ron—Dad—Me

Ron—Me

If it was dark at milking time, Dad would light the kerosene lantern and set it on the ground out behind the cows. This setup was the source of quite a startling experience for all of us one night. At one end of the stanchions was the old garage. Dad had set the lantern on the ground as usual. Sometime later we were all startled to see the shadow of some type of gigantic creature passing across the wall of the garage. After the initial shock Dad discovered a large frog walking on its tiptoes between the lantern and the garage thus casting its shadow on the wall!

On one occasion when we kids were toddlers and the weather was so stormy that it was next to impossible to keep our tent in tact, Dad and Mom decided to try leaving us in the house. The stanchions, being quite close to the house, made it easy for one or the other of them to check on us

Me—Ron on Cry Baby. Note cow in stanchion in background

between milking each cow. All went fine for a while but then I guess Ron became bored. Being a creative little rascal, he discovered it was great fun to get a hand full of beans from the bean jar and throw them onto the linoleum floor. Not only did they make a great racket but they scattered marvelously! He would throw and I would stand by, clapping, squealing, and laughing! It was all great fun until we got caught!

Ron picked up beans, one at a time, until he had blisters on the ends of his poor little fingers! Needless to say, it was back to the tent for us during milking time!

On another occasion when we were a little older, they tried leaving us in the house again. Well, Ron didn't get into the bean jar; he had learned his lesson, but I attacked the goldfish! I don't remember where the goldfish had come from but I did realize that it was considered a great thing to catch fish. Having Joseph Creek running through our place, Dad and Mom fished often. We kids would sit along the bank watching and witnessing the exuberant joy the catching of a fish provided. I guess I stored this image in my little brain because I proudly met them at the door when they came in from milking. I had the two goldfish stabbed through with a paring knife!

Phil Attebury—Me

When we were still very small, Dad and Mom would leave us with Grandma Berthe for a little while during haying so Mom would be free to help Dad in the fields. Mom soon became a good hand with the team, so mowed and raked hay for Dad.

At the mouth of Sumac, on Grandma Berthe's place, was the Harris-Pine Logging Camp. I remember so well one of the loggers. His name was Phil Attebury. He took a liking to me so he would take me fishing in his spare time. He nicknamed me his "Little Fisher Woman." I can remember being so embarrassed when he called me that, but I really liked him and was always ready to go with him.

Phil had a wife, Mary. I remember she was tall, very pretty, and a redhead! She didn't like living in the country so she chose to live elsewhere. She came occasionally to visit Phil.

One time she and Phil gave Ron and me presents. I don't remember if it was a special occasion or "just because." Ron and I didn't get many things so usually were delighted with anything. I don't remember why I reacted the way I did on that particular occasion. Maybe it was because we had so few toys. They gave Ron a toy, I don't remember what, and gave me some pretty lacey panties. I had been taught to be polite and to be appreciative of anything, but for some reason I absolutely could not control myself. I was so disappointed!

I was able to compose myself long enough to thank them before I slipped off to hide and cry my eyes out! I knew how bad it was to not be grateful for the gift, and I knew how embarrassed my folks would be over this behavior. I knew the embarrassment would probably turn to anger when Phil and Mary were gone, so my intent was to hide and not let anyone know how I had felt. I probably would have pulled it off if Phil had not insisted on telling his "Little Fisher Woman" goodbye!

Me—Ron Note: road builders camp and equipment in background

When he couldn't find me, they all realized I really was missing and started a serious search. After some time I was found in the back of the storage room under some boxes. Of course no one had any idea what had caused all of this. I also had been taught that when an adult asked you a question, as a child, you sure as the world had better answer, so I told them why I was crying, full well knowing that the "sky would probably fall." I remember Phil sweeping me up in his arms and his wife apologizing and apologizing for having been so out of touch with children's likes and feelings. They had no children of their own. Of course this made the folks feel so bad for her, and made me feel even worse and afraid. By the time Phil and Mary left, the whole situation was totally defused and I don't remember even getting scolded! The next time Mary came she brought me a toy!

There weren't many logging roads in our area at that time but there was a lot of harvestable timber. A road crew was brought in to improve the Joseph Creek and Crow Creek roads and to also build a lot of new logging roads. A camp was set up at our place.

Mom was hired to cook for the road crew. Dad pulled in an old shed and, in a make-shift fashion, attached it to the backside of our house, just off the kitchen. This served as the dining room for the crew.

Because of the war, some things like sugar and coffee were rationed. I can remember the margarine coming in a bag and we had to add a little tablet to it, to make it yellow. Ron and I loved squeezing and squeezing the bag, working the coloring through the margarine.

Joseph Creek was the source of a mixture of pleasure and fear. The creek was over along the hill on the far side of the canyon from our house. With the calf pasture and a couple of fences being between the yard and the creek, the creek didn't seem to be that immediate a danger but you know how fast and far an unattended toddler can go! One day Dad was up a draw haying on the bench and Mom was busy putting out a wash. Doing a wash meant running it through the old wringer washing machine which had a gas motor, if you were lucky enough to get it started, or doing it by hand on the scrub board. The washing was then hung on the line in the backyard.

Mom was so intent on her wash that more time slipped by than she realized before she went to check on us kids. Ron was nowhere to be found. Mom immediately ran to the creek, searching along its banks, to no avail.

In a state of hysteria she headed up the draw, carrying me on one hip, to go get Dad. As she reached the hayfield, there was Ron. He had decided to go find "Daddy and tractor." When the relief was over the anger set in. Mom cut a little switch and marched that boy home switching him on the legs ever so often. He never ran away again!

Poor Ron! He made the mistakes and got the punishment. I stood by observing it all and learning from his mistakes! Oh, that is not to say I didn't get my share of lickin's, 'cause I did! But I would have gotten more, if he hadn't preceded me in the school of hard knocks!

One source of trouble we neither seemed able to resist was playing trucks in a dirt pile at the end of the house. With washing clothes being such a task, it was a major infraction to deliberately get dirty! We would always plan to play just a little while then get out before we got caught, but invariably we would become so engrossed in our fun that time would slip by and Mom would come looking for us. It was a given that if you intentionally disobeyed, you would get a switching. That was a quick, convenient source of punishment because an enormous willow tree grew in our front yard.

I loved and hated that tree all at the same time. It was wonderful to climb, but oh, the switchings we got from its twigs and branches. Nothing stings worse than a willow switch! As we got older, humility was added to the pain because the folks would make us kids climb the tree and select the instrument of punishment.

We exhausted all possibilities of sizes that would hurt the least. First we got tiny twigs, thinking that they wouldn't hurt so much. Wrong! They sting like fire! Next we got great big ones thinking that the folks surely wouldn't use anything that big on us. Wrong again! We finally came to the conclusion that no matter how you "sliced it" a whipping was going to hurt. The best thing to do was just to stay out of trouble!

Our punishment didn't always come in the physical form. I suppose my greatest pain came from feeling that my dad was disappointed in me. Once Ron and I were playing up on the hill above the house. To little kids, maybe three or four years old, it seemed like a long way back down to the house. We both had to go to the bathroom and didn't want to go clear down to the outhouse so we reasoned that if we both wet our pants, Mom would feel it couldn't have been helped.

She had some old rags she fashioned into diapers! I remember her saying, "If you're going to act like babies then I will treat you like babies," and she diapered us up! I remember being so ashamed of having Dad see me in diapers!

Once Mom had to get the cows in for milking from the field across the creek. Ron and I were too young to leave alone so she put me in the very front, Ron next, and then herself, on the back of Nibs, Dad's horse. We were riding bareback, as usual. All went fine until we had crossed the creek, then for some reason we all fell off with Mom kind of landing on top of us kids. I remember how worried she was that she might have hurt us. I never remember us riding "trio" again!

Thus the years ticked by, the experiences added up, and the hard work continued. It was all a fact of life, a part of living, a necessary part of "Getting Started!"

Mom said we were poor, we just didn't know it!

Mom and "Friday,"
a Brown Swiss heifer

Mom, Ron, Dad, Me

Me in buggy under
the willow tree in
the front yard

Anna & Dave Hearing when they owned/lived
at "our place." They were Gertie McFetridge's
parents—Bud & Mac Birkmaier's great-grand-
parents. This barn was gone by the time Dad
bought the place.

Preschool Years with Dad

I am not sure how old Ron and I were when Mom started teaching at the Lewis School. I do know that we were still taking afternoon naps. We didn't have the money to replace our cribs, and with all of us sleeping in the same room, there wasn't room for bigger beds anyway! Ron and I slept in cribs until we were as tall as the cribs were long! Ron's crib was a blue metal one and mine was natural wood. Mine had a slat missing toward the foot of it. When I wanted to get out of it I would just slide out feet first.

Dad used to put us down for an afternoon nap right after lunch. He would sit in the living room until he thought we were asleep. He would peek in to make sure all was calm, then he'd go out to do some work that would not take him far from the house. When he figured it was about time for us to wake up he would come back to the house for a cup of coffee and wait. The only thing that confused him was the fact that at the end of our nap time, more often than not, the bedroom would be in shambles with blankets, pillows, and clothes thrown everywhere. One day Dad decided to play detective. He peeped in, as usual, to check on us to see that we were asleep, then he slammed the living room door as though he was leaving the house, but instead, he stayed quietly in the house. Just as he suspected, in a few moments the bedroom exploded with laughter, shouting, and things flying through the air. Of course it all stopped as suddenly as it had begun when Dad burst through the door!

This was the era before baled hay, so it meant a lot of forking to get the cattle fed. One haystack was in the middle of the field across Joseph Creek. We would ride the bobsled, pulled by Dad's team, Tim and Tom, over to the stack where Dad would pile it high with hay. Riding atop that load of hay, Dad would sing all the way back. Dad was happy; he was content; he was fulfilled; he was complete. He had his health, his family and his ranch! One of his favorite songs was *"Forever and Ever!"* I can still close my eyes and hear him singing from the top of the load of hay on a crisp winter morning!

Ron and I were always baffled as to how there were new calves on the feed ground. Being too young to be told about "the birds and the bees," Dad explained it away by saying that the cows found them in the hay. As Dad pitched off each fork full of hay, Ron and I were worried for the baby calves; afraid that Dad would "fork" one!

One time they found me pawing through the hay for all I was worth. When they asked me what in the world I was doing, I confidently told them that I was going to find me a baby calf!

With Mom at school, Dad had to prepare lunch for us kids. We didn't have a great variety so Dad had to be creative to fix things we would eat. One year we must have had an abundance of canned peaches because to us kids, it seemed that was about all we ate! By the end of the winter we were so tired of peaches, we almost refused to eat them! Dad discovered that if he would put a bowl of them right next to the block of ice in the icebox, a few hours before lunch, the juice would have slivers of ice in it, and we loved it!

Mom took Ron and me to school on special days such as picnics! On the days when there was a special evening function at school, Mom would stay at school so she could prepare. Dad would get Ron and me cleaned up, then he would go out to do the milking and chores. On one particular occasion, while Dad was out doing the chores, Ron and I decided it would be a great idea to surprise Mom by baking a cake and taking it to school with us.

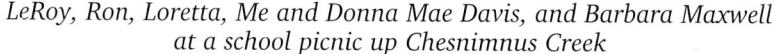

LeRoy, Ron, Loretta, Me and Donna Mae Davis, and Barbara Maxwell at a school picnic up Chesnimnus Creek

Dad came back to the house to find us, one on each end of a bench with a large bowl between us. We were adding flour, eggs, milk, and anything else we thought we had seen Mom put in cakes. We had about as much flour on us as was in the bowl.

That is the only time I can remember getting whipped with the razor strap, and do you know, as much as that strap hurt, the thing that hurt most was that Dad threw our "cake to be" out to the pigs! I was so sure it would have been delicious and Mom would have been delighted.

When it came time for the spring fieldwork, Dad had to figure out a way to take us along. Up on the bench there was a rocky "neck" which ran between two fields. There were some logs there that formed a square. I think they were the remains of an old feeder. Anyway, Dad would spread blankets out in it and tell us not to get out of the logs. He could see us from both fields except for one small section of one field, which dropped down into a draw. We played, ate snacks, and napped in our "log square" and watched Dad go around and around the field. Once we woke up from our nap at a time when Dad was down in the draw where we couldn't see or hear him. I started crying. Ron took me by the hand and we started out across the field. I really don't know where we thought we were going but at about that time Dad came out of the draw. We went straight for him and he for us! When he had stopped my crying, we told him we thought he had left us. That was the first time I saw Dad cry. I never again ever worried that Dad would leave me!

We didn't have thermal jugs so for the hottest part of the summer Mom would hand sew layers and layers of burlap over a glass jug. We would then soak the burlap with water and the evaporation would keep the drinking water slightly cool. Most of the time though, we just drank from an old mason jar. Even today, if I drink from a mason jar, I have a flashback of those childhood days. No water tastes and smells quite like water from a mason canning jar!

Our first riding experiences were on Dad's horse, Nibs. Dad would saddle him, put us on him, then turn us loose in the yard. If we weren't careful, Nibs would go under the clothesline. This would scrape us kids off or the saddle horn would catch on the clothesline and bust it. If there were any clothes on the line, they would end up in the dirt with us kids!

As we got older, the folks started assigning various chores to us. They taught us to milk cows by starting us out on cows that were ready to dry up. If a cow wasn't milked dry, she would cut back on her production of milk. If this continued for a length of time, she would completely quit producing, or "dry up." Of course when we were so little, we couldn't get a cow milked completely dry, but we could get enough

Preschool Years

Me—Ron, on Nibs, in front of bunkhouse that burned.

out of her to take the pressure off her bag so we accomplished two things—the cows dried up and we learned to milk!

On one occasion, Ron and I were milking on the same cow. Ron was on the "milking side" and I was on the "off side." The cow we were milking was gentle, but the cow next to me was a kicker. I don't know if my back touched her side or what but I never knew what hit me! I just remember being rolled over and over until I hit the pole fence out behind the cows. This was when we were still milking cows in the outside stanchions before Dad built the barn in 1949.

Immediately a large "goose egg" appeared on my forehead. I remember Mom running to the house, practically hurdling the large wooden gate into the yard. She brought back a cold wet cloth to put on my head and all was well!

Probably the chore I hated the most was feeding the bucket calves. In those days we didn't have bottles or buckets with big calf sized nipples. To get a calf to drink we would dip our fingers in the milk then let the calf suck our fingers. As the calves were sucking, we would immerse our hands into the milk. As the calves sucked our fingers, they would also be sucking milk. After doing this several times, the calves would learn to just stick their heads into the buckets and start drinking the milk.

It is the natural instinct of a calf to bunt the udder of its mother as it is nursing, to supposedly get her to "let down" more milk. This instinct carried over into the bucket feeding process. The aggravating thing was that sometimes they would bunt when there was still lots of

My curls

milk in the bucket, causing the bucket to go flying, and the milk to be splashed over us from head to toe, literally! We would be drenched in the sticky, smelly milk. It would be in our hair, our eyes, and if it caught us just right, in our mouths! Mom kept my hair in curls and one "bunt" of a calf could undo all the work she had done to fix my hair!

Milk, fresh from the cow, is very different from the homogenized/pasteurized milk from the store. It is called raw milk and has its own peculiar taste and smell. I had quit drinking milk long before this time so it was really offensive to me. People who drank raw milk all their lives didn't mind it, but we had many town guests who turned their noses up at it!

My Grandma Berthe had blamed her being overweight on her consuming so many dairy products as a kid. I guess she had passed that theory on to Mom, because Mom really didn't care that I didn't drink milk.

When Mom weaned Ron from the bottle, she weaned me at the same time. It was just easier than having him begging for my bottle. He, being ten and one half months older than me, was able to drink well enough from a glass to retain his liking of milk. By the time I was old enough to drink well from a glass, Mom said I had lost my taste for milk! So having that terrible stuff splashed into my mouth when we were feeding the calves was really disgusting to me!

Me—Ron, feeding bucket calves

Another chore I hated was helping castrate the baby pigs. Dad kept the brood sows

Preschool Years

in little pens, each of which had a small shed. Dad would put the old sow out so she couldn't get us, then Ron and I would crawl into the shed, catch the baby pigs and hand them out to Dad. Mom would hold them and Dad would castrate them while standing there at the doorway of the shed. The high pitched squeal of a baby pig was bad at its best, but when it was echoing around in a small shed, it was deafening! And the odor! Oh, I can remember as a little girl, thinking it was the most horrible smell in the world. I remember it smelling something like what I now think of as a formaldehyde odor. I can remember becoming quite nauseous before the job was done.

Before Dad bought Roamy for Ron, we had to share Dan, the only horse we had that us kids could ride outside of the yard. We always rode bareback because Dad didn't want to have to worry about us getting hung up in the stirrups.

Each evening before the milk cows were brought in off the hills for milking, Ron and I had to get the calves into a pen, from the calf pasture so they could be bucket fed and so they wouldn't get mixed with the cows. The cows would then be put in the calf pasture for the night after they were milked.

Because Ron was the older, he felt he should be in front and do the reining. That would have been fine except for the fact that the faster we would go, the more Ron would curl his legs back, rather that let them hang down. When he curled his legs back it forced my legs back too. We eventually would be practically standing on our knees on Dan's back. Of course the outcome was that we would fall off, usually in a patch of thistles! When Dan felt us going off he would stop suddenly and stand there until we gathered ourselves up. I always ended up bawling, more out of anger toward Ron for making us fall off than from any hurt I experienced from hitting the ground!

In those days we never went to the doctor except for serious injuries. One time a cup of hot coffee was knocked off the table and scalded my shoulder and arm. It must have been pretty bad because I can remember lying on the couch with that arm sticking straight in the air. I found if I kept it elevated, it didn't throb so badly. Because it just wasn't the practice to go to the doctor, it was a very frightening thing to have it even mentioned. I was horrified when Aunt Mary came in and asked if the folks were going to take me in. They decided I would be fine with home remedies and clean bandages.

Another time there were several of our cousins eating at our place. I was so excited because I was going to get to sit by LeRoy. Mom gave me a little bowl of cream style corn to carry to the table. I fell, broke the bowl and cut a gash in my wrist. I can still remember how at the very

Dad—Mom—Ron—Me, ready for the Chief Joseph Days rodeo in our new outfits!

first the gaping gash looked white like pork fat, with what looked to me like a little blue worm at the bottom of it. Quickly beads of blood appeared along the edges of the gash and instantly it filled with blood which started running down my arm. Mom bound it up with a cloth and it healed fine but left a scar I carry to this day. Later I came to realize that "the little blue worm" I had seen at the bottom of the gaping wound was an artery!

One time Dad got his little finger caught in the combine and almost cut it off. He did have to go to the doctor that time! There were many times he was very sick with what we called a cold, but now I am sure it must have been pneumonia. Mom would put boiling water in a bowl with some strong menthol smelling stuff. Dad would drape a towel over his head and put his face over the bowl, breathing in the steam. This would get him breathing well enough to carry on with the work that had to be done.

We never got a lot of new clothes; with our life style they weren't necessary, but we always got a new outfit for Chief Joseph Days. We would be decked out from head to foot, including hats and boots. I can remember how very proud we were of those outfits!

Because of all the time we got to spend with Dad during those preschool years, my life was filled with memories. A bond was formed between us that lasted to the day of his death!

WINTERS

Most winters were blessed with a heavy snowfall so Dad shoveled snow up high on the walls around the house to help keep the house, especially the floors, as warm as possible. This snow bank also acted as a freezer. Meat was put in cream cans, then the cans were buried in the snow bank on the north side of the house, thus frozen meat was enjoyed all winter.

Winters were a great time for sledding parties, card parties, fudge making, taffy pulling, and making popcorn balls. As rough times tend to pull people together even now, so it was back then!

Winters were harsh but also offered a change of pace for the adults and much fun in the snow for us kids. The snowfall was much heavier back then, piling to a depth of two to three feet and at times even more. I can remember Ron and me digging down until we reached the ground then standing up and not being able to see out. We were probably around three feet tall at the time.

Our house was built on a little bench that dropped off into the swamp and pasture below. We spent hours sledding down this slope then trudging back up only to do it all over again. If we became

Ron—Me

Me—Ron

Me—Ron

bored with this, we rolled snowballs and built jumps which added to the excitement. Larger snowballs were made, on which we would play "King of the Mountain." Once Ron and our cousin Lyle, who lived three miles on down Joseph Creek, were dancing around on top of one of those large snowballs. Lyle slipped, falling onto the hard, packed, frozen snow, breaking his leg.

One winter the snowfall was exceptionally heavy and it was complicated by high winds. The Pass had drifted in and kept drifting back in faster than the county road crew could plow it out. (The Pass meaning the Crow Creek Pass). Uncle Don, who lived three miles on down Joseph Creek from us, was the mail carrier. He carried the mail every Monday and Friday; that is when the roads were open! When he had missed several runs with the mail, the post office notified, I'm not sure who, but "they" sent Ray Dunsmore in by plane. Our place was the only one with a large enough field, and a place where the canyon was wide enough to allow a plane to land. Dunsmore, being an experienced canyon pilot was able to land without incident.

The plan was for Uncle Don to fly out with the mail. He also was going to pick up a few, a very few, supplies. Uncle Don was a large man. As he climbed into the plane he started to kick the snow off his boots but at the first kick he put a hole in the plane! Later he said, "Do you have any idea how I felt crawling into that flimsy contraption?"

Each family was allowed to order several items of food. Mom ordered a side of bacon. (We must have been out of our home-cured meat.) At that time bacon came unsliced and still on the rind. She felt it would be very useable because she could use it for breakfast meat and also use the rind to cook with beans.

Uncle Don's trip went without further incident and the much appreciated food and long awaited mail was delivered. To celebrate our good fortune, Dad and Mom decided we would go down to Uncle Don's and Aunt Mary's to play cards. Dad hitched up the team, loaded some hay on the bobsled, then Dad and Mom bundled us kids up and stuck us down in holes in the hay to keep us warm. With a joyful spirit, we started down the canyon.

The Joseph Canyon is quite crooked at Uncle Don's place thus the wind didn't reach down into the canyon bottom with much force. When the card playing finished and we headed for home, we noticed that there was a stiff breeze but thought it nothing to worry about. As we proceeded up the canyon to where it started to widen, the wind continued to get stronger. By the time we reached home, the wind was coming with quite a force; in fact, with such force that doors were banging and gates were swinging!

With having no refrigerator and the back porch being the coolest place to store food, Mom had put the slab of bacon on the porch. The wind had apparently been blowing strongly for quite some time because the yard gate had blown open as well as the back porch door. An old sow pig had discovered this and had helped herself to the bacon. All that was left of that beautiful slab of bacon was the rind, cleaned off slick as a whistle! Mom just started crying.

The only hot water we had was heated by coils in the cook stove. The water was stored in a large tank behind the stove, with the cold water coming into the coils through a pipe coming out of the bottom of the tank. As the water heated, it would return to the tank through a pipe going to the top of the tank. Thus as the water circulated through the coils, eventually the whole tank of water would become hot, that is, as long as you kept a fire going in the stove. This was considered a real luxury but there was a price to pay! When it was very cold in the winter, it was a battle to keep the coils from freezing and bursting during the night.

With the firebox of the cook stove being so small, the fire had to be fed often. I can remember Dad staying up through the night, sleeping in a chair, so as to keep the fire going. If the extreme cold persisted for several nights, he would become sleep deprived and very exhausted. On more than one occasion he finally became so exhausted he simply couldn't stay awake. He would go to bed for a few hours only to awaken to the horror of finding the fire out and the coils frozen and busted. This would happen in the course of only a few hours. The old house was that cold!

There was a doorway between the kitchen and living room but no door. When the coils would burst we couldn't use the cook stove until Dad got the coils fixed. We would hang a blanket over the doorway then live in the front room, cooking on the heater stove.

We kids would get into our pajamas next to the heater stove. We would then turn round and round to get as warm as possible on all sides. Dad and Mom would hold blankets up to the stove to get them warm. They would then wrap them around us like a cocoon, then pack us to bed. We learned to dress and undress very quickly while trying to keep warm by that stove.

Occasionally a bunch of the neighbors would gather for a fun filled coasting party. A location would have been chosen that had a long, gradual slope with no obstacles such as timber or fences at the bottom. A large bonfire would be built, around which some of the adults would sit and visit, keeping an eye on the cocoa and chili.

In later years we had the luxury of my Uncle Don's jeep, which he used to pull or haul us back to the top of the slope. We really thought we had it good then!

Me—Ron

One Christmas Ron and I got a seven-passenger toboggan. Dad said he should be the head man so he could steer it. I still think it was just a good excuse to be one of the kids! He would yell out for all of us to lean to the left or lean to the right. He was always careful to make sure each passenger's legs were wrapped around the person in front of him and tucked safely into his lap. As each person hung onto the side ropes, it kept all the legs safely tucked in. We never did break a leg on that ol' thing.

Once our sledding party was up Chesnimnus Creek on a slope at the mouth of Pine Creek. Chesnimnus Creek was at the foot of the slope but was frozen over so posed no problem. Mike Dunbar was a young man who worked for Uncle Don at that time. He came to the party bringing along his skis. One child had a bad sled wreck about halfway down the slope. Mike came skiing down the slope, swooped the youngster up into his arms, then came flying on down the slope, shot across the frozen river and came to a sliding stop at the bonfire. Understandably, everyone was dazzled!

Needless to say, at the top of our next Christmas list was a pair of skis! I don't remember if it was that very next Christmas, but we did get those skis! They were of the crudest design but none-the-less, they were skis! They basically were pointed boards, turned up at the tips, with a groove down the center of the bottom side. There was simply a leather strap to keep them on.

We never even knew there were such things as snow suits (and maybe there weren't back then), so to keep warm we would put on layers and layers of clothes. Of course as they became wet, they got heavier and heavier. There was no such thing as insulated boots either. We had buckle-up overshoes to slip on over our shoes. How cold we were willing to get usually determined the length of the sledding party!

Later when we kids were older and we had a pickup, Dad would let us drive from Uncle Don's place back to our place to check if any cows were calving while he and Mom continued a card game with Uncle Don and Aunt Mary. We had to cross an old bridge over Joseph Creek and then follow a road that was nothing more than tracks beaten out along the edge of a field. In the winter, we bucked the snow and later when it started thawing, we slipped and slid through deep, slick ruts in the mud! We soon learned that it is much easier to steer with only one hand on the wheel when slithering through the slimy ruts!

When the spring thaw came, Joseph Creek would get so high that it would actually go over the old bridge. Mom was so afraid that our rig would be swept away, that she refused to ride but would get out and walk across. Some of the planks had lost the spikes that nailed down the "down river" end of them, so as the river got high enough to go over the bridge, those planks would float and bob. It is amazing that Mom did not slip and fall on those wet, slick planks, but Dad could not persuade her to stay in the rig!

In later years when we lived in the new house after coming home from The B&H, a ranch Dad worked on up Chesnimnus, I can remember the blankets of my bed freezing to the wall on the back side of the bed where it was shoved tight against the wall.

Bridge crossing to Uncle Don's during spring runoff—1950's

The B&H Ranch

I was impressed by the B&H Ranch even before it was the B&H. The first I remember of this ranch was the folks talking about it at one time being owned by a Frenchman, Mr. Armand Vigne, and his wife Leoncie. They ran sheep. They sold it to Jim B. and Nellie L. Chaffee on Dec. 31, 1942. The first I can remember of actually visiting the ranch was when Jim Chaffe owned it. He turned it into a cattle ranch. I remember thinking how big and elegant the house seemed. The living room was so big that the couch could actually be in the middle of the room and you could walk all around it!

Henry Braun

Helen Horton—Me

When Dad and Mom went there to visit, Ron and I would play outside. Out behind the house was the abandoned lambing shed. It was long and narrow with lambing jugs on each side. Lambing jugs are small pens in which ewes and their newborn lambs are put for a few days before being turned out with the rest of the sheep. I remember the jugs being double decked, though after being around sheep later in my life, I can't figure out how it would have worked.

My next memory of the ranch was when we went up there and tried out a horse for us kids. I couldn't make the horse do anything, but Ron managed him fine so Dad bought him, Roamy, for Ron.

In 1951 Henry Braun and Bud Horton bought the ranch, naming it the B&H, which it has been called ever since. Henry Braun was from the Clarkston, Washington/Lewiston, Idaho area. Bud Horton was from the Seattle, Washington area. Bud also owned a meat processing company called the Inland Meat Company. The

B&H Ranch brand was I N L. Horton also had a feedlot in Clarkston, Washington, down by the Snake River.

The B&H became a part of my life when I was in the first or second grade. Dad was hired as the ranch foreman, and Mom was hired to cook for the ranch crew.

One of the most memorable experiences of the B&H was the raising of a fawn deer, Princess. The men had been out riding when the dogs jumped a newly born fawn. Dad rescued her and brought her home to us kids. She quickly learned to drink from a bottle with a lamb nipple. She immediately became a favorite of everyone, including the ranch hands. She would wriggle in between their legs and hide under the large crew table. She waited patiently for tidbits from the men's plates. One man, Orie Dunbar, would purposely take more syrup than he planned to eat so he could hold his plate under the table and let Princess lick it clean.

Ron, Princess and Me

Princess—bunkhouse in background

Bread was a favorite of hers. One morning Ron and I were making our lunches. Ron had put his bread on the counter and went to the refrigerator for whatever it was he was going to put in his sandwich. When he returned to the counter his bread was gone. He, of course, accused me of taking the bread, then he went to get some more. He again turned his back to do something, and again his bread disappeared. He was just ready to lay into me when he saw the last of a slice of bread disappear from the corner of Princess's mouth.

Probably Princess's favorite, though, was watermelon. Mom would hold pieces high and Princess would walk on her hind legs to get them!

In the morning, Dad would open the front door and Princess would come bounding into the house. He would then open our bedroom doors. Being an old house that wasn't insulated, the bedrooms were cold, so we slept buried down under the covers. Princess would come into our bedrooms, poke her head in under the covers, lick us, then give that uniquely darling little cry that only a fawn deer can give!

Men from the Game Department came more than once to take her away, but unsuccessfully. Princess slept in a very dark corner of a big old woodshed. When any of us would walk to the door of the shed she would jump up and run to meet us. The first time a "game man" came, he walked right to that shed door, stopped and glanced in momentarily, then went on. Princess knew he was a stranger and never moved a muscle.

Later the Department sent another man to get her; again to no avail! By this time she was bigger and spent most of her daytime up in a thick north behind the barn. She would follow us to the car every morning and watch as we drove off to school. She would then bounce along the road to the barn, duck under the fence and disappear into the north where she would stay until we got home from school.

Once when a man from the Game Department came to take her away, Orie Dunbar was building a corral up by the barn. The man quizzed Orie as to where the deer might be. Orie swung his arm in a broad, sweeping motion toward the north and said, "She's probably somewhere up there in that north." The man then asked Orie to help find her, to which Orie replied, "If you want to take that deer from those kids, you're going to have to do it on your own because I'm sure as H____ not going to help you!" The man left empty handed and they never came for her again.

Another highlight of experiences we had while at the B&H was riding in the Chief Joseph Days Parade. I rode Dan, Ron rode Roamy, and Dad rode Nibs. Three of the ranch hands rode ranch horses. Dad knew that Dan would be fine but was not sure how Roamy would react so he put Ron in the middle, between Dad and me, with the ranch hands right behind us. We were right

Dan—Me

Ron—Bill McCrae, Dad and Glen Ollis

behind a float with some pretty girls and I can remember how they were so impressed the way Nibs pranced, seemingly in time to the music of a band that was nearby. As little kids we were so proud; we were sure we were the star attraction!

Me, Ron, Dad, (Bill McCrae), Glenn Ollis, Chet Mastrude

There was a crude airstrip up on McCarty Ridge. Often when the bosses came, they would fly in, buzzing the house, before heading for the airstrip. Not having a phone at the ranch, we never knew when they would show up, but it was always a time of excitement. As soon as the plane buzzed the house, we would jump into the jeep, go up Chesnsimnus about a mile then work our way to the top by way of a washed out logging road.

We had quite an assortment of hired men pass through the ranks while we were at the B&H. Some of the more colorful of them were Cody Dodson, Cleve Sandlin, Chick Beeman, Orie Dunbar, Swede Larson, and "Rawhide" Robinson. I also remember Percy Winters because sometimes we kids would go into the barn unexpectedly and see Percy currying a horse and singing, "When My Blue Moon Turns to Gold Again," as tears ran down his cheeks! The rumor was that he had had his heart broken recently! Also I remember Percy getting his arm caught in the baler. It tore the sleeve off his shirt and did some damage to his forearm, but it could have been far worse! There were also quite a few younger men who didn't leave the lasting impression on me that the older men did, except for Keith Shevlin—Ron and I really liked him because he was such a tease!

Most of the men got along pretty well, but I remember one feud that brewed for quite some time. It was between Chick and Rawhide (I don't remember his real name but he liked to be called Rawhide; I guess it made him feel tough). For some reason they took a strong dislike for each other. Rawhide always had a lot of "big stories" to tell; maybe Chick got tired of them!

One winter Dad sent them up to a place in Pine Creek, to winter some cattle. I don't remember if B&H owned the place at that time, if they had leased it, or if they had just bought the hay and were going to feed it up there rather than haul it down to the ranch. Anyway, Dad sent Chick and Rawhide up there to batch and feed the cattle. They got to

Chick Beeman

hating each other so much that they wouldn't stay in the house together. One of them would go out and do some of the work while the other one fixed himself something to eat, then they would switch.

One day they had some major disagreement. Rawhide got so mad that he saddled up one of the horses and rode down to the ranch to complain to Dad. It was almost dark when he got to the ranch and he was scared to death! A cougar had run across the road in front of him. I don't remember if Dad made him go back that night or let him wait 'till daybreak, but Dad did tell him to get back up there, and "get along" or he could consider himself fired!

Another time Rawhide told us he could play the fiddle and asked if we wanted to hear him. The folks couldn't very well turn him down, so they agreed for him to come into the ranch house one evening and play us a few numbers. Ron and I had heard "ho-down" music on the radio so we were looking forward to it. He must have played classical music because it sure wasn't "ho-down!" I am sure it was beautiful music, but we simply were not educated musically so as to appreciate it!

The rumor was that Chick got his nickname as a young man because anytime his friends got a craving for fresh fried chicken, Chick could always come up with the fryers, though he never raised a chicken in his life!

I remember him as toothless, good natured, and always wearing garters around his upper arms to hold his sleeves up. I knew him before we went to the B&H because he had worked for my Uncle Don. Once when he was working for Uncle Don, Donna Mae, Lyle, Ron and I went into the bunkhouse where Chick stayed and we found his chewing tobacco. We didn't know what it was so we took a big bite of it. We decided that it was such terrible stuff that it should be disposed of so we threw it into the creek. Maybe Donna Mae and Lyle got blamed for it because when we were at the B&H, Chick was good to Ron and me.

I must admit there was one thing we did when he was at the B&H that irritated him to death. Mom had laying hens that ran loose. They helped keep down the earwigs, spiders, and other bugs around the house.

One day the bunkhouse door was left open and a big old red hen went in, jumped up on Chick's bunk and laid an egg. Every morning thereafter she would stand on the bunkhouse step and sing and sing until we kids would let her in. When an egg was found on Chick's bed every day, he became the target of a lot of teasing, to the point he became irritated! We kids named the hen "Miss Beeman."

On one occasion Bud Horton brought a couple of young men with him when he came to visit the ranch. I believe one was his nephew. Anyway, they joined forces with some of the young hired men and planned a snipe hunt for Ron and me.

They took us over by the creek and got us all set up in amongst the river willows on a large gravel bar; then they went back to the bunkhouse. We pounded our sticks faithfully for what seemed an eternity! We decided that we weren't going to be successful but realized that every hunt doesn't end with success so we weren't too disappointed.

We trudged back across the field to the bunkhouse and reported our lack of success. The guys were a great encouragement and assured us that we had just given up too soon as it was just then getting dusk and the snipes were sure to be coming out anytime! They took us back over to the creek and got us all set up again; then they went back to the bunkhouse. We feverishly pounded those sticks until darkness really started setting in! We may have only been six and seven years old. but we weren't stupid! We realized that we had been had, and it made us kind of mad! Now this was late spring and cattle had been fed all winter in the field between the creek and the house, so on our way back, we filled the gunny sack almost half full with dried and partially dried cow piles. We then marched up to the bunkhouse door and knocked loudly. When the door opened we burst past the "doorman" and announced, "We got a whole bunch of 'em," at which time we grabbed the bottom of the sack, slung cow piles all over the bunkhouse, then ran like the devil for the house! A couple of the guys followed us to the house and wanted to give us a whipping or at least have Dad whip us. Dad just laughed at them and said that their joke had backfired—live with it!

I realize now what a mess it must have been for them to clean up. The bunks were around the edge of the room with a large rug in the center. With no vacuum sweeper, it must have been a chore!

The bunkhouse was near the main house with the well right in front of it. The well was our only source of water when we first moved to the B&H. Our only bathroom was an outhouse a ways out back. It wasn't long until Dad put in a cistern on a hillside about half a mile on up Chesnimnus. The water was then piped to the house, which really made it easier for Mom cooking for the ranch crew. The urgency of clean water was realized when Dad caught the hired men stepping out of the front door of the bunkhouse and relieving themselves just feet from the well, before turning in for the night.

When we were at the B&H, the benches on what is now called Poverty Flats, were all hayed. It was a real job to get the hay put up and hauled down the draw to the ranch before the elk got it. Elk were a real nuisance as they would actually lie and roll in the hay, mashing down even more than they ate. When it was baled, it had to be hauled almost immediately, otherwise the elk would paw the bales, breaking the strings.

Many a night, just at dusk, we would jump into the open topped jeep and make a run on the benches. Dad and the guys would shoot over the heads of the elk to scare them off. The elk would run back up into the timber, but if the truth was known, they probably were back in the hay before we were back to the house!

Dad shot an old 30-40 Craig, which we had named Meat-In-The-Pot. On one of these runs was the first time I had seen Dad shoot when it was dark enough to see fire shoot out the end of the barrel. I was impressed! It was a rifle with a lot of "umph," but at times Dad must not have held quite high enough because we harvested a few!

The ranch boss complained that Mom was spending too much money on groceries, so Dad decided that one way to bring the bill down was to furnish some of the meat. He decided to kill some of the deer that had been hanging along the road near one of the feed grounds. I guess he was confident that he would get some because he loaded up several of the ranch hands and us kids on the back of a stock truck that had had the racks taken off of it. They had been using the truck to feed the cattle.

It was snowing like crazy—those big flakes that look more like feathers than snowflakes! Dad figured this was to his advantage because it would cover up tracks and blood. It was one of those days when it seemed that Dad just couldn't miss! I swear a deer dropped every time he shot. I think he got caught up in the excitement of it all and maybe just wanted to see how many he could get—show off a little for the young ranch hands! When he stopped shooting, there were five dead deer.

The ranch hands climbed up the hill and drug them down and threw them on the bed of the truck. Of course there was blood everywhere, but it kept snowing so the blood was soon covered. Then it just kept snowing. It snowed so much, in fact, a grader was sent out to plow the road. Well, as the grader cut the snow bank you can guess what showed up! Bright red blood! The man running the grader was one to help himself to a little meat once in a while too, so he just laughed it off, saying nothing to anyone.

The plot crumbled though when some time later Dad fired one of the young ranch hands. He went straight to town and turned Dad in. By then the meat was all gone so there was no evidence!

There were many exciting adventures while we were on the B&H. Many times when we were within a mile or so of the barn on our way back from riding for cattle all day, one of the guys would say, "Race ya" and the race was on! It didn't matter if we were on the road, out in a pasture, or crossing a field, we went like crazy for the barn. Ron and I were right in the middle of it all, and I never remember a time when we were eating too much dust!

Once Ron and I were riding alone up Chesnimnus from the ranch headquarters. We had a couple of dogs with us. One of the dogs heeled Ron's horse. Ron's horse started to run and mine wasn't to be left behind! Not expecting to run, we hadn't gathered up our reins so we had a true run-away! Our horses never stopped until they reached the corral where they skidded to a stop with their noses inches from the corral poles. I can remember feeling pretty loose in the saddle, but we neither one came off. We tied the horses up, walked across the corral to where Dad and Mom were. Dad asked, "What was that all about?" That's when I started to cry! Ron didn't!

The ranch house would get quite hot in the summer with cooking for the crew and all, so in the evening the screened windows would be opened. One night Ron and I were sent out to do something after dark. As we passed under the open kitchen window, the folks heard me say, "Don't worry Ronny, Sissy won't let anything happen to you." That was one time I was braver than Ron so I don't let him forget about it!

At this point in my life I had never gone to church and Sunday School and had heard God and members of the Deity referred to only in vain. But from somewhere within me, I knew there was a God and I knew He lived somewhere up in the sky.

At that time, Jello came in a box that had an inner piece of wax type paper folded around the powdered Jello. When Mom would make Jello she would leave just a little on the opened paper and Ron and I would get to lick it off. No matter how much she left, it never was enough! Our dream was to someday be able to eat a whole package of Jello!

Ron on Roamy—Me on Dan

I had never stolen a thing in my life, but the day came when we could resist no longer. We sneaked into the pantry and each took the flavor of our choice. We then climbed the hill to a cave that overlooked the buildings below. It was a small cave, not deep enough but what you could see a piece of the sky no matter where you were in that cave. We just knew that if we could see the sky, then God could be looking in on us. We became so nervous we spilled a good share of our Jello. Of course there wasn't much dirt on the cave floor and the Jello was bright colored so we had a terrible time trying to conceal the evidence! That was a real example of how guilt can eat you alive.

One winter we ended up with a couple of bummer calves. Bud Horton said that if Ron and I would raise them on the bucket, he would buy each of us a bicycle in the fall when the calves were sold. Fall came, the calves were sold but we never saw the bikes. I remember Mom expressing her lack of respect for him from that day on.

When we left the B&H and moved back to our place on Joseph Creek, there were many things I hated to leave behind. By far the hardest, though, was Princess. She was grown by then and there was no way we could uproot her and take her with us. I remember the horribly sad empty feeling I had whenever I thought of her so I would consciously make myself wipe her out of my mind.

When we had moved to the B&H, Dad's mom, Grandma Katie, had talked Dad into letting her move into our place on Joseph Creek. She brought her cows with her and settled in. All went well for a while then one day Grandma built too big of a fire in the heater stove.

Me on Blacky—my bucket calf

The stovepipe came out of the back of the stove, went straight up, then made a 90 degree turn into the flue. The problem was that where the stovepipe ran horizontal, parallel to the ceiling, it was too close to the ceiling. If an extremely hot fire was built, the stovepipe would overheat, causing the ceiling above it to get too hot—possibly catching on fire. That's exactly what happened!

Grandma tried to put it out but when she saw it was hopeless, she started grabbing some of her personal items and then packed beds, dressers, and other furniture out into the yard. About that time

Bud and Zuah Birkmaier came by. They had been up to Mac Birkmaiers, a mile up the canyon, and were just headed back to their place down Joseph Creek. Bill Poulson, from up Crow Creek about eight miles also showed up. By this time the house was too far gone to get anything more out of it. The fire had spread to the bunkhouse, which was over the cellar. Bud and Bill started packing canned goods out of the cellar while the bunkhouse burned above them. Grandma Berthe could see the smoke from her place a mile down the canyon. She had no vehicle so she walked up the canyon as fast as she could, but everything was pretty well gone by the time she got there.

When all was done that could be done the attention was turned to Grandma Katie to see if she was all right. They then realized her hair was badly singed!

It was a mail day so later when Uncle Don came home from running the route, you can imagine the horror he experienced when he saw the smoldering remains of the house.

Grandma Berthe told Grandma Katie she could move down with her, so Grandma Katie moved her cows down and they lived together in the log house the rest of that winter.

Grandma Katie had six sons. They went together and bought her a little place in the valley with each of them making two months payments each year. They moved her on to it and she continued to live there until her health made it impossible to live alone.

When we were ready to leave the B&H, we had no house to go home to! We moved in with Grandma Berthe in her log house. (Grandma must have felt like she was running a shelter for the homeless!)

Dad bought a bunkhouse from Uncle Don. They put it on log skids and pulled it up to our place, to a knoll above where the old house had been. Dad turned the bunkhouse into a living room and two bedrooms. He then built on a large kitchen/dining room, pantry, and a small room that would initially serve as a bedroom for Ron but later would be a bathroom. It was never made into a bathroom while we lived there— all we ever had was an outhouse! The house was finally finished and we moved in and settled into life on Joseph Creek again!

Lewis School and Grade School Years

Mom, ?, ?, Huffman boy, Barbara Maxwell, ?, Loretta and Donna Davis.

LeRoy Davis, Barbara Maxwell, Mom, Loretta and Donna Davis

Walter Maxwell, Dad, Uncle Don, Uncle Roy, and Ron

Mom's first year of teaching was at Liberty on upper Prairie Creek in the Wallowa Valley. It was a small, one-room school with grades one through eight. One of her favorite students was a cute little boy, Ronny Repplinger. Later she named my brother, Ron, after him.

When Dad and Mom met, she was teaching at Wallowa. They were married six weeks later, October 2, 1942. She immediately handed in her resignation, to be effective at Christmas break.

Her next teaching experience was at the Lewis School, which was up Chesnimnus three miles from where we lived at the head of Joseph Creek. She started teaching there when Ron and I were preschool ages. The school was the social hub of the community. Mom put together Christmas programs, pie socials, basket socials, etc. I can remember as a little girl being so embarrassed when my pie or basket dinner came up for auction—Dad was the auctioneer. At Halloween we had a mini-carnival. A corner of the room was partitioned off with a sheet pinned to a wire, which had been stretched across the room. The little kids could "go fishing" there. We were amazed as to how the girls always hooked girl things and the boys hooked boy things. There were sack races, three-legged races, and other contests for all ages. One contest was for the wives to toss jellybeans to their husbands who would catch them with their mouths. This was all great fun until Dad sucked one down his windpipe and almost choked to death. I can remember him hanging over the porch railing coughing, red as a beet, with men taking turns beating him on the back while we kids stood around in complete shock or crying. We didn't know the Heimlich maneuver back then.

Me, Ron, Lyle and Donna Mae. See cistern upper right by tree.

    A concrete cistern was up on the hill. It was the school's water supply. Each fall just before school started, the men would drain the cistern and clean it. There would always be frogs and salamanders in it. MOST of them were alive! When the cistern was empty the men would scrub down the walls then pour straight Purex on them. They would then catch the water coming into the cistern from the spring and throw it against the walls to rinse the Purex off, but hard as they tried, the water at the beginning of the school year always tasted of Purex.

Me—note heavy cotton stockings

    There were swings, teeter-totters, and a slide to play on but no mowed lawn. Each fall the students would have to trample down the dried grass and weeds. The girls always wore dresses back then, and heavy cotton stockings. The dried seeds and stickers were a miserable thing to deal with as they stuck to and in our stockings.

    Starting to school seemed like a real milestone to Ron and me. We really had the feeling that overnight we had grown up. I remember very shortly after starting school, Dad was headed down to Grandma Berthe's with the tractor. The tractor had a farmhand with a hayfork on the front. This was a frame to which were attached long tines used to haul hay. Dad had never let us ride on it for fear we would slip and fall down through it. Well, on this particular day Dad decided we could ride on the hay fork. I can remember us discussing the fact that we were big and how great it was that Dad would let us do more things now!

When my brother and I became school age, some of the people thought Mom would be partial to Ron and me so she was asked to resign. A lady, Miss Neal, was hired. As a child, I did not realize the extremely difficult position in which Miss Neal was put. There was no teacherage at that time so Miss Neal had to board with various families. Jerry and Virginia Fine had no children and had an extra bedroom. They lived over a mile up Calf Creek, which was a small canyon across Chesnimnus from the school. When Miss Neal's work was done, which in the short days of winter would be after dark, she had to wade across Chesnimnus Creek to start her walk home. The creek had ice in it all winter but seldom froze over completely so she couldn't walk across on the ice. She must have been terrified walking up the dark, timbered canyon with all of the sounds of the wild; sounds with which she was unfamiliar. After one year of teaching at Lewis, she was asked to resign. As I look back I wonder if she wouldn't have resigned anyway! I am sure it was a miserable year for her. It certainly was a miserable year for us kids!

There were three of us in the first grade; Ron, our cousin Lyle, and me. The very first day of school I was seated by myself in front of a boy who immediately started pulling my pigtails. Ron and Lyle were seated across the

Miss Neal, Me, and Ron

aisle on a bench. Mom had stayed at school for a while that morning to see how everything went because she and Dad were concerned about how I would do since I was only five. (They wanted Ron and me to be in the same grade so I started early.) After a few minutes of having my pigtails pulled, I started to cry. Mom took me outside and asked me what was wrong. I said, "I want to sit by Ronny." We went back in, the teacher seated me by Ron and everything was okay after that.

We were later assigned to desks, with mine being between Ron's and Lyle's. This was done to keep the boys from talking and playing. The boys thought it was great fun to stick Kleenex to their faces, tear out holes for their eyes and mouths, then make faces back and forth at each other. They would roll their eyes and stick out their tongues. Well, if I looked forward I would see one of them, if I looked back, I would see the other.

I was always one given to laughter and getting the giggles! Once we all got to giggling over those "masks" so Miss Neal stood us up in front of the room and said, "If you want to laugh, then laugh for everyone!" We were so frightened at that point that we couldn't laugh, so she would hit us with a thick yard stick while yelling, "Laugh, I said laugh!"

Miss Neal was of the belief that it was very bad to be left-handed and all measures must be taken to break any child of such a habit! Ron was left-handed so he became her crusade! For a while she kept patiently taking the pencil from his left hand and putting it in his right. Finally she became exasperated and tied his left hand behind his back. As little kids, our interpretation of the situation was that Ron was being disobedient so would really be in trouble if Dad and Mom found out. We kept it a secret for some time before one of us slipped and said something about it. Of course the folks quizzed us to get the whole story, then took action! As already stated, Miss Neal left after her first year at Lewis!

It became apparent that if we were going to get a fine teacher who would stay for several years, she would need to be provided with a better situation. It was decided to build a teacherage, and also a horse barn for the kids who rode horses to school.

My cousins, LeRoy, Loretta, and Dan Davis rode to school each day. They lived out on top, up toward the head of Gooseberry Creek. They rode one especially smart old mare, Flame, who would paw her way across Chesnimnus Creek when it had ice on it. She would paw the ice with one foot until it broke, take a step forward, then paw with the other, stepping forward again when the ice was again broken. She would continue this until she had made it safely across the creek.

LeRoy rode a palomino mare, Snooks, that he was especially proud of. He would impress us little kids by crawling under her belly and between her legs.

Loretta wore long pants under her dresses to help keep her warm. She would slip them off when she got to school. On one occasion when they were headed for home, for some reason Loretta fell off while crossing the creek. The creek crossing was in sight of the school so they came back to the school where Ron was stripped of his clothes and wrapped in a blanket. Loretta then wore his clothes home.

After Miss Neal left, Mrs. Gladys Quinn, the wife of Ed Quinn, came to be our teacher. She and Ed had a ranch on Alder Slope, out in the Wallowa Valley. If the roads were bad, Ed would drive Mrs. Quinn out to Lewis on Sunday evening or early Monday morning. He would come again on Friday afternoon to pick her up. We were so accustomed to saying "Miss Neal" that we called Mrs. Quinn "Miss Quinn." I don't recall her ever correcting us.

Mrs. Gladys Quinn

Mrs. Quinn was a good teacher. She also was a fun teacher. Once while she left the room to go to the rest room, some of us removed the thermometer from its holder and held it next to the stove. We then quickly replaced it just before she returned. We started commenting how overly warm the room was so Mrs. Quinn checked the thermometer. Of course she immediately knew what had happened! She apologized for having let it get so hot, threw open the windows, refused any requests to go to the cloak room to get coats, then let us sit there and freeze! Boy did that one backfire! Another time I remember her chasing Ron around the room with a broom, all in fun. Mrs. Quinn taught at Lewis my second through fourth grades.

Ron and I had never gone trick-or-treating so some of the kids from up at the Daggett Logging Camp invited us up, to go around the logging camp. The older kids set the scene by telling us lots

*In back: Ron, Lyle, Barbara Maxwell, Mrs. Quinn—Middle: Me and Donna Mae—
In front: Loretta Davis, Doretta Huffman, Marjorie and Marie Crisp*

of spook stories as we waited for it to get dark enough to set out.

We stayed in a group and went to every cabin in the upper camp. We felt pretty smug about all the loot we had collected as we headed back down the road to the lower end of the camp where our friends lived. At one place along the road there was a swamp with cattails about ten feet below the road. It was a dark night with just a little starlight so it was difficult to even see the potholes and rocks on the road. Just as we were right by this swamp, we heard the most horrible noise behind us. We looked back to see a "ghost" floating about three feet above the road, and coming right at us! We screamed and started running. I was along the edge of the road next to the swamp. As I turned to look at the ghost, I ran off the side of the road and rolled down toward the swamp. The rest of the kids didn't even realize I was missing and just kept running for home. I waited a little while, listened, then crawled up the bank. I peeked around and seeing nothing of the ghost, I high-tailed it for the cabin too!

Later we learned of the fun one of the loggers had had scaring us. He was wearing black pants and had draped a sheet over his head, thus giving the elusion of a ghost floating above the road!

Along with the place on Joseph Creek, Dad had 800 acres over in Peavine. The easiest way to get to it was to go up Chesnimnus to the Daggett Logging camp and turn up the draw by the Hinton Place. The road went up a canyon to the Foster Place (what now is called Poverty Flats). It then followed a logging road that went along the benches to our place.

Dad pulling a combine similar to the one used in Peavine

Some years Dad hayed it and some years he raised grain. No matter what the crop was, it was a battle to keep the elk out of it. When Dad raised grain, he would have Uncle Ray Thompson (Dad's sister's husband), come out and help harvest it. We used an old combine that had to be pulled by a cat. Dad would drive the cat and Uncle Ray would be on the combine. There was no holding tank for the grain so as it was threshed out of the heads, the grain would come out a spout. Uncle Ray would hang a sack under the spout to catch the grain. As that sack was filling, he would be sewing up the previously filled sack. He would stack those filled sacks on a platform until he had about six of them, then he would release a lever and the filled sacks would slide off the platform, down a chute and onto the ground. We kids would ride that dirty old combine all day just so we could ride those sacks down the chute! At the end of the day, all of the sacks of grain had to be picked up or the elk would come in at night and paw them until they ripped open. They would then eat the grain.

The years that we cut hay up there, we had to immediately pick up the bales or the elk would bust them open too. We had an old truck that did not have brakes. We used it to haul the grain and hay. Dad took the doors off of it so in case the truck got to going too fast and we had to jump, there would be nothing for us to get hung up on!

There were a couple of the old style wooden boxcars not far from our Peavine land that we camped in when we were up there haying or combining. They were mouse and rat infested and even had holes in the floors and doors where the porcupines had chewed their way in, but they did provide a roof over our heads in case of a shower. To us kids it was great fun and quite an adventure!

When I was about nine years old, my Uncle Roy who lived up on top at the head of Gooseberry, where Dad and his mom had lived when Dad met Mom, had a heart attack. While he was in the hospital a minister from a little church in Joseph visited him. As a result, Uncle Roy and his family started attending church. They were so excited about their newfound knowledge of who and what God is, and God's love for them that they came down and invited us to go to church with them. It was late on a Sunday afternoon and there was no way we could get ready for the evening service, but Dad and Mom promised to go the next Sunday.

The folks kept that promise and that was the beginning of my knowledge of and love for God! I can still remember the night when, as a little girl I knelt by my bed and asked Jesus into my heart!

Living so far out, it took us quite a while to drive in to church, and we always allowed some extra time in case of a flat tire or some other problem. We usually didn't have problems so arrived at church early—usually the first ones there!

The church had many gatherings, picnics, and potlucks. I remember one Easter egg hunt in particular. Each family was asked to bring a dozen cooked, colored eggs.

We were in the car when Mom remembered the eggs. She sent Ron back into the house to get them. After church there was an Easter egg hunt on the church lawn. As we kids started finding the eggs and putting them in our baskets, some of which hadn't been colored, Mom made a comment about people being too lazy to even dye the eggs they had brought. Later one of the undyed eggs broke—it was raw; hadn't even been cooked! What a low down trick to play at a church Easter egg hunt!

The next morning Mom grabbed a carton of eggs from the refrigerator to make fried eggs for our breakfast. There were our Easter eggs! Those undyed, raw eggs at the egg hunt were ours! Ron had grabbed the wrong carton! Talk about embarrassed—Mom really "had egg on her face!"

We always had our own Easter egg hunts. Ron and I would hide them from each other or we would get together with Donna and Lyle. We would carry a saltshaker with us so when some of the eggshells became too broken to keep hiding we would sit and eat them. We hid the eggs time after time over the course of a couple of weeks, without them ever being refrigerated, and we ate every one of them. (When we were sick of them, our moms would use them in salads or make deviled eggs!) We never once got sick from them!

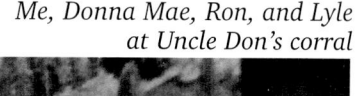

Me, Donna Mae, Ron, and Lyle at Uncle Don's corral

Mom again started teaching. She taught my fifth through eighth grades. There were kids from the Daggett Logging Camp and lots of "Davis cousins!" I am sure Mom felt a lot of pressure, knowing the previous apprehension some of the Davises had had about her teaching her own kids.

Long before Mom had become our teacher, she and Dad had told Ron and me that if we ever got a spanking at school we would get one twice as hard when we got home. One day Aunt Mary visited school at a time when we were having music class. For music we kids would sit on benches and chairs in a semicircle beside the piano. Mom would play the piano and lead the singing. On this particular day Ron happened to be sitting by me. My chair was a couple of inches higher than his chair so he just cocked his leg up on my chair, and I, of course pushed it off. I swear that was all that happened, but Mom saw it. When class was over Aunt Mary left and the rest of the students were dismissed for recess, but Ron and I were told to stay in. Mom then proceeded to tell us that people would think there was no way she could control a school full of students if she couldn't even control her own kids. She then gave us a good hard whipping. I remember being totally shocked at her reaction to the incident, but of course knew better than to try to plead our case. As the sting of the whipping subsided, the fear of facing Dad mounted.

When we got home that evening, we changed our clothes and got right in and did our chores. We then went up into the hayloft waiting our summons. Dad got in from work and still we weren't called. After what seemed like an eternity, Dad stepped out the back door and called, "Supper." We slowly and solemnly trudged to the house, washed up, and silently took our places at the table. Mom and Dad carried on their usual conversation, but I don't remember us kids having much to say. Supper ended and, as was the custom, we kids did the dishes. Still nothing! The evening was spent reading until it was time for bed. Still nothing. We went to bed figuring Mom would tell Dad after we went to bed. We anticipated the "ax to fall" at breakfast the next morning. Still nothing! As the days passed the worry moved a little more to the backs of our minds, but there was always that questioning fear of, "When's it going to happen?"

I guess Mom knew enough psychology to know the dread of getting the punishment was far worse than just getting it over with! She never told Dad for six weeks and then he said, "It has been too long for me to do anything about it now! Besides, when I told you about the whipping at home, I didn't know your mom would be your teacher!"

Having read *Tom Sawyer* and *Huckleberry Finn* at school, Ron and I decided to build a raft. There was a good swimming hole under the

Chesnimnus Bridge where we played a lot. Not knowing what we were doing we selected logs that weren't completely dry. After days of labor we had Dad drag it up to the swimming hole with the pickup and help us put it in the river. That was when we discovered that it would barely float! This flaw in the design actually turned out to make the raft even more fun than it would have been if it had floated really good. We discovered that if we both got on one side, that side would sink, causing the raft to stand almost straight up and down. Then just before it toppled over on us we would scramble up it to the high side, which would then crash down to the water surface. This side would then begin to sink and the fun would start all over!

One fall was especially warm. In fact it was so warm that we would take our swimming suits to school and have Mom drop us off at the bridge on our way home from school so we could swim. One night was especially warm and there was a full moon. Donna and Lyle were staying with us that night so we all stopped for a swim. After it was dark and the moon was quite high, Dad came looking for us to see why we hadn't come home!

The Chesnimnus Bridge was made with pilings going down into the river bed. There were stringers over those pilings that extended out beyond each side of the bridge. To keep cattle from passing under the bridge, the fence had been extended out and attached to the pilings in the river.

There was a slough close to the bridge and there were loads of cattails growing in it. In the autumn the cattails got really ripe. They would burst into, literally, millions of little "fuzzies" if hit against something.

One day Donna, Lyle, Ron and I were playing at the bridge and having a lot of fun with the ripe cattails when we heard a car coming. We all climbed over the edge of the bridge, each crouching on one of the four stringers that stuck out from under the bridge. It was a warm day so the folks in the car had the windows down. As they drove across the bridge we pelted them with the cattails. The car was instantly filled with a cloud of fuzz and we realized, too late, that our practical joke had gone too far and we were probably in a lot of trouble! The driver screeched to a stop, jumped out and started shouting at us! Of course, the instant we saw the mess we had caused, we were out of there, each of us finding his own way down off that bridge and up under it. This was a prime example of what a person can do when the adrenaline is pumping. I dropped down to the wire fence then tight-wire walked about six or eight feet on the top wire of the fence over to the bank where I crawled in a hole up against the bottom of the bridge. I had never before, and have never since, been able to tight wire walk!

The man stood up on the bridge, screaming at us and throwing large rocks over the side and down into the creek. After some time, he drove up the road just a little ways and started shooting a gun. We were certain that he was trying to kill us so we stayed under the bridge for a long time after we heard the car drive away. We thought that maybe he had stayed behind and was just waiting for us to come out so he could get us!

When we finally had the courage to crawl out, we high tailed it for home and told the folks the whole story. Dad asked us what the car looked like and when we told him, he burst into laughter. With there

Mom, Me, Ron and Darlene Bennet

being so little traffic down there, everyone took notice of any car that went by and Dad had done just that when our "future victim" had gone by our place earlier that day. Dad knew who it was! It was a car dealer from Enterprise who was just as big a practical joker as we kids were! He was having just as much fun scaring us kids as we thought we were going to have by pelting his car with the cattails! We didn't get into too much trouble, but the folks told us to never do that again because of the terrible mess it must have made—and we never did!

Mom planned a field trip each spring for the end of the school year. We put together a picnic and mothers helped drive all of us to Cove for a fun day of swimming in the hot spring pool. All of the little pre-school brothers and sisters went with us so we had quite a party! Cove is a small town in the Grande Ronde Valley. It is approximately one hundred miles from the Lewis School so it truly was an all day trip! Even after the number of students diminished the last few years that I went to Lewis, Mom still continued those trips to Cove. She knew how few special things we got to do!

As my older cousins became high school age, they were moved to town and the younger siblings went with them. The logging camp "dried up" and our numbers at school dropped drastically. There were no longer enough students to put on school programs so school settled into the hum drum of pure academics!

We couldn't afford to buy pop so we would make our own root beer. Ron and I had gathered bottles and had bought our own bottle capper. Mom would buy a little bottle of root beer extract that had the directions of how to make it. After making it we had to lay the bottles on their sides in a place that was warm and draft free. After about two weeks it was ready to drink. As it aged it got more and more fizz to it. In fact it would finally get to where when we opened a bottle, about half of it would spew out!

When I was in the seventh or eighth grade, I had my first crush. He, Raymond Reel of Wallowa, was a few years older than me. We had met through the youth group at church. He was tall, dark, and handsome, and very shy! My folks liked him very much and trusted him completely. He also was a friend of my brother so he would come to Joseph Creek to see us and the three of us had a lot of fun!

On one of his visits we told him about our "strong" root beer. We complained to him about the fact that every time we opened a bottle, half of it would be wasted! He assured us that he knew how to remedy that! He said all you had to do was open the bottle and VERY quickly put it in your mouth. He proceeded to show us how it was done, but it didn't go as he had planned! When he put that bottle in his mouth, I swear he had root beer coming out his eyes, ears, nose, and mouth! He started gasping for air and coughing! When he got past the worst of it, we all had a good laugh.

Most of our place at the head of Joseph Creek was not nearly so steep as the country on down the canyon but the hill over across the creek, on the west side of the canyon, was steep. This hillside had several draws coming down the face of it. Each of those draws had norths that had dense timber and brush.

One fall we were missing some cows so Dad went to the top on the west side looking for them. He rode his horse, Nibs, who was not sharp shod, which is having shoes with sharp prongs on the bottom to give traction. It was late enough in the year that the hillsides were frozen and the norths were frosty even during the warmest part of the day.

Dad was coming off the hillside by way of a trail that followed the crest of one of those frozen draws. It was so slick that Dad had gotten off and was leading Nibs, for his own safety and also to make it easier for the horse. Nibs lost his footing and slid into the draw. A mass of small trees and thick brush finally stopped him. When Dad got down to him, Nibs was still down and so tangled that he couldn't get on his feet. The only way Dad could get him untangled was to get the saddle off by cutting some straps. He got Nibs on his feet and started leading him out of the north when Nibs again lost his footing. He slid into the draw again but this time it was a large tree that stopped his skid with his back taking the full force of the impact. With the saddle being gone there was nothing to protect his spinal column. He immediately seemed to have lost use of his hind legs. Dad tried in vain to get him to his feet. Hoping that he was just stunned, Dad left him and walked home, planning to go back the first thing the next morning to get him.

When we got home from school that next day Dad met us at the car. He didn't say a word; he just broke down and started sobbing. We immediately knew what he had found! With his front feet and legs, Nibs had pulled himself on down the draw a ways. He still had no use of his hind legs. It was very evident that his back was broken. Dad had to put him down. That was the second time I ever saw my dad cry!

Ron was always looking for a way to make a quick buck so one time Dad told him he could earn ten dollars if he could suck a raw egg and keep it down. Ron asked if he could break it into a bowl and spoon it out. Dad said, "Sure, do it anyway you want to but you have to keep it down!" Ron broke the egg into a bowl and got a big serving spoon full of the egg white. He wasn't sure how it would taste so he thought he would just sip a little of it out of the spoon before he tried the whole spoonful. Well you know how egg white "hangs together!" He didn't get just a little of the white but instead the whole spoonful slipped out of that spoon and down his throat before he knew what had happened! Then the egg white came back up just as quickly as it had gone down but with it came ALL of his lunch he had just eaten. It went all over the table and everything that was on it! Dad roared with laughter but Mom was totally disgusted. She was even more unhappy with Dad for goading Ron into it than she was with Ron for the mess he had made. She just walked out the door as she said, "Clean it up, and you had better do a real good job of it!"

Back then a dollar was really worth a dollar! You could get a hamburger with fries for $.35-.40—a dozen maple bars for $.55-.60—and mail a letter for $.023-.03.

Wool was at that time worth a lot more, in comparison, than it is presently so when one of our ewes died, Dad said we had to "pick" her (pull the wool off). When a sheep dies, if you let it lay a few days its body will release the wool and you can pull it off as easily as you can pluck the feathers from a well scalded chicken! Because this ewe had been sick, we had her in the barn, so that is where she died. It was the middle of the summer and quite warm. We let her lay for a few days then something else kept us busy so we didn't get to the "pickin" job for a few more days! When we did go to pick her she was starting to get "ripe" so we found an excuse to put it off for even a few more days. Of course each day we put it off the problem only worsened!

Finally Dad said, "Today is the day!" When we entered the barn we knew it was not going to be fun! We put the wool sack outside the barn, and opened the doors to get some airflow. Then we went to work. We took a deep breath of fresh air outside the barn, filling our lungs to an absolute maximum. Next we ran in, grabbed handfuls of wool and dashed out of the barn, gasping for air! After stuffing the wool into the sack we took another deep breath and started the process all over again!

As we proceeded with the project, things only became worse! The more of the body that was exposed the worse the ordor became! The sight of that carcass—it was totally digusting! It was a purplish color and covered with a layer of greenish slime! What POOR kids wouldn't do for a buck or two!

Our grade school years ticked away and before we knew it, it was time to go to high school. This required many changes and things were never the same!

Farm Animals and Pets

Farm animals were not only a source of income but often a friend and playmate. With the lack of close neighbors, playmates, TV, phone, etc., these pets became very important to Ron and me. Not only did we have many litters of puppies and kittens, but also bummer calves, lambs, and piglets. All pets were kept in the house until they got too big and/or too messy!

One of our first house pets was a little piglet named Pork Chops. He was born during the cold of winter so of course he came to be a house pet. He loved to get under the heater stove in the front room. He would stay there until he could stand it no longer, at which time he would scramble out, squealing for all he was worth. He would then shoot into the bedroom, slide under the bed, and stay there until he was cooled off. Slowly he would mosey back out to the heater stove where the cycle would start all over again!

Grandma Berthe had one little pig that loved to root around our necks, ears, and hair as we lay on the floor. Talk about a tickling, hair tangling experience!

Our second house, which Dad built after the first one burned, was arranged such that there were two bedrooms, mine and Dad and Mom's, off the end of the living room. Ron's bedroom was a small room off the kitchen which was supposed to later be made into a bathroom, which never happened while we lived there!

All the rooms had linoleum on the floors since the lack of electricity made it impossible to keep carpets clean. Each night about an hour before bedtime, we would open the bedroom doors to let them warm up a little before going to bed.

We had a house cat and a bummer lamb, Annie Laurie, who would entertain us each evening with their antics! The cat would go in one bedroom, the lamb into the other. Pretty soon the lamb would come bounding out, at which time the cat would come streaking out of the other room. The cat would grab the lamb around the neck and "steer wrestle" it to the floor. They would then jump up and run back into "their" respective bedrooms. They would repeat this time after time in the course of an evening. Occasionally the lamb would get sidetracked by a bedspread that needed some nibbling. The cat would get impatient, sneak into the "lamb's bedroom" and flush it out, just to throw it to the floor once again!

Ron and Annie Laurie, the lamb who followed us like a dog

Annie Laurie became one of our favorite bummer lambs. As she got older she followed us everywhere and played with us more like a dog than a lamb!

We milked cows, separated the cream, then fed the separated milk to the calves. Ron and I would take this opportunity to have a little "calf riding." When the calves got to hating it so badly that they wouldn't come in for milk, Dad would put a stop to it!

Ron and I started our little flock of sheep when we were probably in about the third or fourth grade. Some of the neighbors, the Bill Poulsons, who lived a few miles up Crow Creek, had a few sheep. Our cousins, Donna and Lyle, from down the creek, got a couple of bummer lambs from them, so then Ron and I begged so persistently that we got one.

The big bands of Snake River sheep would pass through the sheep driveway on down Joseph Creek at the Vacant Forty. They were on their way to the Wallowa Valley and the Wallowa Mountains each spring. Occasionally the herders would have a bummer lamb they would give away. Sometimes an old ewe would stray from the band and be left behind. If someone spotted her before the bears, cougars, or coyotes got

Ronny, Donny, Jackie and Me

her we would have a sheep roundup. This entailed running her down, roping her, and throwing her in the back of the pickup.

One such old ewe was up Sumac. We went through the usual procedure of tiring her out, at which time she holed up in the creek bed next to a steep bank that had a bush growing out of it. I am a firm believer in the saying, "Dumb as a sheep," but this one, at least in this instance, was smart! Dad was trying to rope her, but each time he threw the rope, she ducked her head under the bush. When the rope had fallen to the ground, she would pull her head out, and I swear, look at us with a grin on her face! We did finally manage to catch her!

These sheep, having been run in a large band, were quite wild so we would take them home where we would put them in a small pen and gentle them before turning them out to pasture. They became Ron's and my source of income. The word "allowance" was never spoken in our household!

Me on Dan

The first purchases we made with our "sheep money" were saddles and sleeping bags. Because the sheep were so good to us, it was only right we take good care of them. I can remember hearing the coyotes howling, just across the creek, on moonlit nights. I would get up and run, yelling and screaming, down toward the creek. They would become quiet and run back up into the trees just to come back down as soon as I went back to bed. This would go on all night!

If the sheep were in the field across the creek grazing during the day, we would call them in before dark. We would do this by giving a loud high-pitched "trill" of the tongue. The sheep would come running and jump into the creek. By the time they were across the creek, they were so waterlogged they could hardly walk!

Dan was my first horse. Dan, whom Dad had bought from Lawrence Rowe, was a little sorrel gelding. Dad bought a big black gelding, Roamy, for Ron, from a guy on a ranch up Chesnimnus— the ranch that later became the B&H. Dan babysat many a kid over the years!

By the time I was about in the fifth grade, I could Roman Ride Dan, but only at a walk. I would get him running but the minute he felt me start to stand up, he would slow back to a walk. I never did master using a switch to keep him running while I stood up.

When I was eleven or twelve, I decided I really wanted to get another horse of my own as Dan had died of cancer. I not only wanted a horse, but I wanted to break and train it. Dad bought a two-year-old filly for me, and a three-year-old gelding for Ron. We got them from Bud Birkmaier, who lived on down Joseph Creek, so they had good feet and were used to the steep country.

We tied them in stalls in the barn and led them to water each day to gentle them down and break them to lead. I loved Gypsy and spent a lot of time brushing her and just talking to her. It was a great experience and a feeling of accomplishment to break my own horse. I don't know who learned the most, the horse or me.

It was early spring and still cold enough to be wearing heavy chore coats. One day I was up in the manger brushing Gypsy's head. I turned my back to her to grab a currycomb and quick as a flash, she bit me. She grabbed me by the back right over one shoulder blade and practically lifted me out of that manger. I was totally shocked, then scared, because I had heard horror stories of studs ripping men's throats open. I went dashing off to find Dad. When we took my coat off and examined my back, she had bitten hard enough to break the skin even through that heavy coat!

Tammy and Ming Toy

Dad and Ming Toy

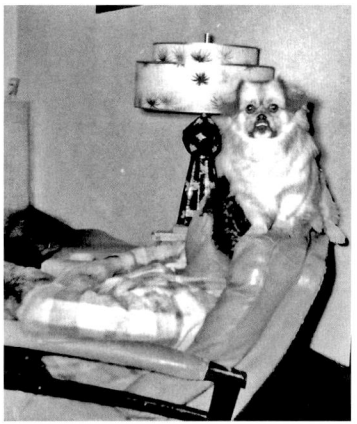

As bad as the bite hurt, what hurt the most were my feelings. How could something I loved so much turn on me? When Dad saw that I wasn't seriously hurt, we went back to the barn. He made me get back up in the manger in front of her. I started brushing her, then she tried to bite me again. Dad was right there and the moment she laid her ears back and started for me, Dad popped her on the nose quite firmly with a stick he had brought along for just that purpose. Gypsy never tried to bite anyone ever again!

All of the dogs we had ever had were stock dogs. Ranchers just didn't have lap dogs, but when we were in the sixth or seventh grade we got a little half Pekinese-half Pomeranian puppy. When we first got him, you could hold him in the palm of your hand. He became a favorite of the whole family! Because all of the other dogs were stock dogs, Ming Toy got to thinking he was a stock dog too. He would go after the cows just as fast as his short little legs would take him. If a cow turned on him, he would do kind of a flip and head back to us even faster than he had gone after the cows!

One summer Dad was finishing up building the fence between the Chesnimnus and Cougar Creek Reserves. We camped up on our land on the back end of Poverty Flats, on the benches along the Peavine Canyon. We had a baby kitten that had to be cared for so we took it along with us. He really adapted to the camping life and actually seemed to enjoy it. He would play around camp all day while we were gone building fence. He was entertained by bugs crawling through the grass or simply a blade of grass dancing in the breeze! He greeted us when we came to camp each night and by the abundance of energy he had each evening, I am sure he probably napped away a good share of each day!

We would spend the evening sitting around the campfire, roasting marshmallows, joking, teasing, and planning the next day's work. On one particular evening, we had let the fire die down to a bed of embers as it was getting close to bedtime. The kitten was still full of energy so was tearing around camp with all of its cute little antics, chasing anything that moved. I guess he must have seen an ember in the fire move because quick as a flash he ran straight into the fire. He ran back out just as quickly but his little feet were burned and his hair all singed! We put ointment on his feet and put him in his bed. Each day we kept food and water by his bed. His playful antics were missed but do you know, before very long he was all healed up and right back at it!

Company

    Our ranch was on a dead end road, so there was not much passing traffic. We found ourselves running to the windows each time we heard a vehicle. Our neighbors did the same, so we had a built-in "community security" long before the establishment of such things in the big cities!

    It was usually a great treat to have company come for an over night stay. I say "usually" because there was one couple who lived up Calf Creek, a draw off Chesnimnus Creek, who didn't always know when to leave. They came quite often to play cards, and we never knew if they intended to stay all night. They probably didn't know either, until the night wore on and it got too late and cold to want to go home, so they simply wouldn't leave. Looking back, I am not sure where everyone slept as we kids would go to bed before the card playing ended and we would get up after the adults were up. I do know it was rumored that at times my dad would say, "Mom let's go to bed so these people can go home!"

    Some company was always truly a delight. My dad's brothers and their families never came often enough. Uncle Vernon and his family were from Emmett, Idaho. He had a milk distribution dairy there. He delivered bottled milk early every morning. They had a nice home and seemed rich to us kids. On one particular visit from them, I stuck my foot up in my dad's lap, while in the presence of Uncle Vernon, and showed Dad that my foot was completely out the side of my shoe. On their way home, Uncle Vernon stopped in Enterprise and bought me a pair of shoes and had them delivered on the next mail run. As a little kid I didn't realize what an embarrassing situation I must have put my dad in.

    Another of Dad's brothers that came was Uncle Claude and his family. They lived at various places on the west side of Oregon and didn't come quite as often as Uncle Vernon's family.

    Dad's oldest brother, Guy, who was almost old enough to be Dad's father, came for family reunions, but I never remember him and his family coming to our house to stay. They lived in S.W. Oregon so it was a long way for them to travel.

    Dad's other brothers, Don and Roy, and his one sister, Vera, lived in the county so we saw them more often. We had family dinners, picnics and camp outs. We usually always went camping over the Fourth of July. Sometimes we camped at what was the end of the road, at that time, up Chesnimnus. It was approximately where the Vigne Campground is now. Other times we camped at Dad's land at the north end of Poverty Flat. Since several families of us had cows to milk morning and night, often we camped on Swamp Creek which was more centrally located. I absolutely loved watermelon and could never get enough of it. The Fourth of July meant the first watermelon of the season!

Mom's only brother had passed away when he was sixteen and her dad passed away after she was out of high school. Her only surviving immediate family was her mom, Grandma Berthe. Grandma was a Womack from Wallowa so Mom had aunts, uncles, and cousins down there. Mom also had some aunts, and cousins on her dad's side, down around the Portland area. Her cousins had kids, most of whom were a little older than Ron and me. Being from the city, they knew nothing about country life. Ron and I felt pretty smug when we could teach them to milk, ride horses, fish, etc. Mom's grandparents, on her dad's side, were German people who had come from the old country. In fact, they had had to flee Germany for political reasons.

Great-Grandpa Mink had a mustache that was terribly scratchy. We always had to kiss him "hello" when he arrived and "goodbye" when he left. I can remember dreading his arrival because of this, then dreading his departure for the same reason!

One of Mom's aunts, Aunt Martha, and her husband, Uncle Bill Larkin, came about every fall for hunting. They brought Great-Grandpa Mink even after Great-Grandma Mink had passed away. Uncle Bill's and Grandpa's pipe smoke would fill our little house!

Great Granddad Mink, Uncle Bill, Dad and "Weiner Dog"

There were no doe hunts at that time because the deer numbers were down. One year Dad and Uncle Bill had been successful in killing a huge buck. They brought it home and hung it from the willow tree in the front yard. Ron saw it and came dashing into the house, screaming, "Sissy, Sissy, come quick, come quick, Daddy finally got one with horns!" Uncle Bill just about collapsed with laughter!

Uncle Bill and Aunt Martha always had two or three "wiener dogs," which Dad detested! One year after another successful hunt, Aunt Martha announced how glad they were to get the meat. They wouldn't have to buy dog food all winter! For some reason, thereafter, Dad just wasn't very successful when hunting for and with Uncle Bill.

Aunt Martha, holding Weiner Dog, and Uncle Bill

...Daddy finally got one with horns!

Uncle Bill and his trophy!

Grandma Berthe

Cabin Grandma was born in—additions to cabin added later

On a cold, frosty morning in February of 1888 in a one-room log cabin on upper Diamond Prairie near Wallowa, my Grandma Berthe was born. She was one of many children born to John William and Martha Jane Thompson Womack, a hard working pioneer family. Martha Jane's father had been a wagon master for wagon trains coming west. When he moved his family west, Martha Jane drove one of the wagons.

There were more than enough girls to help with the household chores, but never enough boys to do the outside work so Grandma became one of the "guys." She had a natural love for the animals and the outdoors, thus she was fine with this arrangement! She became a skilled horseman and farmer. By the time she was a young lady, her mother had passed away. Many of the older siblings had married and/or left home so her dad found himself shorthanded. At this time in Grandma's life she had household responsibilities as well as outdoor work to do.

Grandma Berthe— headed for Pendleton

To become a teacher at that time, all you had to do was pass a test. Grandma

Grandma's homestead on Marr Flat

took and passed the test, much to her dad's objections. He wanted her to stay home to cook, clean, and work for him on the ranch. She taught at Promise, north of Wallowa, boarding with various families. She rode horseback to and from school each day as well as back to Wallowa each weekend so she could help her dad.

On September 15, 1915 there was a picture of Grandma and her horse in the "Wallowa Sun" stating that she was headed to the Pendleton Round Up to compete in the cowgirl events. She never told us about this, and I did not find out about it until I was in the process of writing this book!

Grandma had pioneer blood in her veins and a pioneer spirit in her heart that spurred her into action. After teaching at Promise, she homesteaded on Marr Flat, east of Joseph, between the Imnaha Canyon and Big Sheep Creek. One of her neighbors was a single young man by the name of Max Mink. They met, fell in love and married.

While on Marr Flat, Grandma rode the mail route to Joseph, carrying the mail and small supplies and provisions for the families on her route, using a packhorse when necessary.

Later both Grandma and Grandpa sold their homesteads and moved to Joseph where they lived for many years. Grandpa worked for the railroad. They had two children, Little

Grandma & Grandpa's wedding day

Max and Maxene, my mom, who became Mickey to her friends. Little Max was born a "blue baby" and due to health problems had to drop out of school at an early age. He passed away as a teenager. Grandpa Max passed away after Mom was out of high school.

When Mom was little, she and Little Max, in the evening, would go to pastures outside of Joseph where their milk cows were grazed during the day. The cows were brought to the barnlot behind the house where they were milked. They were kept there until after the morning milking then they were driven back to the pasture.

The day Chief Joseph's bones were buried

In 1927 the Nez Perce Indians moved Old Chief Joseph's bones from where he had been buried down by Lostine, to the foot of Wallowa Lake. Mom said the Indians had the bones wrapped in a small parcel on a travois. As they proceeded through Joseph, the little Joseph kids followed along. Mom ran along barefooted, and Grandma followed with her camera. Grandma took pictures of some of the Indian women sitting around the fire while the men buried Chief Joseph's bones where the monument now stands.

Grandma's place

After high school, Mom went to Normal School, as it was then called, at La Grande, to prepare for teaching. At that time you had to get only two years of training. You would then receive a life certificate. Mom completed this training and taught some before she and Dad met.

As previously stated, after Dad and Mom bought the place we lived on, on Joseph Creek, they also bought

Grandma's log house, previously the Chico Postoffice

the next place down the canyon, the Bill Fine Place. It had a log house, which had been the Chico Post Office. The Chico School was on the other side of the road.

Well, seeing that vacant log house rekindled the pioneer spirit in Grandma and she wouldn't let up until the folks agreed to let her buy the

Chico School House in later years

Grandma

Grandma's root cellar

place. She, like every other small farmer, milked a few cows, separated milk, sold cream, slopped a few hogs, and raised a few bucket calves.

There also was a large chicken house where she kept laying hens. I can remember many times we kids would be in bed with Grandma and not yet asleep. We would hear an owl's hoot getting closer and closer. This would tell us that the nocturnal creatures were starting to move around. It would also remind Grandma that she had not shut the chicken house door for the night. She would get out of bed and go out to shut the door because if she didn't, a skunk, weasel, or coon was sure to make a raid during the night. They all love chicken!

After Grandma moved to town, Dad moved the chicken house up to our place because we just had a little chicken coop.

Out behind Grandma's house was the smoke house. It had a dirt floor with a small fire pit in the center. We made lots of jerky and smoked a lot of hams and bacon in that smoke house. Ron and I used to go and just sit in the smoke house, savoring the wonderful aroma. For smoking, Dad usually used alder as there was lots of it along Joseph Creek.

Behind the back porch of Grandma's house was a large root cellar which was half buried, half above ground. The part of the walls that were above ground were banked up to the eaves with dirt. This was held in place by a shale rock/dirt wall, set at a slope toward the cellar. There were two doors into the cellar—one was very heavy and hard to lift as it was on a slant over the stairs that led down to the other door, which was the actual entrance to the cellar. The cellar was cased, to keep the dirt from caving in. There were shelves on both sides and the back end. The roof of the cellar extended beyond the front of the cellar and the sloping door.

The corner of this roof came within a foot and a half to two feet of the corner of the back porch roof. On days when we felt especially daring, we would jump across the chasm!

Sitting on top the cellar roof was a wonderful place to daydream away a lazy afternoon. From atop this roof we could sit and look up Joseph Creek to our place and watch for the folks to come and get us, on those occasions when they left us with Grandma. On one such occasion they went to the Lewiston Round-Up and came home with a blue tricycle for me and a red wagon for Ron.

It was always a treat to spend the night with Grandma. She slept in a regular double bed which was pushed into one corner of her bedroom. She slept on the outside edge of the bed, putting one of us kids next to the wall and the other in the middle. Looking back now I can't believe she could have gotten very much rest! I never remember her complaining, but I do remember her telling us that if we would lie very still our feet would warm up faster. In the winter all of the beds were icy cold when you first crawled in!

When we were a little bigger and it was too crowded for all three of us in one bed, she put Ron and me in a bedroom on the other side of the living room. We shared a double bed when the feather tick bed wasn't made up.

Grandma's house was made of squared logs for the exterior walls but the interior walls were framed. There was an upstairs above the kitchen and Grandma's bedroom, but just an attic above the front room and that other bedroom.

As Ron and I would lie in the bed, we could hear not only mice scurrying around, but also the thump, thump, thump of pack rats in the attic. We also could hear them crawling up and down in the walls.

There were holes in the walls so it was possible for the mice and rats to get into the main part of the house. We always wondered how many of them came visiting while we were asleep.

Ron decided to demonstrate his ingenuity by devising a way to catch one of those rats, if they really were prowling around our bedroom while we slept! Rats were a common nuisance around the old homesteads so we were raised with a knowledge of how to trap them and what to use for bait!

Ron knew that rats loved dried prunes, so he got a very large fishhook and baited it with a prune. He tied a long fish line to the hook, ran the line up through the foot of the bed, and tied it to his big toe. The whole plan was just to wake him up so he could see the rat!

Well, it worked but not exactly as he had planned! The rat ate the prune, getting the hook caught in its mouth. When it hit the end of that line it went ballistic and Ron went straight in the air, coming down on top of me. Of course we were both hollerin' by then so it wasn't long until Grandma was there to the rescue. She had some big tongs designed to move logs around in the fire. She was quite a sight, jumping around that room trying to catch that rat with those tongs!

Grandma was experienced at trapping and killing pack rats. Grandma's kitchen was small with a very low ceiling. Once she found a rat in her kitchen. She quickly shut the doors, grabbed a broom and started after it. With the ceiling being so low it was impossible to get a good swing at the rat. All she was able to do was to make the rat really mad—to the point that the rat became the aggressor. He jumped from the sink to the table, to the hoosier, and back to the table. When Grandma moved toward him he lunged straight toward her face with his teeth bared! She diverted his attack with her arm and the broom handle. At this time she realized it might be wisest to just let this one go! She opened the outside door and out he ran!

Grandma's house had a front and back porch, both of which were screened in. The back porch was off the kitchen, so was used to store the kitchen firewood and also food. She had a couple of pie cupboards out there. On the front porch were rocking chairs where we would enjoy the cool of a summer evening. It was a long porch so sometimes in the summer when Ron and I were little, Grandma would make up a bed for us at the far end. We slept some wonderful "sleeps" out on that porch with summer breezes dancing across our faces. It was on this porch that I learned to love electric storms. Grandma's house was not in the canyon bottom but up on a bench above the Joseph Creek Road, at a place where the canyon took a sharp turn to the west. This provided for a little more sunshine in the evening and a grand view both up and down Joseph Creek and up into Alford Canyon. We would sit on the porch watching the lightning and listening to the thunder. Grandma said the lightning was God's way of purifying the air, and it sure did always smell fresh after a thunder shower! She explained that the rumble of thunder was the tater wagon in heaven turning over and the taters rolling across the floor of heaven!

Across the canyon from Grandma's was a densely wooded hillside. Again and again Ron and I would hear a boom, boom, boom, becoming faster and faster and faster, louder and louder and louder, until it reached a crescendo, then stopping as suddenly as it had begun! As little kids we were sure it had something to do with Ali Baba and the

Forty Thieves! We were sure the mouth of his cave had to be over there somewhere! Later we realized it was just a ruff grouse beating his wings.

Grandma's barn was about halfway between her house and Sumac Creek. It was a big old barn with a ground-to-roof hayloft in the center, horse stalls on one side, and stanchions for milking on the other side. The milking section was the only part of the barn with a plank floor. The rest was just dirt. The barn was built with beams that were hewn with a broad ax. The beams were put together by drilled holes and driven wooden pegs.

Out in front of the barn was one gigantic pine tree. Dad climbed that tree once to attach the high line of the derrick. When he looked down, he froze—he absolutely could not move. Mom had to go down to Uncle Don's and get him to come up, climb the tree, and talk Dad down. Uncle Don was a large man, but he wasn't a bit afraid of heights. After that, we stacked Grandma's hay in the barn. I can remember her leading the old derrick horse out behind the barn.

She had a team of blacks, a gelding, Bill, and a little mare, Nell. Bill was lazy but Nell would work her heart out. Nell was faster too, so you had to keep after Bill to make him keep up.

Grandma turned them out during the winter to save feeding them. There was lots of bunch grass and they did fine all winter. They came in sight of the house occasionally, but it was not unusual to not see them for lengthy periods of time. One spring there was a terrible infestation of ticks, but since we had not turned any stock out, we were not aware of this. One day Bill came in alone. Grandma immediately knew something was wrong so she went looking for Nell. When Grandma found her, it was too late. The ticks had gotten her! So Bill became the derrick horse. I don't remember what happened to him after that.

Grandma kept her milk cows in a pasture across Sumac Creek until the hay was put up, then she'd move them into the fields. Sumac never ran much water except during spring run-off, so we could walk across on the rocks. In the driest part of the summer, it would sink and rise, producing water holes with completely dry streambed between them.

During spring run-off, Sumac would spread out over a big gravel bar, becoming very wide and shallow right where we crossed to go get the cows. Back then the creeks were full of steelhead each spring. Often we headed to the Sumac Pasture to get the milk cows, and when we started wading the creek there would be fins sticking up out of the water. Grandma would yell, "Kids run to the barn and get the pitchfork!" Then there we would be, one gray haired lady and two little kids, pitching fish out of the creek!

Grandma had a garden over by Sumac. There was a little ditch that brought water to the garden from on up Sumac, but it never was able to provide water during the dry part of the summer.

On a flat, up Sumac from the garden, was where Harris-Pine set up a logging camp. One day Grandma and we kids were just bringing the cows in for milking. As we came off the hill, some of the men grabbed us, pulling us behind a truck just before there was a gigantic explosion. They were moving camp and needed to do something about the outhouse. All of the equipment had already been moved so to fill in the outhouse hole the men would have to shovel it in by hand. It seems some ingenious guy decided the easy thing to do was drop a stick of dynamite in it, so that is what they did! Of course it blew_____ everywhere and left an enormous hole, but that is the way they left it! Needless to say, Grandma wasn't very happy!

As a preschool child my security was Grandma, and I probably loved her more than anything on earth. She was jolly, fun, patient, understanding, and very kind! At the same time she was strong, daring, and exciting!

She would take Ron and me up to the top of a hill behind her house to practice shooting a .22 rifle. She put a big piece of paper on an old pine tree to use as a target. She took us back about thirty-five yards and then got down on her hands and knees so we could rest the gun across her back. As we got better, she moved us farther from the tree and target. I suppose this was the beginning of my love for hunting. When I was too young to carry a gun, I would follow Dad all day when he was hunting.

Once when we were staying with Grandma, Ron stepped on a nail. The puncture worried Grandma so much that she felt she needed to get him to Dad and Mom. Grandma never had a car—she had never learned to drive. Luckily we had taken Ron's wagon with us to Grandma's, so she loaded Ron in it and we started up the road; Grandma pulled the wagon with me traipsing along by her side. It got dark before we got home, so we could clearly see the light in the house, which was a real encouragement to me as a little kid. Just as we got to where our driveway dropped down toward the house from the main road, the house lights went out. I remember being completely terrified! Somehow in my little mind, it seemed that when the light was gone, Dad and Mom were gone too! I started crying and this scared the folks to death, hearing me out there in the dark when I was supposed to be at Grandma's! I can still remember the warm, secure feeling I had when the story had been told, and I was assured Ron would be fine and we were all safely together!

Grandma Berthe

The sight of blood can be a traumatic experience, and to a small child it can be horrifying! They say hindsight is 20-20, and as I look back now, I can't believe that we didn't have some emergency signal system worked out so Grandma could signal us if she needed help, but we didn't. We could see her place from ours, so it would have been easy to put up a flagpole or something of that sort, from which she could have flown an emergency banner.

We didn't make a point of checking in on her every day and days would slip by so quickly! After not seeing her for several days, all of us, Dad, Mom, Ron, and I went down to her place. I can still see the sight of her kitchen with, it seemed, blood everywhere, and Grandma sitting at the table with her head held over what appeared to be a bowl of blood. Actually she had put some water in a bowl and was letting her nose bleed into it. Her nose had been bleeding for a couple of days, yet she had kept milking her cows and doing her chores instead of walking up to our place for help.

Grandma Berthe in yard of our "new house" —barn Dad built in '49 in background

We loaded her into our car and headed for town. Up Crow Creek there were some men and equipment blocking the road. I don't remember if they were a road crew, loggers, or what. After what seemed like a long time, my dad became upset and yelled out the car window, "I have a woman in here bleeding to death. You had better let me through!" We were let through in no time at all! I know Dad never realized how terribly he frightened me by that statement. I was sure Grandma would die! We got her to the hospital where she had to stay for a few days. They cauterized and packed her nose. Later when I started having terrible nosebleeds, at first I was terrified, but learned to deal with them.

Mom, Dad, Ron and Grandma—Christmas at Homan Place in valley

When Ron was four he had to have surgery for a hernia. Doctor Gregory was to do the surgery in the hospital at La Grande. Grandma had a sister, Pearl, who lived at Cove. It was arranged for Pearl's family to come to the hospital and get Grandma and take her to stay at Cove. I remember crying and begging to go with her. I felt so alone and scared when she was gone. Mom later told that one of the nurses, more than once, looked at me, then at them, and said, "This is the one I feel sorry for!" I don't remember that statement, but I do remember a nurse taking me down the hall and getting me a bottle of pop, which was a REAL treat to me!

Aunt Pearl's granddaughter, who was probably twelve to fourteen years old at that time, would come to the hospital, sit on Ron's bed, and read to him for hours. We all thought she was beautiful and an angel!

Grandma used to take us swimming in Joseph Creek. In the summer when the creek was at its lowest, it was hard to find a place deep enough to really swim, but I swear, Grandma could float in six inches of water! She would get to floating on her back and be unable to get her feet down to set up again. She would start giggling and hollerin' for us kids to come and push her feet down so she could sit up! We were sure that if we hadn't been there to rescue her, she would have floated away!

I can remember only one time when Grandma hurt my feelings. I had always been very interested in the livestock and so I was Dad's little shadow. Going with him to feed, I was with the cows and calves every day. I would memorize all the pairs, the cows with their babies. Not only did I know which calves were Dad's and which were Grandma's, but I knew to which cow each calf belonged.

When it came branding time in the spring, we would have all the calves together, Dad's and Grandma's. As each calf was roped and drug to the fire, Dad would ask me if it was his or if it was Grandma's. At one particular branding all was going fine until one big beautiful calf was drug in. Dad asked me the usual question and I told him that it belonged to old "so and so," one of Dad's cows. Grandma became very upset and insisted the calf belonged to one of her old milk cows. It went back and forth, back and forth, several times with Grandma insisting it was hers and each time Dad asking me if I was sure that I knew what calf it was. It was finally settled by turning the calf loose to go find its mom, which was the cow I had said it was! I then slipped away and cried and cried. It absolutely broke my heart to think Grandma would think I would try to steal one of her calves.

Grandma had worked much harder than any woman should have all her life. Coupled with the fact that no one back then realized the harm that could come from an over indulgence of cream, bacon, eggs, and butter, it took a toll on her health. She developed what was then called hardening of the arteries. She had what apparently were several mini strokes. She had to give up all of her outdoor activities. She stayed on in the log house, but we piled her wood on her porches and she ventured out only to go to the outhouse.

Grandma continued to become feebler, so by the time I was probably in the sixth or seventh grade, Dad and Mom bought her a little house in Enterprise and moved her to town. She enjoyed being in town and being able to go to midweek services at church. Even then she continued to weaken until she was confined to a wheelchair.

At this time, the folks bought the place on Joseph Creek from her. They rented the log house out to various people the next few years.

She stayed in the little house in Enterprise until one day she fell in her kitchen and could not get up. She had just put a frying pan, with grease, on a burner of the electric range. It continued to get hotter and hotter until the grease burst in flames! Grandma kept calling out but there was no one close enough to hear her. Finally her neighbor lady, Bonnie Sasser, came out of her house to get in her car, and through Grandma's backdoor window, could see the flames. At this point Grandma had to admit it was no longer safe for her to be alone.

When Ron and I were ready to go to high school, Dad had rented a valley ranch and we had moved onto it. We had room for Grandma so she came to live with us. She and I shared a bedroom, and a bed, and I didn't mind at all! Mom felt bad because she wanted me to be able to have friends over.

Mom also worried about Grandma being alone in the house all day. My dad's only sister, Vera Thompson, and her husband Ray, lived on up Alder Slope a couple of miles from our valley place. Mom paid Aunt Vera to take care of Grandma and have her live with them. I would drive up and see her as often as I could. Grandma stayed with them, interspersed with hospital stays, until she passed away in the hospital.

I remember her last trip to the hospital. As I drove her in, I remember how small and frail she seemed. I remember her saying, "Honey, I know this is it." I was so frightened and hurting that I could say nothing in reply. We visited her everyday on our way home from school and I know she knew how much we loved her, but there still are always those things that a person wishes they would have said. The night before she passed away, I was in to see her and she was asleep. Later I wondered if she wasn't in a coma. The nurses asked me if I wanted them to try to wake her. I said not to bother her; I would come back the next day. I know I was afraid of the truth. I was afraid she might wake and tell me goodbye and I was terrified of that. I wanted to avoid it!

She did pass away that night and I immediately regretted that I had given up the opportunity to tell her one more time how much I loved her.

Dad was working for Uncle Don up on the Dunbar Place on the Lewis Road, out on top from the pink barn on Crow Creek. It was the fall of the year so Mom had to stay in the valley during the week to teach, but she would go out and stay with Dad on the weekends. I got the call that Grandma had passed away. The drive to the hills that morning to tell Mom and Dad seemed a never-ending journey! Grandma was gone!

Grandma was gone but her pioneering spirit lived on in me! As I look at myself, I recognize so many of my characteristics, qualities, and interests are a reflection of Grandma!

Grandma swimming with a friend in an irrigation canal—not Joseph Creek

MOVING TO THE VALLEY

Dad and Mom had the foresight to realize that if you lived in the hills and had children, there would come a time when some changes would be required. There was a country school for grades one through eight but the only high schools were in the valley.

As a kid, when we would go to town and I would see the mountains as we went through the Crow Creek Pass, I never got over the wonder of how beautiful they were. I didn't stop to realize that at some point in my life I wouldn't live in the hills anymore—that I would probably live in the valley and see the mountains every day.

Crow Creek Pass

The folks had started me in first grade at the same time Ron started so that we would both be ready for high school at the same time. Dad had always said that when we kids were ready for high school we would all move to the valley. He said he wasn't going to have us "farmed out!"

When the time came for the big move, Mom cried and cried and said that things would never be the same again! She was right! Ron and I were filled with excitement at all the adventures that lay ahead, and Dad, well I just remember him doing what had to be done.

Dad rented a place on Alder Slope, the Homan Place. The house would not be vacated until late summer but the hay needed cut prior to that so Dad rented a one-room cabin up Hurricane Creek. We lived in it all summer. It was a wonderful summer—it was like camping.

We could hear and see Hurricane Creek just below the cabin and we heard the mill whistle in Joseph. Ron and I had cots out on the porch;

Hurricane Creek Cabin

Dad and Mom slept inside where we also did the cooking. Our only source of water was an irrigation ditch that came out of Hurricane Creek a little way up the canyon. A cable and pulley system was rigged up whereby we could let a bucket down the cable to the ditch below the cabin. The timing had to be perfect to yank on the rope at just the right time, causing the bucket to dip full of water. We would then "hand over hand" it back up the cable to the cabin. The mountain water back then was pure—we never gave a second thought to drinking it! We used an outhouse and we bathed in a galvanized tub. Things weren't that different from being on Joseph Creek!

At the end of the summer we were able to move into the house on the Homan Place. Now that we could move in, we started moving all the household items, the rest of the equipment, Dad's tools, and the small animals, such as cats and chickens. We had left them at Joseph Creek and had gone back and fed them every few days. With it being summer, they were accustomed to foraging for themselves, so did very well.

I was thirteen at this time and had been driving tractors and vehicles at the ranch for years. On one trip of moving things, Grandma Berthe went with us. We had more tractors and vehicles to move to the valley than Dad and Mom could drive so it was decided that I would drive the old pickup and haul some fuel barrels. Ron drove a tractor.

It seemed best for me to take the less traveled route which went up Johnson Canyon, over Elk Mountain, down Beaver Creek to Swamp Creek, then into the valley. Grandma was to ride with me. All was uneventful until we started down Beaver Creek. The pickup had no brakes and I had not shifted down quite low enough. We got to going faster and faster. We went over a small bridge that was higher than the road on each side of it, thus giving us quite a bump. I glanced back through the rear window to see the barrels go airborne, but they settled back in, rather than bounce out! I asked Grandma if she was afraid, to which she replied, "Honey, as long as you're not acting smart, I'm not at all afraid." Grandma was such a sport and she knew I wasn't acting smart. I was working really hard just to keep that pickup on the road!

We made several more trips to move odds and ends. On one of these trips we were able to capture one old hen, which had managed to escape us on previous trips. Mom had the back seat and trunk of the car full of various things so she, Ron and I all had to ride in the front seat. Mom decided the best way to transport the old hen was to put her in a gunny sack and cut a hole just big enough for her head to stick out so she could get air. We then laid her on top of the things in the back seat. Mom decided she needed to stop at the grocery store as we passed through Enterprise. It was a hot summer day so we had the car windows down. Well, that old hen had never been to town before and when she saw all the cars and the commotion, she started cackling! This, of course, attracted the attention of everyone, much to Ron's and my embarrassment! When one little boy

Me, above Grandma Berthe's place

Our Ranch

Looking up Sumac—Grandma Berthe's Place

Dad branding

Dad, Me, Ron branding

Bill Stevens, Dad, Uncle Don on Lady, Mike Stevens in background

MD shouted, "Look Mama, those people have a chicken!" Ron and I dove for the floorboard, vying for the lowest spot!

Mom had gotten a job teaching fourth grade in Joseph so Ron and I enrolled in the Joseph High School. The Homan Place was in the Enterprise school district so Ron and I rode with Mom to school each day.

One day just as we were leaving for school we saw one of our bulls go down with bloat. Dad was gone so Mom and we kids had to take care of him. I don't remember if we ran a hose down his throat or "stuck him" to relieve him of the build up of gasses. We were late to school but Ron and I thought it just another adventure! Mom didn't get fired and the bull lived!

After a couple of years we moved to another valley ranch—the ranch that is presently owned by Dick Boucher. Because it was milder at Joseph Creek, Dad stayed down there to calve out the cows. Mom and we kids had to stay in the valley during the week but then we would go to the ranch on the weekends. Sometimes Ron and I would go to the ranch and stay for the weekend and do the feeding and take care of the calving cows so Dad could take a break and he and Mom could stay in the valley.

The Bud Birkmaier family, from on down Joseph Creek, had school

Moving

aged kids by then and needed to be closer to school so the folks rented them the ranch house. We moved the milk house up from down at Grandma's place. Dad set it up down under the big willow tree where the house that had burned had been. He batched in this cabin during calving season. We also stayed in it during the summer when we were putting up the hay and any time there was ranch work to be done. Brandings were always turned into a social event.

Lyle, Bill Stevens and Dad

Dad went back to farming just the ranch on Joseph Creek. To make it easier to feed the cattle in the winter, where Dad was by himself, he borrowed a team from Melvin Brink.

Along with the work of the ranch were the fun times. Ron bought a boat so we had a lot of fun at the lake water skiing, fishing and just boating. We also took some pack trips into the high mountains. Some were with the church youth group, led by Wayne and Meleese Cook; others were family trips!

Dad with Molly and Polly

Dad kept renting the valley place until Ron and I graduated from high school and went off to college. Dad and Mom then bought a few acres in Joseph and put in a trailer house. Later they built a house on the property.

For a few years we all went back to Joseph Creek for hunting, and Thanksgiving dinner. Mom was right in her prediction that things would never be the same. They never were! The ranch never again was our primary place of residence!

Coming out of high mountains, Me, Mike Stevens and others

Me—water-skiing on Wallowa Lake

SLIPPING AWAY—CAN IT BE?

Years slipped by with the usual happenings of attending high school and college. After two years of college I got married, then finished getting my teaching degree as my husband finished a degree in Agricultural Science. We had a common goal of getting back to Wallowa County, and eventually getting a place of our own.

Upon receiving our degrees we were able to get jobs in the Ontario/Vale, Oregon area. He worked for the Farmers Home Administration and I taught sixth grade in Vale.

We moved our cattle and sheep to the place we had rented—an old feedlot between Ontario and Vale. We hauled in hay and got setup for the winter.

The house we lived in was so old that each time there was a dust storm I had to literally scoop the dust off of the windowsills. It had a full basement with an unfinished cellar room. That room had a dirt floor and there was no door to close it off from the rest of the basement. My washer and dryer were in the basement, not far from the unfinished cellar room. One weekend Dad and Mom were down to see us. My husband, Dad, and Mom had just gone to bed. I went to the basement to throw in a load of clothes. The clothes had been in a pile on the floor. I just scooped them up in my arms and dumped them into the washer. As I started to add the detergent I noticed something on top of the clothes that I had just thrown in the washer. I looked closer and there was a big scorpion flipping his tail over his back! I screamed bloody murder and immediately I heard feet hit the floor above. My dad was down in a matter of seconds to see what was wrong!

In early spring of the next year, my husband got the opportunity to be assistant manager/grain buyer for the farm co-op back home in Enterprise. With our goal being to get back to Wallowa County, of course he jumped at this opportunity. He moved back to Wallowa County and lived with his folks. I had to stay and finish out my year of teaching at Vale. The livestock had to stay with me, to eat up the hay we had bought and hauled in. I had no tractor or pickup to use for feeding so I would stick the pitchfork in a bale and hoist it up onto my back. I would carry it to wherever I wanted to feed then I would scatter it. This system worked great until one day when I stepped on a board with a nail in it! Having been a feedlot, the old manure was quite deep and all kinds of junk was buried in it. Because of the weight of the bale on my back, I couldn't quickly shift my weight to save myself. The nail went through the soul of my boot and into the arch of my foot. I finished feeding then drove myself into the emergency room at the Ontario hospital. The staff cleaned the wound, applied medication, gave me a tetanus shot and sent me home.

I didn't sleep very well that night but intended to go to school the next day. When I dropped my leg over the edge of the bed the next morning, it felt like my leg, from the knee down, would actually explode. I then noticed a reddish-purple line about half an inch wide, running up my leg almost to my knee.

I called school and explained my situation then again drove myself to Ontario where I drove the streets until I found a doctor's office. The doctor was an old man who seemed quite concerned. He cleaned the wound again, pumped me full of antibiotics and fitted a bag type contraption onto my foot, in which I was to keep a boric acid solution. He sent me home instructing me to keep my foot elevated.

My principal and superintendent came out after school the next few days and fed the livestock for me as I stood in the back door and gave instructions.

It was getting on toward spring so the spring work had begun. My husband and his dad had planned to brand calves that next weekend. I called them explaining what had happened and said that I just couldn't drive all the way home even though they wanted me to come and help.

Spring slipped by, the school year ended and I moved back to Wallowa County. My husband had rented a house and a few acres on Alder Slope where we could live and also have our livestock and feed a bunch of bucket calves. This place later became the Alder Slope Nursery.

I was able to get a job teaching third grade, the next fall, in Enterprise. During that school

Kurt

Katrina

year I became pregnant with our son, Kurt, so I resigned from my teaching position. We moved to yet another place in the valley, close to the Enterprise Livestock Auction. Kurt was born the following September and the next September our daughter, Katrina, was born. They spent a lot of time playing in the old buggy or propped up against hay bales while I was cleaning lambing pens, or loading hay to feed.

We moved to yet another place, the old Julius Allison place, now owned by Randy James. Dad's health continued to fail so he sold his cattle and the summer range over in Peavine. My husband and I bought the ranch on Joseph Creek, except for the house and forty acres, which Dad and Mom kept. We retained the rights to the Peavine pasture and had use of the ranch house and the folk's forty acres, so for management purposes, it was as though the place was still all one unit. A dream had come true—once again Joseph Creek was a part of my life!

We bought a place in the hills, in Arkansas Hollow, a tributary of Swamp Creek, and moved out there. We also were partners in High Valley Grazing Association. We ran the Joseph Creek ranch in conjunction with the Arkansas Hollow place for several years.

Upon resigning from teaching I had become a "stay home mom." As the kids got old enough to take with me, I became more and more involved in the ranch work. (My husband was still working at the co-op.) The years we lived out on Arkansas Hollow and then later when we had moved back to the valley, were wonderful years. I was able to be with my kids all day, every day. They became my little buddies and little helpers. When we were in Arkansas Hollow we had no T.V. Sometimes the days would get pretty long so I would load the kids up in a two-wheeled cart hooked onto the John Deere crawler and we would head up the draw. We could go about anywhere without worrying that we would get stuck, even through the snowdrifts!

The kids in a cart

The kids started driving the tractor for me to feed when they were barely big enough to hold the steering wheel to make the tractor go straight.

I soon learned that if I took a few toys, plenty of food and drink, and clothes to keep them comfortable, they would go with me all day. Many times we must have looked like "Sanford and Sons" as we headed down the road with the day's provisions. If we had the pickup or trailer full of

Kurt

Katrina

Katrina under blanket, Kurt

Kurt and Katrina bathing in double sink at Joseph Creek ranch house

Katrina and brown swiss bull

Slipping Away

Arkansas Hollow

Barn in back, house in front

Kurt and Katrina at Arkansas Hollow Place

Katrina sleeping on wagon

Katrina, Tom Birkmaier, Kurt at Birkmaier's on Crow Creek

Katrina (2 years old) and Kurt (3 years old)

horses or cattle, we would put our stuff up over the pickup cab in the "dog catcher." We generally had an ice chest, a water jug, and when the kids were very little, we even took a potty chair! The kids went with me everywhere possible, whether I was fixing fence, salting, or just checking cattle. On the occasions when I needed to ride for cattle I would leave the kids with their grandma or one of my friends who had children about the same age.

The spring the kids finished kindergarten, we sold the place in Arkansas Hollow and bought a place back in the valley and leased land nearby so we could have a "home place" where we could bring the cattle for wintering and calving.

When the kids became school age, I became totally involved in the ranch. I was again able to spend a lot of time on Joseph Creek, which I thoroughly loved. When we had the cattle on the feed grounds, I would have the hay loaded, then would feed just as soon as the kids were home from school to drive for me.

Several years slipped by, then the summer before the kids' fourth grade, my husband lost his job at the co-op. Our financial situation required that one of us be employed so I went back to teaching and he took over the ranching. I still helped with the ranch work on weekends, vacations, and during the summers. As the kids got older they helped with more and more of the ranch work.

The kids soon became more involved in sports and other school activities and our lives became very busy. The years slipped by, then in February of the kids' sophomore year of high school, a long brewing separation came to pass. Property was divided with me keeping the valley place so I could continue with my teaching job and the kids could go to school. He got the cattle and the ranch on Joseph Creek. Again I felt "My Joseph Creek" slipping away—the place of my childhood memories and adult dreams. I was resigned to the fact that I would more than likely never be directly involved with the Joseph Canyon again!

The kids had various jobs to make some spending money and take care of car expenses.

Katrina and Kurt helping move cattle

While working those jobs and participating in school sports and activities, they kept their grades up and were co-salutatorians of their graduating high school class! After graduating from high school, the kids went off to college but came home in the summers to work.

Over the next few years I visited the Joseph Canyon occasionally by riding into the canyon from the North Highway. I would always jump at the chance to be guide for friends who had never been into the canyon. The most common trails I used were the Wilder Trail, the Vawter Trail, and the Joseph Creek Trail, between the Wilder Place and the Vawter Place. With no ownership, there was always an unfilled feeling on those returns, and yet there was also that feeling of "coming home" each time I went back into the canyon!

On one such trip I took Joanne Lathrop, Judy Sanders, and Carolyn Witty. We parked our rig at the Vawter Trail Head, out along the North Highway (Hwy 3), and rode our horses along the brakes to the head of the Wilder Trail and headed down it. I took the lead because I knew the way and also so I would be the first to come upon a snake, in case we ran across one.

The gals had been a little reluctant to go into snake country, but I told them that we might get lucky and not even see one! If it were really hot, the snakes would hole up. If it were really cool, they would go into a hole to keep warm. As luck would have it, the day we went, it was kind of overcast so neither hot nor cold!

We were almost to the bottom on the Wilder Trail and were on some switchbacks. Judy was right behind me at that point. Joanne and Carolyn were on the switchback above us. That snake must have really been sleeping because Judy and I rode right past him, but when the other two gals came

Joanne Lathrop, Judy Sanders and Carolyn Witty

along, he gave a little buzz and shot down the hill! In that steep country they can really go down hill! Carolyn and Joanne yelled, "Snake." Judy looked down just in time to see the snake shoot under her horse's belly. The horse never even knew what had happened! All was well and we never saw any more of the snake, but by now the gals were kind of "jumpy."

We went on to the bottom and crossed the creek. I showed them some of my favorite places down there, then we took the Joseph Creek Trail which zigzagged up the hill, on the east side of the canyon, until it was above the rims overhanging the river below!

We proceeded up the trail without incident until we topped out onto the Vawter field. Where the trail entered the field, the trail was on the brink of a cliff that dropped hundreds of feet to the river below. There was only one tree in the field and it was several hundred feet down the field.

It is funny how fast the mind processes information. As I topped out onto the edge of the field, I immediately saw a large "limb" on the ground along the edge of the trail. I thought, "How did that limb get clear up here from that tree?" At that moment the "limb" started to move. It gave a loud buzz and started toward my horse. I guess my horse didn't see it because he acted like he thought it was under him. He tucked his nose between his knees and started backing. My greatest concern at this point was the fact that he was backing toward the cliff! I pulled his head around so he was backing along the cliff instead of right toward it!

The snake turned and started out into the field where the grass was a little thicker and taller. As he slithered away, he raised his

This is what my horse was backing toward!

head above the grass, and wagged it from side to side as he looked at us. He slithered away a little farther, and again raised his head and wagged it at us again. After doing this several times he disappeared into the field, much to our relief! His body was about as big around as my forearm just below the elbow and his head was about four inches across at the widest place! He was probably close to seven feet long. In all of my years in snake country, I never saw another snake anywhere near his size!

At this point, the gals were wondering why they had ever let me talk them into going into the canyon! We went on down the trail that crossed the field and then down around the hillside toward the barn at the Vawter Place. As we went around this hillside, there was another snake coiled in the trail taking a nap. He felt the jar of our horse's feet on the trail and quickly moved out of the way. I never even told the gals about him until we were out of the canyon!

Vawter Place from West side

We stopped at the Vawter Cabin to eat lunch. There was a big rim just across the creek from the cabin with a deep swimming hole under it. On the cabin side, the creek was shallow with rocks sticking up out of the water. The gals waded out and sat on those rocks and ate lunch. When I asked them what they were doing, they said, "We are watching out for snakes!" When we were through eating, I suggested that we go for a swim but the gals weren't interested in swimming with the snakes!

Wayne and Ival on Vawter cabin porch

Wayne and Ival Clark, who had previously owned the ranch that

Wayne and Ival at Vawter Cabin

Ival and Wayne Clark

Wayne and Ival—Vawter Trail Ridge in back

included this part of the canyon, had moved back to Wallowa County and were always anxious to go back into the canyon. One time we rode into the Vawter Cabin by way of the Vawter Trail then went on down Joseph Creek and back to the top via the Wilder Trail.

They were both in their seventies at that time. They also were riding horses that were not well broken. Ival was riding a five year old that had come off the tracks and Wayne's horse was a big mare he had raised and just had never gotten her ridden as much as she should have been! I look back now and shudder to think of all the things that could have gone wrong!

When we were back out on top, we had to ride along the highway a ways to get back to our rig. A chip truck came along and just as he got to us, he flipped on his jake brake. Ival's horse spun but Ival stayed with her! If she had gone off and hit her head on the highway it could have killed her! I always wished I knew who that "smart" truck driver was!

I busied myself with developing a hog operation to supplement my teaching salary. I no longer had a ranch but did have a sizable ranch debt that had accumulated over my twenty years of marriage. Things were financially very tight and each month my paycheck would be gone immediately upon paying the month's bills. I never even dreamed of being rich, but I sure thought it would be nice to be able to go out occasionally. I can remember having to juggle the budget to take up the slack after spending extra money for special dinners such as Thanksgiving and Christmas. I didn't have people into my home for meals because of the extra expense it incurred.

Then it happened! One day in May I walked into Safeway and saw a man I knew, visiting with a cowboy. As I started to pass, he called me over and introduced me to this cowboy. The cowboy and I struck up a conversation, a conservation which proved to be the beginning of a ten year friendship—a friendship that was cut short only by his death.

This cowboy was Lee Scott. Lee was working on a ranch out on Day Ridge. We had a mutual love of the cowboy life and the ranch life style. Throughout the early summer I visited Lee on the Day Ridge Ranch. We witnessed the arrival of the elk calves in June and I rode with him on the swather during haying. We experienced some real gully-washer cloudbursts and viewed beautiful sunsets. We climbed the lookout tower and drove all the logging roads on the ranch, one which provided a spectacular view of Troy, Oregon, far below, down on the Grande Ronde River.

Lee Scott on Wilder Trail—rims of Table Mountain breaks at top right

Lee on Wilder Trail—The Gap at upper left and Water Canyon at upper right

Upon making a new friend, my burning desire, if he or she rode horses, was to take them into "my canyon," the Joseph Creek Canyon, so of course I had to take Lee. We unloaded on the North Highway then headed down the Wilder Trail to Joseph Creek.

Lee on Wilder Trail by one of the few junipers in that area—Baker Knob at upper right

I was breaking a young mare, Candy, so I decided to put a pack outfit on her and take her along. I wanted to give her some trail experience in the canyon before riding her in that steep country. Candy was young, green, and pretty soft.

We made it down the Wilder Trail without incident. Candy was obviously tiring so we stopped quite often to let her breathe. On the Joseph Creek Trail there was one place between the Wilder Place and the Vawter Place where there were switchbacks to climb above the rims overlooking the river below. Those switchbacks were in a somewhat brushy draw. We had stopped for a breather and as the lead rope tightened when we started on, Candy rather than stepping ahead, balked, reared back, and went off the trail. Fortunately she went into a

Lee by Vawter barn. My saddle horse and pack horse in forground.

patch of thick brush, which broke her fall. Of course in the brush a little thrashing around sounded like a herd of elk coming through. She ended up on her feet but quite tangled. After breaking out some limbs and brush, we were able to lead her back farther into the draw then onto the trail. She was scared and trembling like a leaf, but had learned a very valuable lesson! She never again stepped off a trail!

We proceeded on up Joseph Creek, stopping at the Vawter Cabin. After a leisurely lunch, we climbed back to the North Highway by way of the Vawter Trail. As we stopped often to give the horses a breather, I pointed out various landmarks of that area—Haystack Rock, Table Mountain, Cliff Creek, Rim Creek, and Baker Knob. Of course I had tales to tell and memories to share. Little did I know that within a few weeks, circumstances would be such that once again the canyon would be calling me home!

Earlier that summer, a rancher on Upper Prairie Creek, Grant Schaefer, had called me, asking if I would bale hay for him. He preferred having women run his equipment because he felt women were more likely to shut down at the first indication of a problem. I took the job, and another woman, Jeannie Lathrop, ran another baler. We baled tons of beautiful hay. We witnessed the Canal Fire with its billows of smoke that rose thousands of feet into the once clean mountain air. To the east were billows of smoke from fires

Canal Fire smoke

Wood Lake with snow

Katrina's and my tent

6 Mile Meadow on West Wallowa River—

in the Snake River country, and to the north, smoke from fires out in the timbered canyon country.

We would stop for lunch, sit in the shade of the equipment and generally spend the lunch break talking "ranch talk." During one lunchtime conversation, the talk turned to things pertaining to the Chesnimnus/Joseph Creek country. Jeannie mentioned that the owner of the Monument Ranch was looking for a cow boss.

Knowing that Lee wasn't content with his present job, I told him about the job on the Monument. Lee interviewed and got the job. He had to give notice to his present boss, so it was decided he would report to work on the Monument in a few weeks.

I had previously made plans to work for another rancher, Rod Childers, driving truck for putting up green chop hay, as soon as I finished the baling job. I had worked at this job each summer since my husband's and my separation. This was another source of income to hopefully help me get back on my feet financially!

During those years my daughter, Katrina, ran the scales for weighing the green chop trucks, changed sprinklers for various ranchers, and worked at a little restaurant in Enterprise. My son, Kurt, changed pipes for several ranchers and also worked at Safeway. The kids knew that if they were going to have cars and go to college, they were going to have to work hard too.

To culminate this eventful summer, Katrina and I packed into the high lakes with some friends, the Les Carlsens. In years past, when the kids were younger, and before my separation, we had gone into the

—Mtn trip with Carlsen's when kids were in grade school

mountains every summer. But with all the changes, it just hadn't been feasible for years.

The trip into the mountains was uneventful, arriving at Wood Lake in the middle of the afternoon. We set up a very comfortable camp, as was our custom, and settled in for what we thought would be a very peaceful, relaxing week.

There was another couple camped nearby and we had some very good visits with them. By the time they left, which was a couple of days after we had arrived, we had exchanged addresses and promised to keep in touch.

The first few days were all we had expected. The scenery was spectacular, the food and company great, and the weather very mild. Then the weather took a merciless turn! Probably the best way to relate the events of that mountain trip is to share the letter I wrote to the couple we had met while there at Wood Lake.

By the time we reached home we had experienced a variety of emotions. We were extremely grateful to have not had any injuries but we also were totally emotionally and physically exhausted. Lee was at my place when we reached home and later he told me he was shocked at my appearance of complete exhaustion and defeat!

The mountain trip experience was behind me. Lee was preparing for his new job and I found myself asking, "Am I really going back to 'my canyon'? Can it really be?"

Following is a letter I wrote to Pete and Lydia, the couple we had met while camping at Wood Lake. It related the events of our trip after they left the mountains.

Pete and Lydia,

I was so glad to hear from you and know you made it out okay. Sorry I have been so slow in answering. It seems I just get busier all the time with school and my pigs. I have just one more sow to farrow then I will be finished with that until next spring.

We ended up having quite an adventure getting out of the mountains. After you left the weather got worse. The rain turned to snow! It snowed most of Wednesday and Wednesday night. All we did was drag in wood to keep the fire going.

By the time we had wood enough for an hour or two we would be soaked to the hide so we'd stand around the fire to warm up and dry out. About the time a person was dried out, it was time to drag in more wood! The snow was so deep we didn't even turn the horses loose to eat. We went to bed, exhausted, at about 9:00 Wednesday night. At 11:00 Katrina's and my tent collapsed on us from the weight of the snow. I beat it off, then did not go back to sleep until about 4:30 the next morning because I had to keep beating the snow off the tent every fifteen minutes. Les stayed up until about 4:00 that morning, beating the snow off the cook area tarps. It did stop snowing at about 4:30-5:00 Thursday morning. We didn't even cook breakfast that morning—all we could think about was getting out of there! It didn't snow much while we were breaking camp and packing the horses, so we were thankful for that.

    Katrina and I had taken wool blankets to make our sleeping bags warmer. We wrapped each of the little boys in a blanket and set one on in front of Les and one in front of Nancy. Blake led three packhorses, Katrina led a saddle horse that had gone lame on the way in, and I led my packhorse. It was then logical that I be the one to go first and break trail.

You weren't around me long enough I'm sure, to realize that I really am pretty "gutsy." I really don't scare easily. I was raised on a cattle ranch where we gathered cattle in steep canyon country. I love the canyons, and steep country doesn't bother me, but I must admit I was really scared this time.

My horse couldn't see to get good footing. He fell with me once and my packhorse fell and did a flip, which messed up her pack so badly that we had to stop and repack her. By the time my horse and packhorse had gone over the trail, it was beaten out enough that the rest of the horses could see where the rocks and holes were.

My greatest fear was in the fact that in many places I simply could not see where the trail was supposed to be. I was afraid each time we went around a steep place that it would be the wrong way; that we couldn't go on, and we would have to try to turn around. That can be difficult when you are leading horses!

It became worse the higher we went—the snow was deeper and we got into the fog. This made it bad because I couldn't look in the distance to see the general direction we were supposed to go. At the pass between Wood Lake and Chimney Lake I stepped off my horse and went into the snow to about six inches above my knees. The danger of going down into Chimney Lake was that, even though the trail was wide, that deep snow gave a false concept of where the trail edge was and a horse could step off the trail.

By the time we got down to Chimney Lake the snow wasn't nearly so deep and by Brownie Basin there was just a skiff. I must admit that it was absolutely beautiful! I said to Blake, "How can anything so miserable and treacherous be so beautiful?"

Needless to say, we really thanked God for a safe trip out. I thought later, "What would we have done if I would have broken my leg when my horse fell." I was visiting with Nancy later and she said she had some really strong painkiller she had gotten from her dentist just in case someone did get hurt.

It is a good thing we didn't try to "wait it out" up there because it stormed through Saturday. I'm sure the snow would have been waist deep in the pass by the time the storm was over.

After it was all over, they said, over our local radio, that the storm had given a record precipitation since they had started keeping track back in 1927. Down here in the valley we got almost four inches of rain in four days. We never get nearly that much even in our wet season—April through June. And of course it stormed more in the mountains than it did here in the valley.

It was a trip none of us will ever forget. We are thankful for getting home safe and for having met you people! Really, those were the very best things of the trip! We sure hope to see you again sometime—maybe in the mountains. Like Blake said, we would have to plan pretty hard to hit worse weather! HA HA It is unbelievable that we could have such weather in August, isn't it?

Keep in touch; we'd love to hear from you! I'll pass any news from you on to Les, Nancy, and Blake.

God bless you!
Julie

The Monument Ranch

Before I tell of the many experiences I had on the Monument Ranch, let me tell of how this ranch came to be—the history of its homesteaders and development!

The Monument Ranch was one of those uniquely remote ranches that are characterized as being "on the back side of beyond," at one time being twelve to seventeen creek fordings past the end of the road. Later the creek fordings were eliminated by the building of the High Road, but the house was still at the end of the road!

Not only was the ranch remote in the sense that it was forty miles from the nearest town, Enterprise, population 2000, but also the last nine miles wound down the Joseph Canyon through the rims and along the steep hillsides that continuously pepper the dirt road with rocks, occasionally accompanied by a full-fledged slide.

There was no phone or other source of communication and the nearest ranch house was up the canyon almost six miles. Though there was no TV reception, we did enjoy the luxury of video films, thanks to the diesel-powered generator that also made possible electric lights and later even a microwave.

In most part, things were done the old fashioned way. In the winter, Dick and Rocky, the team of Belgian geldings, were used to feed the cattle. Pack strings were used to scatter salt and fence material on much of the ranch which couldn't be reached by motorized vehicles. All supplies for the Vawter Cow Camp had to be packed in on horses or mules.

There was a substantial variation of altitude, and climate, from the canyon floor to the pastures on top. The elevation of the canyon floor at the lower end of the ranch was 2,480 feet, whereas the pastures on top reached an elevation of 5,240 feet, making a difference of almost 2,800 feet!

In the summer the canyon was hot and full of snakes, but on top one could enjoy cool summer breezes and find snakes only on the breaks. In winter, the top would be blanketed with several feet of snow while the canyon walls at the lower end of the ranch might be basking in their bareness. Quite often though, there was some snow at the ranch house and on the feed grounds.

The ranch boasted of twelve miles of Joseph Canyon beauty, eight miles of which had been designated as a "Wild and Scenic River!"

The ranch as we knew it, ran cattle on 42,000 acres of canyon walls and "on top" rangeland—12,000 acres of this had been classified by the Forest Service as being too rugged for livestock and accessible only by wildlife. Realistically, there was a lot more of the ranch that was so rugged that cattle should never have gotten on it, but all too often some extremely courageous, or stupid, cows would venture onto those places then we would have to go after them!

Back in the time of homesteading, the Joseph canyon was dotted with scattered homesteads. Each had its own unique history and set of memories, which brought character and charm to the ranch they would become.

Most of these homesteaders had a milk cow or two, fed a few pigs, and raised their own beef, but their main source of income was sheep ranching. At that time, the sheep ranchers were unaware that they were paving the way for the canyons becoming cattle country. Sheep could graze on much steeper range than could cattle. Only after the sheep had grazed on the steep canyon walls for years and had "honeycombed" the hillsides with their trails, could the cattle get around on them!

The Monument Ranch was made up of six of these homesteads, each of which was surrounded by public land. The reason for this is that the homesteaders settled only where the canyon widened enough for a few buildings and at least a small field in the canyon bottom or on a nearby bench. Much of the canyon was so

Alvin and Gertie McFetridge's wedding day

Gertie and Alvin with Bernice and Orva

Monument Ranch

Chico flume at Green Place, built by Alvin—1917

narrow and rugged that there was no place for buildings, much less fields, thus it was never homesteaded.

Permits to graze the public land surrounding each homestead were issued thus making the total usable acres far more than just the deeded land.

The Monument Ranch did not burst into existence as quickly and easily as each new day is born with the breaking of the dawn.

The ranch was the fruit of many years of hard work, dedication and sacrifice! The Monument Ranch, as most ranches in the steep canyon country, also originally was a sheep ranch. Its development began back in the early 1900's with the efforts and dreams of Alvin McFetridge.

Alvin homesteaded in the Wallowa Valley on lower Prairie Creek about a mile north of the where the Pratt School later was built. His place was between the Getting Road and the Swamp Creek Road. He received the deed to this land from the U.S. Government in

Chico flume—1917
Alvin's father-in-law, Dave Hearing, Glen Whitmore and Alvin in flume

Alvin mowing hay at the Green Place

Original Townley buildings

House at Townley Place built by Alvin

Buildings at Townley Place, as Bud and Zuah knew them

Townley Place as Bud and Zuah knew it from top of "Shitter" Ridge

1914. In 1915 he sold this 160 acre homestead to Horace Chenoweth and bought a 760 acre ranch on Chesnimnus Creek, the buildings being about a mile or mile and a half up the canyon from the Chesnimnus Bridge.

Realizing the necessity of getting the maximum production from his land, Alvin built a flume to bring water to his largest field. This meant going up Chesnimnus a ways to gain elevation so that there would be enough "fall" to get the water to flow to the field. Not only did this flume have to carry water for the better part of a mile, but it also had to cross Chesnimnus therefore, this meant it had to be built high enough and sturdy enough to not be taken out by high water in the spring.

While living there, Alvin and Gertie's daughters attended the Chico School, down Joseph Creek. Some years later, one of their daughters, Bernice, met a young man, Ed Birkmaier, who worked for the Forest Service. They later were married and were the parents of two sons, Alvin (Bud) and Mack Birkmaier.

In 1918 Alvin bought 160 acres, down Joseph Creek about ten miles, from the man who had homesteaded it—Benjamin M. Townley. Townley had completed the homesteading requirements and received the deed in 1917. Although there were only 160 acres of deeded land, there were grazing rights for public land which surrounded it.

Townley Place as we knew it

In 1928 Alvin sold the Chesnimnus ranch to W.H. Green. The place has since been known as the "Green Place." Alvin and Gertie then moved down to the Townley Place.

Townley had built log buildings when he homesteaded the place. When we were on the ranch, the original log buildings were completely gone and there was a large hayshed at that location. When Alvin bought the place, he built a frame house on down the canyon about a quarter of a mile and

Townley Place as we knew it from top of "Shitter" Ridge

Barn at Townley Place

Mac and Bud Birkmaier at Wilder Place

Stoney Stoneman, Alvin, Gertie, Ella Stoneman, Ted Howerton at Wilder cabin

across the creek from the original buildings. He also had T.K. Edgeman build a frame barn right close to this new house. This same man also built the barn at my Grandma's place up Joseph Creek, and the barn on Cougar Bench. These are the buildings that were there when we were on the ranch.

The Townley Place became the ranch "headquarters", the "home place" for the ranch. The Home Place was at the mouth of Townley Basin and was between the mouth of Cougar Creek and the mouth of Baker Gulch. This was the first of what would eventually become The Monument Ranch! By the time we were on the ranch, at the Home Place were the house, bunkhouse, barn, hayshed, and corrals. When Alvin was running sheep, there were also lambing sheds.

In 1929 Alvin bought the Wilder Place, which was eight miles, by trail, on down Joseph Creek from the Townley Place. Harold Wilder was

Alvin McFetridge and Ed Buchanan at the Wilder Cabin

an English teacher from back East. For some unknown reason he felt he had to get away so he came west and homesteaded, being issued the deed to the land in 1903. It is told that he was an alcoholic, possibly a recovering alcoholic, because he would walk down the middle of the street when he did go to town, so he could stay as far away from the bars as possible. He corresponded with his wife and daughters but seemed to have no desire to go back East to see them.

It is told that once his daughters did come all the way out from back East to see their dad. They sent word into the canyon to their dad that they were up on top and wanted to see him. He sent back word that they knew where he was and if they wanted to see him they could come into the canyon!

His cabin was lined with cardboard and had writing all over it. Alvin told that Mr. Wilder did not cut his fingernails so they got really long. When Mr. Wilder would make bread or biscuits, the dough would get under his nails. He would sit really still and the mice would come and eat the dough out from under his nails!

Mr. Wilder apparently intended to stay on Joseph Creek until his death because he constructed a "funeral pier". It included a huge mound of burnable materials. He requested that his body be burned on this. Windy Burleigh lived on the next place down the canyon, which was about one and a half miles. Windy said, "By G__, I'll burn him if that's what he wants!" but when the time came, the authorities said otherwise. Mr. Wilder was found in his cabin in real bad shape. Some say he was unconscious, and some say it was the result of a snake bite. He was carried out to the top. He never recovered so never went back into the canyon!

Burleigh Cabin

Burleigh Place

Later Jake and Ruth Berland lived on the Burleigh Place. I can remember Ruth telling that she was fine with living there until one day she

Wilder Place from Joseph Canyon View Point on Highway 3

saw a rattlesnake trying to climb the screen door. When Jake came in from work that night, Ruth, in a matter of fact way said, "Jake, you have got to get me out of here!" Then she told him why. From the way she told it, I think they did leave before much longer!

After Mr. Wilder died, Alvin bought the place from Mr. Wilder's widow and daughters, with the exception of one acre which was to be kept as "The Wilder Monument." Because of the irregular shape of the desirable land in the crooked canyon bottom and its benches, homesteads were often not an exact 160 acres. The Wilder Place was 149.14 acres. After Alvin bought the place, he expanded his sheep operation. He sent some of his crew down there to lamb out some of the sheep, take them to pasture on the canyon walls, then later, to pasture on top—to Table Mountain. The Wilder Place had the grazing permit for the Table Mountain area.

There was no cook stove in the cabin at that time because the original Wilder cabin had burned then another one built, so Alvin decided to bring one in for the sheepherders. A stove was purchased. They partially disassembled it then loaded it on a travois type contraption pulled by a big old workhorse. The Wilder Trail, because of the steepness of the terrain, is a series of switchbacks. When pulling the travois it was impossible to go around the hillside, thus they had to go down the bottom of the draw.

The Wilder Place was near the north boundary of the ranch in the canyon bottom, but out on top the ranch went even farther north, taking in Horse Pasture Ridge and the Tamarack Canyon over next to Broady.

The Wilder Place was below what we called "The Gap," which was a gap in the rims along the breaks of Table Mountain on the east side of Joseph Creek. From the west, the Wilder Place could be seen from the Joseph Canyon View Point on the North Highway, (Highway 3), that goes from Enterprise to Lewiston, Idaho.

After "proving up" on his homestead for several years, Alfred "Swede" Larsen received the deed to his land on Cougar Bench in 1920. The place changed hands a couple of times, then Alvin purchased it in

Monument Ranch

Lee glassing breaks from Wilder Field—Haystack Rock on skyline

Wilder Monument

Horses under cliff at The Gap

Looking down at Joseph Creek through the Gap

Cliff near the Gap

Larsen Place on Cougar Bench

Bunnie Kincaid

1939. After selling his homestead, Swede worked for various ranchers, one being my dad when he was the foreman of the B&H Ranch up Chesnimnus Creek.

The mouth of Cougar Creek is about a mile up Joseph Creek from the Townley Place. Cougar Bench is, by trail/road, a couple of miles up Cougar Creek.

When Swede lived on Cougar Bench there wasn't even a wagon road in to the place. He had to pack all of his supplies in on packhorse. Later a road was punched in which was passable only by 4-wheel drive rigs.

With the Wilder Place being eight miles, by trail, down Joseph Creek from the Townley Place, Alvin's operation was pretty scattered, so of course he jumped at the chance to buy the Larsen Place on Cougar Bench which was closer to home.

Bunnie Place about 1946

Bud Birkmaier is Alvin McFetridge's grandson, who became Alvin's partner, then later the sole owner of the ranch. Bud tells of when he owned the place, he hayed the fields on Cougar Bench and stacked the hay there. When winter came he would take a team and sled up to the bench and leave them there. He would also take as many cattle as he figured it would take to eat up the hay. Each day he would then ride a saddle horse up, harness the team, which had been tied in the barn, pitch a load of loose hay onto the bobsled and feed the cattle. When he had finished, he would take the team around to a spring in a draw and water them. The

Bunnie House from the back

Bunnie House as we knew it

team would then be put back into the barn where they were fed and tied for the night. Bud would then ride his horse home just to do it all over again the next day!

Bud continued to hay the benches. When a better logging road was built he then hauled the hay to the bottom rather than feed it there on the bench.

All that remained of the buildings at the Larsen Place when we were on the ranch, was a heap of rotten logs, poles, and sawed lumber that once had been a big impressive barn, and a one-room shack that used to be Swede's home!

When arriving at the Monument Ranch via the Joseph Creek Road, you first came to "The Vacant Forty" which was between Uncle Don's place and the first piece of deeded land of the Monument Ranch. The Monument Ranch had the permit for the use of The Vacant Forty.

The Vacant Forty was a piece of land in the bottom of the Joseph Canyon which had been set aside from any homesteading. It was to be used as a stock driveway. It was through this driveway that the bands of sheep passed when traveling to and from the Snake River country to the Wallowa Valley and the Wallowa Mountains.

A bridge had been built across Joseph Creek so the sheep could cross in the spring even when there was high water. Bud says this bridge was stout enough to ride a horse across while leading a pack string. The bridge eventually washed out and a much less impressive, make-shift bridge replaced it. When the bands quit passing through, this second bridge washed out and was never replaced.

A guy by the name of Ed Buchannan worked for Alvin. One day he was making fence material there at The Vacant Forty when he had a heart attack and fell over dead.

After passing through The Vacant Forty, the next place you would come to was the Tippett Homestead. William P. Tippett homesteaded this place in 1915. It was made up of 141.5 acres. He apparently had hard times because the place was put up for sale as a Sheriff's Sale in 1925. It was bought by a Berthe Wolff who must have been a real business woman, because the records show that she bought up numerous Sheriff's Sales. She then sold the place to Lee Jacobs in 1940. In 1943 Jacobs sold it to J.W. Rutter. In 1945 Rutter sold it to a Bernice Elaine Huff, a single woman from down around Battle Mountain, Nevada. This lady later became known as "Bunnie" Kincaid. This is the place that had the three-room cabin, in which my dad and mom spent the first winter after they were married.

When Bunnie first came to Joseph Creek she had a guy by the name of Dave with her. He started building her a log house but only got up a few logs before winter set in. They went back to Nevada where Dave died. The next spring she came back with a husband—John Kincaid. They continued to come to Joseph Creek each summer and go back to Nevada each winter. He finished the log house for her and when they went back to Nevada for the winter he died! She came back for the summer and got hooked up with a guy by the name of Joe Shannon. He worked for Alvin and lived in the Cussins' cabin. He fed her a big line of owning lots of land and hundreds of cattle but Bunnie saw through him pretty fast—they were together only that one summer. She sold the place to Alvin in 1948 and went back to Nevada where she eventually died.

Arthur Cussins' Cabin

Root Cellar at Cussins' Place

Bud tells of the first time they ever saw Bunnie. They looked up to see someone coming across the flat on a single-footing Appaloosa stud! Bud said Bunnie spent a lot of time at Alvin's and Gertie's and they came to think a lot of her though she was a pretty tough ol' gal!

One day when I was a small child, I was thrilled when my folks announced that we were going down to "The Bunnie Place!"

As a child, of course my imagination ran wild, and I was sure that I was finally going to see where the Easter Bunny lived! I was terribly disappointed when we arrived and I realized it was just a "people house," a ranch style, one-story log house. It was very impressive when compared to any of the other houses in our area so all of the adults were "oooing" and "ahhhing," but I was inwardly grumbling with disappointment and disgust!

Another mile or so down Joseph Creek from the Bunnie Place is the Cussins Place. It was called the

Cussins Place even though Cussins didn't homestead it. A guy by the name of Martin Dunleary homesteaded it; received the deed from the US Government in 1917, then sold it to Arthur Cussins in 1920. This homestead consisted of 133.58 acres.

Arthur Cussins was living there when Dad and Mom were living in the little cabin on the Tippett Place, later known as "The Bunnie Place." Mom said Mr. Cussins would come up the canyon quite often. As he approached, he would always be singing or whistling very loudly. It seemed that with them being newlyweds and all, he didn't want to arrive unexpectedly.

Uncle Don bought the Cussins Place from Mr. Cussins in 1948. (After Cussins moved out is when Joe Shannon lived in this cabin and worked for Alvin). Uncle Don hayed the place and stored the hay in the barn. When Dad was a young man he was helping stack hay in the barn. They had put in enough hay that it was up to the cross beams. To steady himself, Dad laid his hand on the crossbeam. He thought it felt surprisingly cool. As he looked he discovered that he had laid his hand on a rattlesnake, which had curled up for a nap! Dad livened things up by forking that snake out to the guys below! Pitching hay all day got to be pretty boring so it was a common trick to pitch a snake at whoever was working with you just to see how fast they could move!

In 1952 Uncle Don sold the Cussins Place to Alvin. So now Alvin owned all the private land from Uncle Don's north boundary to the mouth of Baker Gulch, plus Cougar Bench and the Wilder Place.

When we were on the ranch all that remained at the Cussins Place was the little cabin with its roof caved in, and a hole in the hillside that was the opening to the root cellar.

Vawter Place from Joseph Creek Trail

Vawter Place from Vawter Bench—note barn across creek

Vawter Place—shop on right

Shop before it was remodeled into a horse barn

Vawter Cabin with shake roof

Vawter Barn across the creek from cabin

In 1963 Alvin added the sixth and last homestead to his ranch. It was the Vawter Place which was five miles, by trail, down Joseph Creek from the Townley Place. The Vawter Place is at the mouth of Swamp Creek, where it dumps into Joseph Creek.

Buying the Vawter Place proved to be quite a challenge for Alvin before it was all done! Alvin had known Clayton Vawter for some time, as Clayton had worked for Alvin off and on whenever Alvin had a special project that required an extra hand. They seemed to get along fine.

All of this changed one day as Clayton rode up the canyon arriving at Alvin's place about fifty yards behind his dog. Clayton's dog ran straight up to Alvin, "heisted" his leg and peed on Alvin, who kicked at him and threw a few choice words his direction. Maybe Clayton didn't see what the dog had done because when he saw Alvin kick his dog and cuss him, it made him mad so he tried to run over Alvin with his horse. Alvin reached down, picked up a rock and underhand, kind of "lobbed" it at Clayton. It went right past Clayton's head and this really made him mad so he wheeled his horse around and headed back down the canyon. Alvin picked up another rock and threw it at Clayton, hitting him right between the shoulder blades. Alvin said it was the only time in his life he was able to hit anything with a rock! Well, Clayton carried on as if he had been half killed! From that time on, Clayton would have sold to the devil himself before he would sell to Alvin!

Clayton had received the deed to the place from the government in 1920. He sold it to Arnold and Edna Smith in 1952. The Smiths sold it to Clifton and Lillian Ragin in 1953. Then in 1963 Alvin was able to buy it from Ragins. It was not a full 160 acre homestead— it was only 127.25 acres.

Clayton Vawter

Photo permission of Signal Mountain magazome, Vol 2 No 6 Summer 2001

When we were on the ranch, the Vawter Cabin was still used as a cow camp. In the cabin was a set of bunk beds, a little heater stove and a table with benches. There was also an old wood cook stove that was no longer functional.

Vawter Place after remodeling shop and with new roofs

Out in front of the cabin was another log building, which originally was Clayton Vawter's shop. It had since been converted to a floorless horse barn. The walls were made of logs that were flattened on two sides and stood on end rather than being stacked horizontally. Both the cabin and the horse barn had had metal roofs put on them by the time we were on the ranch.

The cabin was tucked in against a steep wooded north hillside so it got no direct sunlight for several months during the winter.

The barn was across Joseph Creek on a flat right across from the mouth of Swamp Creek, where the winter sun heated it and warmed Vawter's livestock. It seems he was more concerned about his livestock than for himself. The barn had not been maintained for years so had become quite dilapidated as we knew it.

With the barn being on the opposite side of the creek from the cabin, it meant crossing the creek several times a day to do chores and take care of the livestock. When it was cold and icy in the winter or when there was high water in the spring, it was particularly unpleasant and dangerous. Even in the heat of summer, a man didn't want to get his boots wet so Mr. Vawter built a bridge. Bud says that it was not just a foot bridge—a person could ride a horse across it.

The Vawter Place was the only private land between the Townley Place and the Wilder Place. Upon purchasing it and its grazing permits, Alvin was able to unite his ranch. He now owned or controlled all the land from The Vacant Forty on the up-river end— the south end of the ranch through the Wilder Place on the down-river end—the north end, twelve miles of rugged, challenging, magnificent Joseph Canyon!

On each of these homesteads the remains of fences that used to enclose small pastures for the milk cows, pigs, and horses could still be found. Also there were abandoned pieces of machinery that had been used to till each "bottom" or bench, now put to rest under a lone pine tree or on the crest of a cliff.

Bud and Bill McCrae packing fence material on Joseph Creek Trail—pack horses were draft horses

Packing salt into Slide Creek —Haystack Rock on skyline

The High Road

The equipment had been disassembled, packed in on horses, then reassembled upon reaching its destination. Each field had had its own set of equipment because it just wasn't practical to disassemble and reassemble it to move it from one bench or field to another. The once tilled fields were later used for grazing.

As Alvin got older, he realized he needed to take in a partner, and who better than his grandson, Bud Birkmaier. Later Bud became the sole owner, as previously mentioned.

Bud married Zuah Botts from out around the Flora area. They moved into the house at the Townley place and Alvin and Gertie moved to town. Alvin and Gertie came back down in the summers and stayed at The Bunnie Place.

Because of the distance, and the condition of the road, when I was a kid we didn't travel down the canyon to Alvin and Gertie's very often. The High Road hadn't been built at that time and to get there you had to ford the creek at least twelve times. At some fording places you could drive into the creek and straight out the other side. At other places, after entering the creek you had to drive up or down the creek bed to a place where you could drive out the other side.

This could be done uneventfully most of the year but during high water each spring it could become extremely dangerous or simply impossible! It wasn't until years later, during the time Bud owned the ranch that the High Road was built. Upon its completion it became necessary to cross the creek only once—right at the Home Place. A bridge was built to make this crossing. The bridge was rebuilt several times, each time a little higher and wider, in hopes it wouldn't wash out again.

Years slipped by with me having no reason to go down the canyon, then Bud and Zuah invited Dad and Mom down for a spring branding. I tagged along, jumping at the chance to get back down into "My Canyon!" The branding was held at the Larsen Place on Cougar Bench.

Through the next span of years, the ranch started changing hands. First Bud took in a partner, then that partner sold his share to yet another guy. Bud eventually sold out completely and the ranch seemed then to go into a perpetual roll of "changes of ownership." During one of these ownerships, in the '70s, the ranch came to be known as "The Monument Ranch" and it has been known as that ever since.

It was rumored that Pearl Ingle, the local realtor who handled all of these changes of ownership had made more money in commissions than the ranch was worth at that time!

In 1977 Wayne and Ival Clark, from Bellevue, Idaho, bought the ranch. My husband and I were running our place at the head of Joseph Creek so we got to know Wayne and Ival. Again I occasionally got to ride in that country. Clarks were unable to sell their ranch back in Bellvue and were unable to keep both ranches so were forced to sell The Monument Ranch and go back to Idaho.

The ranch changed hands a couple more times with George Darnielle finally owning it. His son, Dub, managed it for several years. It was under this ownership that Lee was hired to be the cow boss. Then in 1992 the Hunting Camp Allotment was acquired. This completed the ranch as we knew it when we left it.

Back on the Ranch

There was a period of time between Lee getting the job on the Monument Ranch, and when he was to report for work. The owner, "Dub" Darnielle, had flown him over the place, pointing out "the four corners" and saying, "Well, there it is." Of course, country looks a lot different from the air, so Lee really didn't have much of an idea how it all fit together.

Lee was one of those guys, though, who could remember the land, having once driven or ridden horseback over it! Of course, with my love of that country, I jumped at the chance to be his guide. Dub gave Lee the pickup he would be using on the ranch and told Lee to go figure the place out!

Our first exploration turned into quite an adventure! Of course the first place I took Lee was to the ranch house. We then headed up Cougar Creek to Cougar Bench. I knew that in the past I had driven up Cougar Creek to the top, Red Hill, so we decided to try that too. Well, as so many things in life have a way of changing with time, so had that road. There were some washouts and water bars that didn't used to be there. We made it across the first washout but then knew we were committed to going to the top because there was no way we could cross that washout from the other direction. We slowly climbed toward the top by way of a logging road, and were feeling quite smug. We had gone about three-fourths of the way when we encountered another water bar which really didn't seem much more difficult than previous ones, but upon crossing it, we heard a loud bang and our forward motion stopped! Upon examining the underside of the pickup, Lee knew that that pickup wasn't going to take us any farther!

The only way out was afoot. We had the choice of going back down the canyon to Joseph Creek then up Joseph Creek several miles to the nearest ranch, or we could go on to the top. As we had come down Joseph Creek earlier in the day, we were sure there was no one at home at the next ranch up Joseph Creek.

I knew that the road we were on would come out near the Red Hill Lookout, if we went on to the top. Our hopes were that someone would be at the lookout tower, but this was not a sure thing as the tower was manned only by volunteers. We decided to go to the top.

By the time we reached the top, the Red Hill Road, it was dark. I mean really dark! As we approached the lookout our hopes were completely dashed! The tower was dark! We were wondering just what kind of a predicament we had gotten ourselves into. The nearest help would be a ranch about ten miles away, down on Crow Creek, but it seemed that we had no other choice.

As we were walking on the road, which was about one hundred yards from the tower, Lee swore he saw a quick flash of light at the top of the tower. He let out a yell, which was immediately answered. At that point we were ready to dance a jig right there in the middle of the road. We hurried over to the tower and after identifying ourselves, and explaining why we were hiking around in the dark, the guy at the top invited us up.

Come to find out, the flash of light Lee had seen was the guy lighting a cigarette. I never thought smoking was a very good idea, but I sure was glad that that guy was smoking that night!

The guy was able to radio into Enterprise to a Forest Service person who in turn called my cousin's son, Mike Falk, who was living in a trailer out behind my house. He worked at the Les Schwab store in Enterprise. Mike came out and picked us up. We got home in the wee hours of the morning.

Red Hill Lookout Tower

Lee still had some responsibilities at the job he was leaving on Day Ridge, so had to go back out there the next morning. Mike was always helping me out so he told us that he would take his pickup and he and I would go out and pull the broken down pickup to town when he got off work the next day. I would get things gathered up so we could leave the minute he got off work. I dug out my old logging chains and discovered that there were some hooks missing, so I loaded them up and took them in to the "Grain Growers" where a friend of mine, Dean Garrett, worked. When Dean saw the old chains and the shape they were in he asked, "What in the world are you going to do with these Juls?" (He always called me 'Juls'). I had to fess up to what a predicament I had led Lee into! Dean could see how upset and worried I was and being the good guy he was, he insisted that he go with Mike and me and help get that pickup out! He would take his pickup.

When Dean and Mike got off work, the three of us loaded up in Dean's pickup and headed out. Dean had some better chains so we took them and also a tire to put between a couple of chains to take the "jerk" out of pulling the rig.

I, of course, was the only one who knew where the pickup was, so told them how we needed to go to get into the canyon. We were able to drive on a logging road for a ways down a ridge but when we got to where the road dropped off into the canyon, I told Dean he would need to turn around right there as there was no place to turn around on down in the canyon. Dean had to back the rest of the way. We had to cross a couple of water bars but they weren't very big so we made it fine.

We had just hooked onto the pickup when I looked up and saw a man walking down the road toward us. My heart stopped! With this person silhouetted against a background of sky and trees I couldn't tell who it was. I feared that Dub (Lee's new boss) had gotten wind of our trouble and had come, or sent someone else, to give us H_____! What a relief and surprise it was when I realized that it was Lee! He had gotten away from his other responsibilities sooner than expected.

We were ready to see if our well laid plan was going to work. Mike got into the broken down pickup and Dean got into his. Dean pulled ahead far enough to tighten the chain then accelerated. His pickup spun and the rear end started moving toward to edge of the bank but the broken down pickup didn't budge! Dean said we had better chain up! After the guys got the chains on Dean's pickup Lee and I stood on the rear bumper to add weight and give more traction. Again Dean tightened the chain and slowly he moved ahead with the other pickup following like a well broke horse! We made it over the other water bars without incident and at last were on the Red Hill Road. It was decided that Mike would drive the towed pickup and Lee and I would follow in the rig Lee had driven out.

With it being August, the roads were dusty so the challenge was in Mike being able to see through the dust from Dean's pickup. Dean pulled him until we got to where the Red Hill Grade starts. The broken down pickup's motor would run so there were brakes and power steering.

House when Lee moved in

Barn when Lee moved to the ranch

Filthy dog run at left

It was decided to unhook and let Mike drive it to the bottom of the grade where we again hooked onto it and towed it the rest of the way to town. Boy what a way to start a new job—hopefully things would get better!

The next task was to complete Lee's move to Joseph Creek. He had been in the process of moving while I was in the mountains. When we arrived at the ranch I was totally shocked at the condition of the place, yet once again I had the feeling of "coming home!" I remember turning over and over in my mind the question, "Can it be, can it really be that God is once again going to allow me to be a part of the Joseph Canyon—the Joseph Canyon be a part of me?"

As you know, in the beginning of any job there are a lot of adjustments to be made, and a ranch job is no different, in fact it is even more so! You have to learn the range, the stock, the neighbors, and the boss. And so it was with Lee on the Monument Ranch. It was a very learning and rewarding experience!

When moving Lee onto the ranch, it was quite apparent to both of us that it was to be a real mixture of excitement and hard work. It was late summer so it would be necessary to prioritize projects that needed to be completed immediately, those needing to be completed before the snow fell, and those which could wait until the next spring and summer.

The prior occupants of the house had left the place in complete disarray! The yard was full of discarded items ranging from tin cans to furniture. Doors were missing on the barn as well as some of the wall boards. The corral around the barn was basically gone. There were only a few posts still standing and they were leaning in every direction. There was a dog kennel, using the term loosely, that was sixteen feet square. It was made with steel posts and plywood. The plywood was laid on its side making four foot high walls, I suppose to keep the dogs from seeing out and barking at game all day and night. The dogs the guy had had were hounds, not cow dogs. The dog poop was six to eight inches deep over the entirety of the pen. I literally became sick when seeing this pen; not just from the horrible odor but also from realizing that those poor dogs had had to stay in such a mess. We tore the plywood off, threw it in a pile and burned it then pulled the steel posts. Lastly we used the blade of the cat to push the poop out onto the feedlot where hopefully it would dry and be trampled in by the livestock, thus becoming less aromatic!

Scotch Thistle across the river from house

The next job we tackled was spraying the scotch thistle. They still had enough green in them that we knew spraying would be effective. When approaching the house by the road, you actually go past the house then switch back, cross the bridge over Joseph Creek and arrive at the house and barn.

Across the bridge from the house, where the road made the switchback, was a feedlot. The scotch thistle had literally taken over this feedlot. It looked like a field of sugar cane! The thistle was so large and tall that the stock would not even attempt to enter it. We put the sprayer on the flat bed pickup, then went to the top of the switchback. The plan was that Lee would sit in the dog-catcher so he would be high enough to spray out over the tops of the thistles, which were in places higher than the cab of the pickup. I was to choose a place and just drop off over the bank of the road and drive blindly through until I came out on the switchback below. This was one of the times when fate smiled on us because everything went as planned.

It was not until the thistles had died and we mashed them down, by running over them with the cat, that we realized the feedlot was littered with boulders about two feet in diameter. I had driven between them, not as much as even bumping a single one!

We were busy all fall completing tasks that had to be finished before the snow flew and before the cattle gathering consumed all of our time. Each thing we did was necessary and a part of ranch life, but Lee and I were both itching to get to what we loved most—riding and pushing cattle in whatever direction they needed to go! We realized that not until then would we have the complete fulfillment of knowing we really were "back on the ranch"!

That First Fall

Since Lee had come onto the ranch in late summer, he had not had a chance to learn the summer range. When it came gathering time, the ranch owner headed up the gathering, calling in people he had had ride for him previously. It had rained a lot, making it impossible to get trucks into the corrals on top so the cattle were brought to the bottom to do the weaning. The calves were trucked out and sold; the cows were left to hang around the corrals for several days until they quit most of the bawling. As the boss left with the last load of calves he said, "I'll bring a crew down on Saturday and we'll push the cows down the canyon." Lee's response was, "You're the boss so do what you want but Julie and I and the dogs can do it!" The boss looked at Lee like, "You've got to be kidding," but after a few more persuasive remarks from Lee, he decided to let us try. We knew he was thinking, "Boy, do they have a lot to learn," but the truth was, "Boy, did he have a lot to learn about Lee, me, and Lee's dogs!"

This was the first chance Lee had had to view the cattle gathered together so he could see what the herd looked like! There were a lot of large exotic bred cattle. In that steep country, a smaller cow seemed to be able to get around better. Lee's goal was to have a smaller cow that was a good milker, so each year thereafter, Lee kept culling those larger, exotic cattle and replacing them with black baldies—a cross of hereford and angus.

The ranch did continue to use some Simmental and Limousin bulls but replaced them as they got too big.

Pushing the cattle down the canyon that fall was Lee's first real task not under the boss's supervision. The first half mile was along a road and then through a brushy, timbered bottom. The cattle spread out but with the help of the dogs, we kept them pushed out of the brush. At the far end of the timbered bottom, the trail

Starting down Joseph Creek Trail

Pushing cattle up through rim to High Trail

Dogs working cattle

zigzagged up through a rim, then wound along the hillside above the river. At the place where the cattle had to climb up through the rim to get to the High Trail, there also was a natural fording place to cross Joseph Creek. We were able to get the cattle up through the rim by Lee and some of the dogs blocking the creek crossing, the other dogs and me crowding the cattle so they would meander up the steep climb. Patience, patience, and more patience were needed when driving cattle in the steep country! When you were trailing cattle on a single-file trail, you could work yourself into a real dither if you didn't develop an abundance of patience!

A good dog was worth a dozen cowboys in that steep country. Lee had several good dogs during his stay on the Monument. After that first drive, I knew I had to get a couple of my own if I was going to be of much help. I got a couple of pups and by working them with Lee's old dogs, they trained pretty easily.

Of all the dogs we had, one stands out as superior to all the rest. That was Ol' Mert. She was two years old when Lee went to the

Cattle strung out on Joseph Creek Trail

canyon and she was well on her way to becoming a wonderful dog! She had been given to Lee by Duke Lathrop who said he just couldn't get her to work.

On that very first trip down the canyon, Mert proved herself irreplaceable, as she did every trip thereafter. When there was a fork in the trail, Lee would simply say, "Get ahead Mert." She would drop down under the trail or climb above it and work her way through the rocks and rims. She would be out of sight for most of the way, then suddenly she would pop up on the trail and stop the cattle, causing them to take the other fork. As I said before, a dog can be worth a dozen men! If you had had a dozen cowboys with you, you still couldn't have gotten past the cattle in that steep country to head them off!

As we progressed down the trail, we dropped off a bunch at Cliff Creek, some at Rim Creek, and some at Slide Creek. The cattle would work their way up those side canyons, feeding on the good grass along

the breaks. We had packed salt in on the mules, putting it at strategic places on ridge points, about two thirds of the way to the top.

The goal was to have the cattle not hang along the fence on top or drop back down into the bottom of Joseph Creek. We accomplished this by doing a lot of riding, pushing them up off the bottom and down from the top. We kept a real good scatter on the cattle and they did well!

That first fall we could see it would be wise to do some trail work to make places more accessible in the future, so as we pushed cattle up those side canyons, we took along a pack mule with a chain saw and some pruners. If the trails were cleared up the canyon bottoms, it was quite easy to push cattle up those canyons then grade them out onto the hillsides and ridges.

The fall passed quickly, then instead of keeping the cattle scattered, it was time to start gathering. As it started snowing on top, the cattle would naturally start coming to the bottom. The main gather was quite easy. We would simply ride down Joseph Creek, counting cattle as we went. When we had seen about as many as we could comfortably push up the trail, we would start back toward home. As we moved up the trail there would always be cattle higher up on the hillsides and ridges. Some would see us and start moving along with us on their own. Others needed encouragement. Lee had one little dog, Jackie, who, if you put her on them, would stay with a string of cows for miles. She would follow them along, pressuring them just enough to make them nervous and keep them moving. She would stop and look down on us occasionally as though she was checking to make sure we were doing our part! Most of the time the cattle she would be following would drop into the bottom of the first main canyon they came to. They would then come down it and we'd pick them up on the Joseph Creek Trail.

Of course there were always those old die-hards that would hole up in a pocket here or there with an attitude of, "You come and get me or I'll stay here and die!" Gathering those critters provided some real thrills!

That first fall it had snowed up high and the cattle were moving down, so we did the main gathering in December, finishing up during my Christmas vacation from my teaching job. We knew the count wasn't right so we kept combing the draws and ridges of the side canyons. The north slope of Baker Knob had burned and had been reseeded with lush grass so it was a real drawing card for a few adventuresome, cantankerous old cows that fall and almost every fall thereafter!

The hillsides down there were not at a continuous slope but were very steep, then not so steep, then very steep again. This gave the hillsides a ripple effect which made it impossible to see very far above or below you.

When gathering the north side of Baker Knob, most of the time Lee would have me stay on the Joseph Creek Trail while he dropped down, crossed Joseph Creek, then worked his way up the other side. When he got to the far side of the canyon, I would signal by waving my arms, as to which direction he needed to go to get to the cattle.

Lee on Joker, crossing Joseph Creek on ice

In late fall and winter this procedure was complicated by the north being frozen and slick! The horses we rode each time were chosen by knowing what would be the task of the day. Most of the horses would not go out on the river ice, but one big bay gelding, Ol' Joker, would go anywhere. Lee stuck a rope on many a cow that wouldn't cross the ice, and drug her across with Ol' Joker!

Lee had been told that the cattle were to start calving in February or early March. We went down the canyon on New Years Day to see if we could pick up some more stragglers. Sure enough, we found a few between the Vawter and Wilder Places, but the surprise came when we saw that one cow had a baby only a few days old. We started home with them, planning to drop the cow with the baby whenever he gave out. That little devil made it all the way home that night! I did walk a good share of the way, encouraging him by a tickle on the back ever so often.

Bringing in the baby calf

It was a very dark night—so dark in fact that I simply couldn't see to walk the trail when it went through the dark draws. At such times I would get back on my horse, knowing he could see better in the dark than I could! Bringing the baby in had really slowed us down so it was late when we got in that night, as would happen many times in the years to come.

Another time we were bringing more stragglers in and again there was a calf just a few days old. We had ridden from the Home Place to the Wilder Place and then had gathered The Gap. We pushed the cattle we had found up to Slide Creek, which was between the Vawter Place and the Home Place. With the days being so short, we knew we could never get home before dark so we had planned to stay at the Vawter Cabin. After dropping the cattle at Slide Creek, we rode back down to the cabin.

The next morning we rode up Joseph Creek to pick up the cattle we had left there the night before. Lee and I always paid close attention to herd markers so we would be able to identify a group of cattle when we picked them up later. Herd markers stood out as different—did not blend into the herd—were colored/marked differently from the rest of the herd. Lee and I both remembered what the cow with the baby looked like. Sure enough she was still there the next morning but with no calf! Cows instinctively hide their young calves. They generally act nonchalant unless the dogs get too near the hidden calf, at which time they come running.

Try as we would, we couldn't break that cow's bluff that morning! We figured we were just not getting close enough to the hidden calf to make the cow nervous. After searching for quite some time, to no avail, we remembered that as we had ridden down the trail the day before, there had been a pair of golden eagles soaring above us among the rims at this very location. Golden eagles have been seen packing off fawns and lambs. We finally figured that either that cow was putting up an incredible bluff or she had witnessed the destruction of her baby and knew there was nothing left to protect.

Me sitting on Cliff Creek Rim eating lunch—iced over Joseph Creek seen below

The hillside was strewn with large boulders that had broken loose from the rims above and rolled to a resting place below. There was a gully coming down from the rims. It was almost full of rocks. As a last ditch effort, I decided to ride up along it just in case the cow had actually taken her baby that far to hide it. Sure enough, when I got near the top, there was the calf in amongst the boulders. It never moved a muscle, though it was batting its big soft eyes. When I got off my horse, picked it up, put it on the gully bank, and made it stand, the cow could see I had discovered her hidden treasure. Her bluff was immediately broken and she came running to claim and protect her baby!

Yet another time we were bringing more stragglers up the canyon. We had gotten to a place between Cliff Creek and Bull Canyon. Having been so busy with bringing in the cattle, there had been no time for exploration. We rode only where we had to, to gather. Up until this time there had been no need to ride this particular area so we had no idea of how the cattle accessed and exited those ridges and basins. While trailing our bunch up the Joseph Creek Trail, we spotted half a dozen critters high up in a basin. There was no trail up to them so Lee said he would just work his way up the ridge, through the rims, and start pushing them toward the Home Place and see what happened. He took three dogs, leaving two with me. I was to wait for about an hour then start on toward home, in hopes that his cattle would come down somewhere ahead of me. I hadn't gone far when darkness overtook me.

I couldn't hear Lee, cattle, or dogs so had no idea where he was, therefore I had no option but to just take my bunch in. All the way I was hoping I would get home and find he had beaten me there. No such luck!

When I got within sight of the house, all was dark. I knew if he was there he would have started the generator to have lights in the barn. Upon getting in, I immediately started the generator. The barn lot floodlights came on and there was Wayne and Ival Clark's pickup parked in front of the house. They had come to see us and upon finding the pickup there, and the dogs gone, they knew we were out riding and figured we would get in sooner or later. They didn't know how to start the generator so were sitting in the dark house waiting for us.

I went in and said "Hi" to them, telling them I needed to go take care of the horses. Down deep, my stomach was churning. I was worried about Lee up there on a frozen hillside he had never been on. He had no idea where the trails were or what their condition was—and in complete darkness!

I knew I had to stay busy to keep my mind off of it. I unsaddled my horse and turned him out. I then loaded hay on the pickup and scattered it out in the horse pasture for all of the horses.

Lee had an unbelievable ability to reason the most likely way a trail would serve an area. He also knew how cattle were most likely to traverse a terrain. At times, I swear he thought like a cow!

Lee and Carolyn eating lunch—looking up Bull Canyon

I had the feeding done and my dogs put away for the night and still no Lee! With nothing left outside that needed to be done, I went in to visit with Wayne and Ival. I certainly was glad to have their company to help pass the time. Several times I left the house and walked far enough from the house to leave the sound of the generator in the background. I went over toward the hill that Lee should have been coming off, and strained my ears for any sound of Lee, dogs, or cattle! I wished I could hear his yelling echoing across the canyon in the darkness! I would have at least known he was okay.

Our dogs very seldom barked when working cattle and we really discouraged them from barking when they were chained up for the night, but when my dogs started barking that night, it was music to my ears!

Carolyn Witty and Lee on Bull Canyon Trail—Joseph Creek below

I went flying out of the house toward the barn, and there in the barn floodlights was Lee, his horse, and his dogs.

I helped him put his horse away as he told me of his ride. Really, all had gone well, it just was a long way up to the basin then around and down to home. Later when we re-rode the trail he had come over that night, we were amazed at how bad one place in particular was, where the trail went

First Fall

around a ledge on a rim. Lee just laughed and said he was glad it had been dark so he couldn't see how bad it was that night! Later a friend brought some dynamite and blew that bad spot for us!

Carolyn and Lee looking down Joseph Creek Canyon from Bull Canyon Trail.

ON THE FEED GROUNDS AND CALVING LOTS

In late fall and during the winter, the elk came down into the Townley Basin. Many a morning I was awakened by Lee coming into my room with a cup of hot tea for me, and announcing, "There are elk in the basin, Jul!" After seeing them in the basin that first winter, we put salt up on one rim the next fall to coax them down even lower.

The second winter Lee was on the ranch started out as a cold one. The cattle were on the feed grounds before Christmas.

My daughter, Katrina, was in Australia on a "Work Abroad" program through the FFA so I flew to Australia as soon as school was out for Christmas vacation and didn't come back until the tenth of January.

Just as I left, the weather was really turning cold. It got to thirty below zero and stayed that way for days. Lee was by himself at the ranch and couldn't get anything started. He had hungry cattle and no way to feed them! Through much effort and frustration, he finally got the pickup started. He fed the cattle then headed straight to the valley place and the boss and announced, "If you don't get me a team to feed with, I'm quitting!" Of course it was not like you could go to the store and buy a team! The boss assured Lee that he would do all he could.

They found a team to borrow for the rest of that winter. The next fall, Jack Ryan, who worked at the Lewiston Livestock Auction, found us a team, Dick and Rocky, in Montana. Later Jack also found us the big gray, warmblood saddle horse which we named Jack.

Upon getting the team, Lee went to work putting together a harness, replacing straps that looked too old. He did the very best he could, with what he had.

The first time we used the team, we loaded a feeding and headed up the Joseph Creek Road to a feed ground a couple of miles up the canyon. This feed ground was an abandoned field along a hillside. Because it had not been tilled for years, there were trees growing in it.

I drove along the top of the field and Lee threw the hay off. When I got to the end of the field I had no choice but to swing the team downhill, turn, and go back along the hillside. As soon as the wagon was headed downhill, all the weight of that wagon load of hay came up against the breeching of the harness. A pole strap broke on one horse and a quarter strap on the other. This eliminated any "hold back" the horses had on the wagon so it started to run up on them and they took off!

Lee was in the very back with the load of hay between himself and me. I was on my own, that is except for a lot of hollerin' coming from the back end of that wagon! I had to think fast! I saw a tree off to the left, just in front of the team. I knew I had to keep going down hill until I got past that tree, even if it meant we would really be picking up speed! If we hit that tree it would bust the wagon to pieces, break the tongue out of the wagon, and the horses would be gone!

As soon as we were past that tree I swung the team to the left and slightly up the hill toward a big swale, where everything came to a halt.

The moment the wagon had started down the hill, Lee had started hollering, "Turn up the hill, turn up the hill!" He didn't see the tree so didn't understand why I had not immediately turned. By the time we had come to a stop, he was pretty "hot" and yelled, "By ___ the next time I tell you to turn, turn!" When I explained my reason for waiting to turn, he realized I had done right so he cooled right off. He said his first fear was that I'd jump and just turn the team

Me driving Dick and Rocky—Dog, Doll begging to get on wagon

Lee with team, Dick and Rocky

Janelle Worseck driving team, and Lee

loose. I can honestly say that it never even crossed my mind! Lee used baling twine to tie things together enough for us to get home.

Some years the winter would be so mild that it would almost be time to start calving and yet there would be no snow in the canyon bottom. Nonetheless, the cattle needed to be close to home where we could keep an eye on them. If there was still plenty of grass along Joseph Creek, we would push them on up toward the Cussins Place, the Bunnie Place, and the Vacant Forty.

By that late in the year the grass was quite depleted of nutrients so we put out tubs of protein as a supplement. One time we decided to put some protein tubs on the bench over across Joseph Creek at the Vacant Forty. Years ago there had been a fairly good fording place but the many high waters since, had about destroyed it. It seemed the best thing to do was to use the team and wagon. There was no gradual approach into the river on the side we had to enter but there was a somewhat gradual incline on the other side where we could pull out.

A friend of mine, Janelle Worseck, was visiting and she was game to go along. I was driving the team. Lee and Janelle were sitting on a bale of hay we had thrown on just for that purpose. The protein tubs were near the back of the wagon bed. I had the team step off into the river at the place we had decided was best, then I turned them upstream. I did my best to maneuver the horses and wagon around and between the largest rocks. Even at this, there were some good-sized rocks that couldn't be missed. When a wagon tire would come up against one of those rocks the team could feel the resistance and would lean into the collars even harder. It is natural for horses to want to increase speed as they feel resistance. They seem to know that if they keep up the momentum they are less apt to get stuck.

I was trying to keep that delicate balance of just enough speed to keep us from stalling, and not so fast that it would become unbearably rough. I felt that I was doing reasonably well until I swung the team toward the bank where they would climb out of the river. They saw that it was going to be a tough pull and they knew they needed to pick up speed to make it up that bank, so that was just what they did—they picked up speed!

After a couple of big jolts, Janelle did a belly flop on the bed of the wagon. You have seen cartoons of a frenzied cat with its hair all standing on end, its four legs outstretched as far as possible and its claws extended, trying to grasp something? That was just what Janelle reminded me of! I swear she was trying to set her "claws" in that wagon bed!

Lee was on the back, down on all fours. As a tub would go airborne, he would grab it in mid-air and yank it back toward the middle of the wagon bed. I had my knees braced against the rack on the front of the wagon to give me some leverage so I could pull on the team to try to slow them down. With each bump, the wagon rack was beating my knees to a pulp!

Of course as the horses left the water and started up the dirt incline, they took a lot of water with them, which instantly turned the dirt to slime! Dick and Rocky were never ones to quit! They dug, scrambled, and clawed their way to the top, Dick actually being down on his knees once. When we were on the flat, we stopped to let the horses breathe, and to regain our composure.

I had to commend Janelle on how quiet she had been throughout the whole ordeal! She had not uttered a sound the whole time! She just kept hugging that wagon bed!

Lee was ashen gray and his eyes were as big as saucers. I tell you, they were two of the funniest looking people I have ever seen! I have never wanted to roar with laughter as badly as I did at that moment, but since I had been the driver and was at least somewhat responsible, I was afraid they would both attack me. It was not love I saw in their eyes!

Another winter it had turned really cold—so cold that the creek was freezing from the bottom up. When this happens, ice starts forming around the rocks on the bottom of the creek bed. This takes up space, forcing the flowing water to a higher level. Many times the water would then flow on top of the ice that already was on top of the river. This made some beautiful ice formations!

The cows had not yet started calving so we had them on a flat across the creek from the upper end of the calving lot. We were crossing the creek everyday with the team and wagon so it kept the ice broke out even though it would freeze several inches thick each night.

For some reason, Lee needed to be gone for a couple of days so he just double fed the cows. On the third day we went back to the ranch and proceeded with the usual feeding routine. I was driving the team and when I made them step out on the ice it didn't break under their weight.

Only when they were out far enough that the front tires of the wagon also were on the ice, did it break. The horses fell through and started stomping their way across, breaking more ice with each step. This was when I made a terrible miscalculation. I noticed that the ripples on the up-creek side of the horses had caused some openings in the ice and the ice didn't seem quite so thick. Thinking I would make it easier for the horses, I swung them slightly upstream until we were about two thirds of the way across, then I swung them back downstream toward the fording. This worked fine for a short while, but just as the horses stepped up out of the creek with their front feet, one front wheel pulled in under the unbroken ice on the down river side.

When that wheel pulled up under the ice, it was like running into a brick wall. Of course this panicked the horses and they lunged, trying to break loose from whatever it was that had stopped us.

When they had stepped out of the water onto the bank they had taken water with them and it instantly turned to ice. There they were, their front feet on an icy bank and their hind feet still in the icy river.

When the horses had lunged, been jerked back and lunged again, a tug chain had come loose. The wagon tongue and the eveners were all under water. Lee climbed out over the front of the wagon, stood on the tongue, and held on to the front of the wagon while he squatted down, reached down into the icy water and hooked the tug chain! I still don't know how he did it! Lee was a large man who wasn't very agile.

At this point we were hooked up again but were still stuck. We tried jumping on the ice to break it away from the tire but to no avail! After several tries, Lee told me to walk back to the barn and get Jim Collier who was there working on the cat.

The unbroken ice was almost level with the bed of the wagon and was about six inches thick so I just stepped off onto it and walked back across the creek.

We thought that with the front end loader on the tractor, maybe we could break away enough ice to free the wagon, or if worse came to worse, we would unhitch the horses and have the tractor pull the wagon out backwards.

It had taken me a while to walk back to the barn, help Jim get the tractor started, and get back up to Lee. We got there just as Lee was coming back across the creek with the team and wagon still loaded with hay, and the cows following.

It seems that after I left, Lee had continued to jump on the very edge of the ice over the stuck tire. It finally gave way and enough broke loose to make it possible for the horses to pull the wagon out of the river. He had gone on up into the flat far enough for the cows to see him. He then turned around and headed back with the cows following him as if he were the Pied Piper.

Since it was almost time to start calving anyway, we let the cows into the calving lot and didn't cross the creek any more that winter.

The team was young but had been broke as a feed team in Montana so fell right into the routine. The ranch hay was stored in a long hay shed. We loaded the hay out of the middle, leaving the hay on each side to the level of the wagon bed. That way we could back the wagon down the middle and load hay from each side. Though we had only 4 to 6 inches of leeway on either side, we could back the wagon the full length of the shed.

Meleese and Wayne Cook—New Year's Day, 1992

Mom driving team—Meleese and Wayne Cook

When the wagon bumped up against the hay at the back of the shed, the horses would wait patiently while we loaded. Even though bales would often tumble onto the wagon with a loud bang and a hard jolt, Dick and Rocky never moved a muscle. They just stood there half asleep,

Feed lot with feed bunks

Lee feeding—Wayne and Ival Clark, previous owners of Monument Ranch

Resting before going around and up to Cussins Bench feed lot seen at top of picture

Cattle on Cussins' Bench feed lot

Resting after feeding on Cussins' Bench, then climbing to Joseph Creek High Road

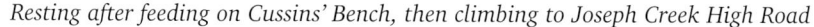

At Bunnie Place—Lee driving, Donna Wilson, and Ray throwing off hay (not seen)

leaning back into the breeching. This developed the bad habit of always wanting to lay back on the breeching when they had to stand, waiting.

The team was great for Lee when he was feeding alone. Rocky was willing to just poke along but Dick was always faster so it was necessary to "stop and go" when throwing the hay off. Lee would "do up" the lines, leaving them with just the right amount of tension. He then could say, "Step" and they would start. After a few steps he would say, "Whoa" and they would stop until again told to step. This was repeated time after time until the feeding was finished.

We scattered the hay in the calving lots as long as we could, but when it got too messy we fed in the bunks along the edge of the lot.

As the calves were born, they, with their mothers, were separated out of the herd and put in another lot. Lee developed a very clever one man system for this. He would put all of the cows in the corral behind the barn. The barn had an alleyway that went clear through it from the corral back out into the calving lot. This alleyway had pens on each side and a gate at each end. Lee would open the gates at each end then stand by the gate at the corral end and let the cows file slowly through the alley and back out into the calving lot. When a cow which had calved, went into the alley with her baby, Lee would pull a rope which was strung through the barn using a series of pulleys and attached to the gate at the far end of the alley. This would close that gate. He would then close the gate at the corral end of the alley, put the mama and her baby in one of the pens, reopen the alley gates and start the procedure all over again. When all the pairs had been sorted off, he would turn the mamas back out into the corral, vaccinate and tag the babies, then put them and their mamas in the lot where the pairs were kept. By using this procedure he was able to work the baby calves and reduce the possibility of getting hurt by a cranky mama.

We always kept big beds of straw in both the calving lot and the "pairs lot." On the weekends we would move the pairs up Joseph Creek to the Cussins Place or one of the other feed grounds. Dick and Rocky were used to feed the cattle on each of those feed grounds so got quite a workout each day.

To cross the bridge, Lee would stop at the bottom of the approach to the bridge. He would get off the wagon, walk up the approach, across the bridge, and open the gate on the other end. He would cluck to the team. They would then, on their own, come across the bridge and proceed on through the gate until he told them, "Whoa." This was a narrow, one way type bridge with no sides on it and was about twelve feet above the river bed. Lee would close the gate then climb back onto the wagon as the horses waited patiently. They would wait until he clucked to them, then they would be on their way!

Whatever the need might be, you could always depend on Lee to rig up a device to serve the purpose. He rigged up an extremely powerful spotlight to use from the pickup to check the cows on the calving lot. It was so bright that by holding it on a cow on the far side of the lot and looking through the binoculars, we could even read the cow's tag number. This gave us a real easy and accurate way to check for calvers.

Lee also had a spotlight that plugged into the accessory plug on the 4-wheeler. We would putt around among the cows, and they got so used to it that they wouldn't even get up.

He made a little slip with low sides of woven wire that we would pull behind the 4-wheeler if a calf needed to be brought in to the barn. The cow could see and smell her baby so would tag along.

Calving time was a busy and stressful time and yet it had its rewards. Having the cattle in on the feedlots gave us a chance to get to really know the cows, which helped us identify them when they were out on the range. We even named quite a few of them. We chose names that correlated with character traits the cows had, or we named them after people they reminded us of!

By the time calving was over we were anxiously awaiting spring turnout!

SPRING TURNOUT

Color photos—page 161

*D*ue to the difficulty of pushing large numbers of cows and their baby calves down the single file trail, several brandings were required each spring.

As weather and grass permitted, cattle were trailed down Joseph Creek, through the rims and draws any time after March 15th. Small bunches were dropped in, and pushed up the major draws along the way. We kept them scattered along the hillsides just up off the bottom from Cliff Creek down to our north boundary, which was about a mile below the Wilder Place. We rode several times a week pushing cattle

The cattle were trailed down the canyon sometime between the middle of March to the first part of April, depending on when the grass was ready. Then they were brought back up out of the canyon usually on Memorial Weekend, as seen below.

Townley Place from Bull Canyon Trail—note the High Road coming around the hillside into the feed lot and the switchback before crossing the bridge

back up the draws and out onto the ridges and points. We carried antibiotics and scour boluses in case we found a sick calf. We would have already salted on those ridges and points with the pack mules.

Lee at Bull Canyon drift fence glassing for critters

In the past the cattle had been taken to the Cliff Creek Flat or the Vawter field, then left to scatter on their own. The first spring that we put cattle down the canyon they went as expected until we tried to push them beyond the Vawter field. It was as though we had hit a brick wall. We worked for hours to get them on around the hill from the field. Once we got them a ways beyond the Vawter field, it was as though they had been conquered so they strung out again.

That spring my daughter, Katrina, helped us push cattle from the Vawter Place to the Wilder Place.

There was one ridge that came down between the Vawter and Wilder Places. The main trail cut across that point and went on to the Wilder Place, but there also was a trail that went right down that point

Lee adjusting salt on Shorty at Vawter Bench

Katrina and Missy on edge of Vawter Bench

Cattle trailing from Vawter Bench to Pole Patch Canyon—rims at left were where Katrina was when Missy was kicked

to the creek. On the hillside just before the point, the trail split with a spur going around above the main trail. By taking that upper trail, I was able to get ahead of the cattle and keep them from going down the point to the creek.

Lee was leading Shorty, a pack mule, with some salt. Shorty was a great little mule who would never kick a person but if a horse got too close behind he would nail it! I had failed to remind Katrina to keep her mare, Missy, back away from him. As they were picking their way through a shale rockslide, she got too close to Shorty and he nailed Missy! Lee and Katrina said it sounded like a gunshot. It caved in her skull in the nasal passage just under her eye. Missy never missed a step! She bled from the nose and also from where the hide was broken on her face.

Spring Turnout

It was a very short distance on to the ridge point. We all stopped there to examine Missy, and it didn't look good! It was decided that Katrina and I would stay there and let Missy rest while Lee took the cattle on to the Wilder Place. Before he got back Missy was wanting to eat!

We came back out of the canyon real slow that night with Katrina walking a good share of the way. On the steep places and the switchbacks we would go just a few steps then stop and rest so as to not get Missy's heart rate up.

Upon taking her to the vet, he said she wasn't damaged

Lee on mule, Katrina leading Missy on Cliff Creek Rim

functionally, but we could have cosmetic surgery done to pull the caved-in bone back out into place. Of course we couldn't afford such a thing so Missy carried her scars to her death. The vet also said that if the blow had been a few inches higher and been in the brain cavity, Missy would have been killed instantly. If that would have happened, we would have lost Katrina too because there would have been nothing to stop them until they hit the creek over a hundred yards below! Again God's protective hand was upon us!

Each spring thereafter, the cattle moved down the canyon easier and easier!

There was no drift fence on the lower end of the ranch so each year some of Duke Lathrop's cattle would drift up onto the Wilder Place. One year we knew there were quite a few of them up with our cattle so Duke agreed to go in with us when we gathered on Memorial Weekend. We trailered out the North Highway and unloaded at the Rimrock Inn. We rode off into the canyon for a ways on a road then dropped off of it onto a trail that went down the bottom of a draw to Joseph Creek.

The plan was that we would ride up Joseph Creek through

Lee, Duke's hired man, and Duke Lathrop near mouth of Peavine, looking up Joseph Creek

Burleigh Place

Joseph Creek Trail between the Burleigh Place and the Wilder Place—a steep, brushy trail

Duke's pasture to pick up any of our cattle that may have wandered down onto his place.

Lee or I had never been down the canyon that far so Duke and his hired man were the guides. It was a good thing that they were because the trail crossed the creek several times and wound along the hillside. In places it was so hidden by brush that if a person did not know where it was you never could have found it.

We found no cattle of ours down on Duke's but there were about twenty pairs of his on the Wilder Place. We helped Duke and his hired man cut them out then they pushed the cattle up the Wilder Trail to the North Highway.

We decided it would be easier to build a drift fence between us than have to ride that country every year. We packed materials in on pack animals and put a fence across the creek at a place where the creek was the only way for cattle to go down country!

Each spring, and often again in the summer, we had to repair, and sometimes almost rebuild, the fence across The Gap. Since this was the only opening in the rims in that area, the elk passed through it on their way from the top of Table Mountain to the bottom of Joseph Creek Canyon and vice versa. When they were being chased in hunting season, they didn't slow down to find a place to jump it but rather just plowed through it. They would get tangled in it and drag it down the hill sometimes a much as 50 to 75 yards.

We would have to hook onto it and drag it back up the hill with the saddle horses. Materials, of course, had to be packed in so keeping this stretch of fence in good repair was quite a chore.

If it wasn't repaired, in the spring some cattle would drift up through The Gap and out onto Table Mountain, then in the summer some of the cattle on Table Mountain would drift off, down through it, and end up in the bottom of the Joseph Creek Canyon. Hard as it was to keep it up, it still was easier than all the extra riding we would have to do if we left it torn to pieces!

When we gathered to bring the cattle out of the canyon each Memorial Day weekend, we would camp at the Vawter cabin. We would pack in one day, staying in the cabin that night, then ride the lower end of the range, which included The Gap and the Wilder Place, the next day. We would bring the cattle back and push them up Joseph Creek past the Vawter Place and drop them there for the night. We would stay in the Vawter cabin again that night, then pick up the cattle the next morning. We'd ride Slide Creek, Rim Creek, and Cliff Creek then take the cattle on to the home place.

The following morning the cattle were pushed up Cougar Creek, then up Thorn Hollow and on to Cougar Bench. The cattle were left in

Lee, Tammy Crawford and Carolyn Witty on edge of Wilder Flat—Haystack Rock on upper left of skyline

Lee and the Peterson bunch

this pasture until in early July when we would put them on the summer range out on top.

Some years we had help for the spring gather. One year a couple of gals I taught with, Carolyn Witty and Tammy Crawford, went down the creek with us. (Carolyn and Tammy rode with us on several other occasions other than the spring gather!) Another spring Randy and Robin

Peterson's camp at the Vawter Place

Warner helped us. A couple of Lee's friends from Burbank, Washington, Jerry and Madge Bjorgo, helped another year.

Whenever we had extra riders it not only sped up the gather but also just made it more fun. The year Carolyn and Tammy went, we were on the hillside above the Wilder Place when we noticed that in one place in the creek the water seemed to be churning. We could easily tell that it wasn't rapids but we couldn't tell what it was. The more we watched the more curious we became so finally we rode down to check it out. We discovered that in a space about thirty feet square there were dozens of suckers. They apparently were following the trout at spawning time and must have been working a spawning bed.

That spring there was a group of guys, the Petersons, most of whom were from western Oregon, that had backpacked from the North Highway to the Vawter Cabin. It seems they had the practice of getting together at least once a year for some type of outing. That spring they were on Joseph Creek for a fishing trip.

We brought the cattle out of the canyon, to the Home Place without incident. The next morning we were taking them up Cougar Creek, then up Thorn Hollow. We were going to scatter some salt that day too, so we took the pack mules. Lee had a young white mule that was ornery and a real kicker. He had her in the front, so he could see what she was up to, then the other mules strung out behind her.

We hadn't gotten very far up Thorn Hollow when we ran into trouble with the cows. I don't remember if we dropped the mules, thinking they would just graze, or what happened, but somehow they got away from us. The mistake was having that young mule in the lead because the good old mules had to go wherever she went. She headed for home! When we got the cattle straightened out, Lee, Carolyn, and Tammy went on with the cattle and I headed back to find the mules. They had gone down Thorn Hollow and hit the Cougar Creek Road. I found salt strung all along the way on the Cougar Creek Road—they must have been going at a pretty good clip! They went through the gate at the mouth of Cougar Creek and headed down the road toward home, but then pulled up on a hillside to graze. That was where I found them.

I was riding my young mare, Candy, who had a habit of "scooting" when something startled her. Now those mules had been no threat to her all morning when they were being led, but when she saw them grazing, with their heads hidden in the tall grass and the packs with ropes hanging everywhere, she freaked out! As we got closer and closer, her head got higher and higher and I could feel her tightening up. I knew she was going to whirl and bolt, it was just a question of "when!" I had the reins gathered up really short and my legs braced, when sure enough, she whirled 180 degrees and back around the hillside we went! I got her stopped, then we turned and headed back toward the mules. With all of the commotion, we had gotten the attention of the mules so they had their heads raised and were watching us. I guess with their heads up she recognized them as mules because I was able to get her over to them, get the lead mule's lead rope and start back up the canyon. I gathered up the salt and repacked it as we went along.

One spring it was time to scatter some salt in the Thorn Hollow/Cougar Bench Pasture. There also was some weed spraying needing done so it was decided that Lee would do the spraying and I would take the mules and do the salting. We didn't have saltboxes so we had to tie the blocks of salt on with ropes. I took salt up Thorn Hollow then came back down a ways to where I could grade around onto Cougar Bench, where I would scatter more salt. I then had to go to the top, into the Dog Fight pasture and get more salt that we had stashed under a tree. When I topped out, the first thing I saw was elk all around the tree and salt. What made it spectacular was that two elk were standing straight up on their hind feet, fighting; striking at each other with their front feet. After watching for a little while I went on and loaded more salt on the mules. I scattered this salt along Shitter Ridge (sorry, but that was what the ridge was named years ago—that was what some cowboys call horses), then dropped down the trail to the house.

I had had a great day with no problems but you know how things always take longer than you figure. Well, Lee had just saddled up and started up the trail to find me when I rode off the ridge.

It was while the cattle were in this Thorn Hollow/Cougar Bench Pasture that we had the experience of doctoring a range bull, thus the inspiration for the following poem.

The Ol' Range Bull

You hear the ol' cowpokes
Tell of things that happened out on the range,
But this here poem will show you sure
That all of that ain't changed.

You see we had this range bull
With a horn growing into his cheek,
If we let him go all through the summer,
Well, by fall he'd be so sick and weak.

It grew so tight against his head,
The skin it had already broke.
We knew there was no time to waste;
It was serious business, not some cowboy joke.

The problem was this mighty bull
Was out on the range for summer,
So rendering first aide to him
Could turn into a real bummer.

But Lee came up with a plan,
A real disaster before it was done.
He said, "This will be real easy, Jul,
If I can just get Dub's tranquilizer gun."

Lee had doctored many a cow,
And knew drugs could change an attitude.
He'd better tackle this like a real cowboy,
Not some polished, citified dude.

He checked with our local vet,
To make sure he got the dosage right,
'Cause he knew if he overdosed him,
The bull could die that very night!

Dave didn't do much to reassure Lee,
Seems he had almost "lost his coat,"
'Cause Dave had overdosed a Parker bull,
Just saving him with $300 worth of antidote!

Well Lee was getting pretty nervous
'Bout how this whole thing will end,
'Cause he knows sure as the world
He don't have no $300 to spend!

Well, we rode up to ol' Cougar Bench,
Lee with gun and drugs in saddlebag.
He says to me, "I'll take the lead,
Jul, you bring up the drag."

You see we had to haze that bull
Back from the edge that dropped off steep,
'Cause if he went down, rolled over the edge,
Well, those range bulls, they don't come cheap!

When we finally got that bull settled
In what seemed like just the right spot,
Lee had his gun cocked and primed,
Whether that ol' bull was ready or not.

Now those tranquilizer guns were a modern convenience,
A right handy little tool,
But if your aim ain't real good, I tell you folks,
You can come out looking like a fool!

Lee was trying to get a good aim,
While still astride his nervous horse,
So it was pretty hard to hit the exact spot;
I understood all of this, of course.

Well, when that dart left that ol' gun,
The crazy thing, it didn't go straight.
It wound around like a confused corkscrew.
The bull saw it coming, but, it was too late!

Some days things all go pretty easy,
But for this ol' bull, today wasn't the day,
'Cause that dart hit him right in the testicles.
And they began to swing and to sway!

That ol' guy never knew what hit him,
But he knew Lee and I were to blame.
After that do you think there was any chance,
That ol' range bull we could somehow tame?

Well we kept a hazing that ol' bull,
It must have been quite a sight!
A hysterical bull with a syringe hanging low,
And I tell you it was hangin' on tight!

All the while we were a wondering,
Why that drug don't start taking effect,
When that ol' syringe, it fell to the ground.
It was the last thing we would ever expect!

Lee dismounted, picked up the syringe,
Then got a big grin on his face.
He said, "Hey Jul, it never went off,
Everything is still in its place!"

Being the kind to never give up
Until the job was done,
Lee took that still loaded syringe,
And he began reloadin' his gun.

Now at this point of the game I can't tell you
What's going on in this poor ol' range bull's mind,
But I can tell you, when he saw us a comin',
He left us in his dust, far behind!

Our horses, they were plumb tuckered
When we finally ran down that ol' guy,
And I can tell you folks that that bull
Had a frenzied look in his eye!

Well this second try was ended
In what you might call a success.
'Cause it hit that bull in the full of the rump—
The very best place, I guess.

He quickly started slowing down,
As he would stagger, and then he would sway.
Pretty soon it seemed he was out cold.
We're going to finish this job right away!

Lee approached that ol' bull in Lee's usual way,
Which wasn't so quiet and meek,
As he yells at the top of his lungs,
"Ol' boy are you finally asleep?"

Well, that bull immediately woke up,
Jumped to his feet and staggering, away he did go.
Where he got the strength to do all of this,
Is far more than I ever will know!

I looked at Lee in total disbelief,
And Lee looked at me with the same,
So you know what our next job would be—
One more time that ol' range bull to tame!

Lee and I, well we would never give up,
We knew what it meant to persevere,
But when that ol' bull went down again,
He kept open one eye and one ear!

This time Lee approached quietly,
I swear he was on his tiptoes,
And quick as a wink he locked some tongs
In that ol' range bull's nose!

Lee said they were just a precaution,
In case that bull tried to scurry away.
I was to hold his head down firmly,
We'd teach him with us not to play!

Sawing so fast to remove that ol' horn,
By the end, made a small billow of smoke rise.
Then you'll never believe what happened to us,
As we looked on with disbelief in our eyes!

Yes, that bull was on his feet again,
And again he did stagger and sway.
But those nose tongs were still locked in,
They wouldn't come out 'till dooms day.

Lee had proved many times in the past
He was quite handy with a lasso rope,
But when the pressure was on, the chips
Were down, well he just couldn't cope!

The bull would lie down so long as
Lee stayed away with his horse,
But if he approached mounted, the bull
Would jump up and take off again, of course!

Lee tried and tried to connect until
With himself he was feeling quite sick,
When I persuaded him to let me try
My old "sneakum up on him" trick!

The bull finally lay down once again.
You could tell he was disgusted with us,
So Lee reluctantly committed to my plan,
Without making too much of a fuss.

At the end of his 60 foot lariat,
The bitter end Lee dallied fast,
While I took the loop end and on my belly
Slithered up through the grass.

As I approached his rear end, over his
Hind feet, the loop I planned to put,
But because of the way he lay,
It was impossible to loop the bottom foot.

So against my better judgement,
For looping one foot I would settle,
Though eventually it would bring me
More irritation than fallin' on a nettle!

Lee backed up ol' Joker,
Taking up slack, pullin' it tight,
And the minute that that all happened,
The bull was up and on the fight!

He still had three good legs under him
To take him wherever he wanted to go.
He went to the left, he went to the right,
That nose rope, it swung to and fro.

It couldn't be that hard to catch
A rope trailing from the nose tong,
Or so I thought, but for the "nth" time
Once more that bull proved me wrong!

Now I admit if I had been younger,
More agile and quick on my feet,
The whole "chase um bull" episode,
Wouldn't have been so seemingly a defeat.

All the while mounted on Joker,
Occasionally on the rope Lee gives a pull,
While at the top of his lungs he was hollerin'
"Get 'im, I said get 'im Jul!"

So once again I rose to the challenge,
I pursued with regenerated hope,
And I outfoxed that ol' jerk of a range bull,
I did catch a hold of that rope!

To loosen the tongs, I worked my way
Hand over hand up that rope.
I looked that ol' bull square in the eye,
Thinking, "You sure are a prize of a dope!

If you could only understand, Jerk,
I'm getting abused trying to set you free!"
But after all that had happened that day,
How could I expect him to have faith in me!

Well after some careful maneuvering,
I did remove the tong, believe it or not.
But just as I did, he gave a great blow
And covered my face with his snot!

Well, our job was almost ended,
There was just one little thing left to do—
Remove that rope from one hind foot,
Oh, it would 'av been easy if Lee could 'av roped two!

Tugging so hard on that ol' rope,
He had pulled the loop really tight.
We thought, "Come off in a week or a month,
If we're lucky, it might!"

Well we followed him 'round 'till that
Rope fell off, Ol' Range Bull was finally free.
Then looking back over his shoulder, I swear,
He ran his tongue up his nose while looking at Lee!

When looking back over the whole ordeal,
We laugh and say, "It's all in a good day's work!"
And in fairness to the ol' range bull I ask,
"Was it him or Lee and I who was the Jerk?"

Summer Range

Color photos—page 170

As the weather warmed and the grass growth crept up the canyon walls, the cattle were pushed higher, their destiny being the top pastures. When the cattle were moved to the top, we moved up too, setting up our summer camps.

Somewhere from the fourth to the tenth of July we gathered the Thorn Hollow/Cougar Bench pasture. We then pushed the cattle to the top, holding them in the Dog Fight pasture. There they were sorted and taken to the various summer ranges.

Some cattle were put on the backside of Table Mountain and others were taken to the lower end of the Tamarack pasture, to Horse Pasture Ridge, and to the Corral Springs pasture. The exact usage of each pasture was determined by a pasture rotation plan that had been developed in cooperation with the Forest Service. As late summer came the cattle were allowed to drift to the front of Table Mountain and to the higher range in each of the other pastures.

We kept the cattle where we wanted them by scattering salt out on the ridge points. In most places the only way to get salt in

Lee and Carolyn on Cougar Bench

Sharing my apple with Candy

The Allen Spring's water trough as we found it. The cattle and elk had displaced the pipe from the water source and mangled the trough.

The new Allen Spring's trough that we installed. We used the team to pull logs in place to brace the trough.

Lee trying to hitch a ride out of the draw by riding in the old trough, but he was too heavy—the team couldn't pull him and the trough up the hill.

was by pack animal. We also rode, to push the cattle into the desired areas and to keep them scattered. We practically lived with them all summer.

When we weren't busy scattering salt or pushing cattle, we were fixing fence or water holes. A lot of the water holes hadn't had much maintenance thus were in pretty bad shape. We would dig out the water source, fence it off, generally with logs, and pipe the water to a trough. Whenever possible we would skid a log along the upper side of a couple of trees then put the trough on the uphill side of this log, thus keeping the cattle from pushing the trough out of place.

The Allen Springs trough was down in the head of a draw that was so steep there was no way of getting a vehicle into it. We took Dick and Rocky, the team, and skidded in the troughs and supplies. We also used the horses to pull into place some logs, against which we placed the troughs. Lee didn't want to leave the old trough down in the draw so he skidded it out with the team. He thought he would hitch a ride out by kneeling

This is the trough we moved from one location to another on Table Mountain

in the trough, but it was so steep the horses couldn't pull it with him in it!

Over on Table Mountain there was a trough, which sometime in the past had been dropped by helicopter. The problem was that it had been dropped about a quarter of a mile from where it was to be installed. We had to do just a little clearing along an established cow trail that had been a skid road. We were then able to, with the team, skid the trough to the new location.

Once any kind of hunting season opened, whether it be bird or big game, we had to constantly check gates to keep them closed. Many people would cuss the "Portland Hunters" but in all fairness, most of the time if we caught someone cutting the fence or leaving a gate open, it was a Wallowa County resident!

It was Labor Day weekend and my kids had come to stay with us at the Hunting Camp cabin so we could celebrate Kurt's birthday. At the end of the weekend Lee and I needed to move camp up to Dog Fight, so the guys, Kurt and my son-in-law Gary, were riding the 4-wheelers. The rest of us were going in the pickup with a trailer load of horses and mules. Before we could get loaded and on our way, Kurt and Gary came back and said they had run into Dub, the boss, and he said the state police had notified him that one of our cows had been shot with an arrow. She was around the Coyote Campground. We hurried to Coyote, unloaded our horses and rode around until we found her. There were people camped at the campground so Lee had an audience as he tried to rope her. Lee never did his best when he had people watching. We ran the cow around for a while. As we did this, the shaft of the arrow came unscrewed from the head, and fell to the ground. Lee roped the cow and we started for the trailer. She was on the fight by now so every time I would try to move in and haze her in the direction of the trailer, she would take my horse. After she took my horse a few times, he got to where he didn't want to get in close to her. We finally got her next to the trailer. We put a second rope on her and passed it up through the trailer and tied it off so she couldn't get away. Next, Lee's rope was run through the side of the trailer and with his horse he pulled her into the trailer.

We hauled her to the vet. After examining her, the vet said the arrowhead was located in such a place that it would probably kill her to operate. We had a better chance of letting it go and taking a chance of it working its way out or chancing that it would form gristle around it, which could cause it to just "stay put." After she was shot full of antibiotics, we hauled her back to the top and turned her out on the range. That cow was still part of the herd when we left the ranch!

The top summer pastures were a maze of a few good Forest Service roads and many logging roads. Some were impassable, others passable but only at a snail's pace with a 4-wheel drive rig. Fortunately we could get to all of the summer camps by 4-wheel drive rigs thus making the transporting of supplies much easier. Though there were many roads, the majority of the salting, fencing, and waterhole maintenance was done by horseback and pack animals.

"The Top" lies across the heads of some deep, rugged canyons, in between which were gently rolling hills, interspersed with draws of dense evergreen thickets. Lush meadows were sprinkled throughout the timberland with some bare bunchgrass hillsides along the breaks of the canyons. Throughout, there were clusters of deciduous trees such as aspen, and various brushes that make it beautifully colorful, especially in the fall!

The ranch had bought a 4-wheeler for Lee to use, so I bought one for myself so I could go with Lee whenever and wherever he went.

A week or ten days would go by without us having reason to go to the ranch house down in the canyon. To check on things down there we would ride the 4-wheelers down a point from Kirkland, catch an old logging road which took us down to Sleepy Bill. We would then climb over another ridge, catch another logging road then follow it down to the Cougar Bench road. We would follow it down to the Joseph Creek road and on to the ranch house. By doing this we were able to check on things down in the canyon without spending hours traveling many miles around the road with the pickup! It would be 10 to 15 degrees hotter in the canyon bottom than it was out on top.

When we moved to the top and there was no activity around the barn, snakes tended to move in. One time we went into the barn and sure enough, there were a couple of rattlesnakes. Lee shot them with a pistol he always carried loaded with snake shot.

One day we were climbing up the Red Hill Grade with a trailer load of horses that we had taken to the valley to have shod. We were heading back to cow camp to move some cattle to a different pasture.

It was the middle of the summer and was a very hot day. With pulling such a heavy load and it being such a hot day, the pickup overheated. We always carried a large jug of water for drinking or for whatever else it might be needed. It was strapped in the front corner of the pickup bed.

When we got to a level place Lee stopped to let the pickup cool off. He thought it seemed like something else could be wrong too, so he got down and crawled part way under the pickup. First he checked toward the back then he rolled toward the front, then he rolled toward the back again. Each time he rolled, his shirttail became a little more "untucked" thus his belly started hanging out.

I was standing right by the pickup and couldn't help but see his bare belly, and right by me was the jug of cool water. I looked at his belly then the jug of water, then his belly again. I swear the devil made me do it! I could not resist! I poured a little of that water on his belly, which caused him to jump, making him hit his head on the bottom of the pickup. He uttered some choice words and started crawling out from under the pickup! I moved away a little distance just in case I needed to make a run for it! Lee was always so fun and good-natured! He "rubbed the hurt out" of his head and just laughed, but did warn me that I had better be watching my "hind side!"

Spring Turnout

Pushing cattle down Joseph Creek Trail

Cattle trailing into Rim Creek

*Katrina, Lee and pack animal (Shorty)
on Joseph Creek Trail across from Vawter Cabin*

Me and Candy on edge of Vawter Flat Rim

Spring Turnout

Me pushing cattle
around hill from Vawter Place

Missy, after being
kicked

Katrina and me above
Cliff Creek Rim—
Haystack Rock on skyline

Katrina and Missy on
Cliff Creek Rim

*Crossing Joseph Creek—
Duke knew where the
trail was in the brush*

*Lee, Duke and hired man
at the Burleigh Place*

*Cave on Joseph Creek
near the north end of
the Wilder Place*

*Finding the trail through
the brush*

Spring Turnout

*Building fence across Joseph Creek at north end
(down river) of Wilder Place*

*Me on Joker, in draw
below The Gap*

*Horses and Lee under rim
at the Gap after unloading
fence material*

Lee pushing cattle into Water Canyon from The Gap

Carolyn Witty, leading pack animals—Tammy Crawford on Noodles

Carolyn, Tammy, Lee and Jackie (dog) looking down Joseph Creek from Wilder Flat—lunch break

Spring Turnout

Madge Bjorgo helping husband, Jerry, fasten chaps at Vawter Cabin

Jerry and Lee and Madge packing out of Vawter Cow Camp after Spring Gather

Bringing cattle out of canyon on Joseph Creek Trail after Spring Gather

Cattle trailing through the mouth of Rim Creek

Cattle on Cliff Creek Flat

Spring Turnout

Coming off Shitter Ridge—Carolyn Witty, Tammy Crawford and me on Candy, leading mules

Tranquilized bull on Cougar Bench— remains of Larsen Cabin in the background

Lee removing horn tip with cable saw. Note nose tongs in the nose.

Lee snoozing after salting and pushing cattle into Thorn Hollow

Lee pushing cattle from Dog Fight Pasture toward Rim Creek Saddle and Table Mountain

Pushing cattle down West Tamarack Ridge below Allen Springs

Summer Range

Lee on Jack pushing cattle down Vawter Ridge

Lee on Jack on crest of Vawter Ridge

Me on Doc on Vawter Ridge— Swamp Creek and Baker Knob in background

*Lee on Joker on Breaks of Horse Pasture Ridge—
Looking across to back-side of Table Mountain.
Dogs—unnamed, Jackie and Mert*

*Horse Pasture Ridge Pond—Highway 3 is on distant timbered ridge—
Blue Mountains, beyond the Grande Ronde River, are on the skyline*

At sunrise—Me on Jack with dogs Tub, Doll, Pet and Mert on the Breaks of Broady

Lee on Joker, coming up out of Broady

*Lee above Peter Springs—looking across
Peavine to Horse Pasture Ridge*

My granddaughter, Jessica and Lee—we had been checking gates

Summer Range

*Me—Lee packing up the salt then...
taking it down the
"Dinosaur Back"*

*Katrina on Breaks of Table Mountain
looking into Joseph Creek Canyon*

*Cliff on back of
Table Mountain*

Me—Lee on the Breaks of Table Mountain looking across Joseph Creek Canyon to Paradise area—Blue Mountains on the skyline are in Washington

Dick and Rocky pulling the water trough with Lee, Katrina and Jessica

Suzy

Fall Gather and "CLEAN-UP" Riding

Color photos—page 193

The "reaping of the harvest" on a cattle ranch was the shipping of the calves and secondly, the gathering of the mama cows and the bulls prior to winter.

Cattle in the Dog Fight pasture headed for the Breaks of Joseph Creek

Lee and I enjoyed the fall roundup, and also there was a pride in a very high percentage of gather. Usually extra riders were brought in to help with the main gather. Some years the boss hired a camp cook.

The calves were shipped, the cows pregged (checked to see if they were with calf) and put on the breaks. We then would start the clean-up riding—riding the summer pastures looking for cattle that had been missed in the main gather. This clean-up riding would extend through the elk hunting season.

When there was any snow, we would drive around on top looking for cow tracks cutting the roads. Upon finding tracks we would unload the horses, trail the cows, find them, then head to the corral at Dog Fight with them.

Other times we would scour the top by horseback, checking out certain pockets we knew to be hideouts for cattle. As we rode the top, we would check at hunting camps, asking the hunters if they had seen any cattle. They would be so excited if they could report having seen cattle!

Once it was reported that there was a group of bulls out on Horse Pasture Ridge. There was probably twelve to fourteen inches of snow on top with a little less down on Horse Pasture Ridge. We chained up, drove down and found the bulls. They were a ways from the road and we knew we didn't dare leave the road because of the chance of hitting a hidden rock or getting stuck. Of course we had a couple of dogs with us, one of

Fall Gather

which was Ol' Mert. As we started the bulls, they went over a knoll to where Lee couldn't see them from the ground so I climbed up into the dog catcher. I could see the bulls, so Lee stood by the pickup and sent Mert after them. I served as the liaison. I would tell Lee what was happening, then he would holler at Mert to, "Get ahead," "Down," "Move up," and etc. By this process, Mert got them on the road and then they were more than glad to follow the beaten out path made by the pickup on our way in. It was a slow process but a necessary one. We always had a deck of cards in the jocky box of the pickup, so as we followed along in low range, first gear, we played Thirty-One while Ol' Mert did what she loved most!

Once the cattle were put on the breaks in the fall, we not only had to check the top but also ride the canyon and keep pushing them back up. Invariably a few would come down, cross Joseph Creek and go up on the north slope of Baker Knob or work around and go up Swamp Creek. Once someone reported having seen cattle on lower Miller Ridge and down in Swamp Creek. Not knowing if they were our cattle or cattle of the Swamp Creek Reserve, Tom Birkmaier volunteered to go with us. Another friend, Randy Warner also went to help. There wasn't much snow at that time so we were able to drive to the top of Miller Ridge. It was decided that Tom and Randy would drop off into Swamp Creek, go down it to Joseph Creek, picking up any cattle along the way. Lee and I would go down Miller Ridge, picking up cattle that we had seen the day before on the north side of Baker Knob. As it ended up, there were no cattle on Miller Ridge. They had already dropped off into the lower country. Lee and I did go on and get the cattle off of Baker Knob.

The ground was frozen and there was about six inches of snow on the north slope. Our horses were sharp shod, as they always were that time of year. As we started around the north we saw cattle on around at just about our level, but also some on a bench quite a ways below us. It was decided that Lee would grade on around and get the higher cattle, I would drop down and get the ones below us. Of course there was no trail going from where I was to the bench below. I asked Lee how I was supposed to get down there. He made a sweeping motion and said, "Just pick your way down through there. Doc will do fine!" He then headed on around the slope. I was thinking, "He is crazy if he thinks I am riding down that. I don't care if Doc is sharp shod!" I kind of fiddled around until Lee was out of sight then I stepped off my horse. My feet had no more than hit the ground until they were out from under me and I was flat on my back! I figured that, as luck would have it, I must have just stepped on a smooth slick rock, so I started to pick my way down and around, holding tight to Doc's reins with one hand and grabbing grass, brush, or rocks with the other hand. I had not gone more than six or eight steps when my feet went out from under me again!

I kept trying to figure out what I could do differently to keep from falling, but do what I might, I simply could not keep my feet under me. Being a slow learner, I fell a couple more times in the next few minutes and my fanny and thighs were getting quite bruised before I realized that once again Lee knew what he was talking about. I got back on Doc and worked my way down to the cattle—Doc never fell once!

The Wilder Monument dusted with snow

I got the cattle to the bottom, crossed Joseph Creek and started up the Joseph Creek Trail. Lee brought his cows off a little farther up Joseph Creek, joined me and we trailed them home. I was thankful he didn't ask me if I had had any trouble coming off the knob, and I didn't volunteer any information! It wasn't until several years after that, that I finally "fessed up" to what had happened that day.

Yet another time, one of the ranchers, who was flying to look for strays, spotted a few head, seemingly hemmed in on a point up Swamp Creek. There was a drift fence running along the side of the Swamp Creek canyon. At this particular place the creek came through the fence, went out around a point, then went back through the fence. The cattle had gotten over on that point then the creek iced over. Some cattle will starve to death rather than cross ice, and it seemed that was what would have happened to those if we hadn't gone after them!

Again not knowing whom they belonged to, Tom Birkmaier said he would go with us. We picked Tom and his horse up at his place, trailered up Elk Creek and out to the top of Miller Ridge.

As we got higher and higher and the snow got deeper and deeper, we all became more concerned, but there simply were no places to turn around until we got to the top! Once you started you were committed! On top there was snow more than knee deep on our horses. Even in this, Lee was able to get the pickup and trailer turned around. We always turned around and got headed in the homeward direction before we started riding so we would know we wouldn't be stuck at the end of the day.

As we rode across the top to start down Nell's Canyon, the snow was really deep because of drifting. I was riding my little mare, Candy. I guess she had never been in that deep of snow and didn't know what to make of it because she kept trying to lie down. She must have thought it would be fun to roll in it!

Not knowing exactly where the cattle were and knowing the daylight hours were short, we knew we had to be able to find the cattle quickly or we would never get them out of there before dark. Our plan was to have Joe Spence fly Dub over Swamp Creek to spot the cows. When we were about half way down Nell's Canyon, sure enough we heard a plane. We rode into a clearing so they could spot us. As they flew over, we weren't sure that they saw us but we waited. In a few minutes the plane returned, buzzed us, and Dub threw out a roll of toilet paper with a note stuffed in the middle. It said the cattle were at the mouth of Nell's canyon; we were headed right for them!

The cattle were in as bad a situation as we had expected. It took a lot of persuading to get our horses to cross the ice. Lee was riding the big gray warm blood gelding, Jack. I saw Lee and him go to battle more than once and it may have taken some time, but Lee always won!

It was absolutely necessary that the horses cross the iced-up creek. First, so we could get over to the cattle, and secondly so a path would be broken out so the cattle would come back across the creek.

We got the cattle and pushed them to the top where we had left the pickup. Then Lee loaded his horse and brought the pickup and trailer out. Tom and I cut cross country and trailed the cows off Miller Ridge and down to Tom's place on Crow Creek.

The cattle turned out to be Duke Lathrop's from down Joseph Creek beyond the lower end of the Monument Ranch. They had drifted up country about eight to ten miles!

When the snow started laying on, the cattle would drift for miles and sometimes in a somewhat unexplainable direction. If they got started up Swamp Creek, they got farther and farther from home and also in higher country, thus deeper snow, but they just kept going!

One winter several of our cattle were spotted clear up Swamp Creek where the Charlais Road comes up out of Swamp Creek and starts down Elk Creek.

We drove up to check it out—see exactly where they were and how many we were dealing with. We had several rustler panels roped onto the outside of the trailer, and a little hay. We found the cattle thin and hungry. Looking at the cows we could tell that one was being sucked but there was no calf with them.

    We turned the dogs loose and sent them into the timber in various directions. The "wet" cow started getting nervous and took off up the hill. She didn't go directly to the calf but at least gave us a general area in which we could expect to find the baby. Sure enough we found where she had hidden it. We put a rope on it so we could use it as bait to get the cows to go into the trailer. It was not until we had the calf up, that the cow came to it—she knew she had been "found out."

    The Charlais Road, in many places went through steep cuts. The banks on those cuts were high and steep, so much so that a cow couldn't get up them. We parked the trailer as close to one side of the road as possible. We then put a rustler panel to the bank on that side. We used the other panels to form a make shift, tiny corral off the back end of the trailer. By putting the calf in the trailer, tying it in, and throwing some hay in the trailer and in the corral, we were able to coax the cows in close enough to the rear of the trailer that we could swing the panels around, enclosing them. Then by pressuring them a little, they hopped right into the trailer.

    The first few years we were on the ranch, Magnums had the Hunting Camp allotment. Ray Wilson worked for them. He stayed at the Hunting Camp Cabin some of the time and at the house down in Tamarack the rest of the time. He and Lee became friends. Since they were running cattle on adjoining allotments, there was always the possibility of the cattle becoming mixed. Occasionally they would help each other ride.

    I got to go on one such ride into Rush Creek. Lee and I were at the Dog Fight Cow Camp so we got up early and trailered down to the Hunting Camp Cabin where Ray was staying. It was a terribly foggy morning—so foggy you couldn't see thirty yards in front of you. We took off out through the timber with Ray leading the way. Having never ridden in that part of the country I had no way of knowing where we were or where we were going. I usually knew my directions pretty well when I was out in the timber, but that morning I would have been doing good to have just told which way was up!

    After riding for some time, we got out of the timber and started down an open ridge. As we dropped lower, the fog became less dense. We then started dropping into Rush Creek.

    It was late fall and there was about four inches of snow on the ground—just enough to ball up on the horses' feet causing the sharp shoes to not be able to get any traction. Still there was not enough snow to hold the horses' feet in place. We were side-hilling around a smooth, open hill. Ray was still in the lead with Lee being right behind him, and I brought up the rear. All of a sudden Lee's horse, Ol'Joker, lost his footing with his back feet. They went completely out from under him and off the trail. As he went down, he kind of rolled up on his up-hill hip to where he had snow clear up on top of his hip. At the same time he was digging in with his front feet. I watched in disbelief as he was able to pull himself, with Lee still on him, back up onto the trail with the strength of his front feet and legs! This was why whenever we were looking for ranch horses, we not only wanted them with a strong rear end, but also insisted they have a really strong front end!

We dropped on into the bottom of Rush Creek and started up it. After a ways we came to a place where a main draw came in. Ray thought there might be some cattle up that draw but felt there would be even more up Rush Creek, so it was decided that I would go up the draw and Lee and Ray would go on up Rush Creek. Later Lee told me that Ray asked several times, "Are you sure Julie will be alright?" Lee always answered, "Yeah!"

I was all right but my only concern was knowing that when I got to the top, I would be back in that dense fog and might not be able to see Ray and Lee. I knew I had to go to the top until I hit a fence then I had to hang to the right. I did this and the timing was so perfect that after a while I could hear cattle bawling so I headed through the fog toward them, which took me right to Ray and Lee!

It seemed that we had to do more trucking in the fall when doing the clean-up gathering than we did the rest of the year. All of the roads out in that area were just an obstacle course of ruts and potholes. They were extremely hard on equipment. The gooseneck stock trailer got a lot of hard miles!

Because of "beating" the trailer over so many miles of rough roads, the u-bolts that attached the springs to the frame would wear thin and break. When this happened, Lee would use a chain and chain binder to hold the axle in place, up against the trailer frame so we could limp home. After this happened several times, we started carrying a spare u-bolt. Lee could figure out a way to fix most anything!

One fall Lee and I were doing some cleanup riding. It was getting late enough in the year that it had started laying some snow on up there on top. We were still staying at the Dog Fight Cow Camp but were anxious to finish up the riding and get moved down to the creek.

When it got late enough in the year that we knew we wouldn't need the mules any more to scatter salt, we would take them back down to Joseph Creek. To be rid of them before the fall gather began saved us having one more thing to deal with.

The mules had been alone down on the creek for several weeks when, for some reason, we needed to go down there. The mules were so happy to see us that they were practically in our hip pockets! They followed us everywhere! As we left in the pickup, they actually ran along with us for a little ways. Lee and I both commented about how lonesome the mules seemed.

We drove back up Joseph Creek the nine miles to where we headed up the Red Hill Grade to go to the top—back to the cow camp at Dog Fight.

The next morning we heard something messing around outside the tent and knew it couldn't be the horses because they were in the corral. We hadn't put any cattle in the Dog Fight pasture so it shouldn't be cows! We looked out and were absolutely amazed to see the mules, Shorty and Suzy, standing there! I guess they thought it was time for us to come home!

They had to have gone up the Joseph Creek road, up Cougar Creek, up Thorn Hollow or around through Cougar Bench, then into the Dog Fight Pasture! Luckily for them we had thrown the gates open so cattle could drift to the lower country. But how did they know where we were?

Suzy and Shorty came to find us at Cow Camp

Cow Camps

Color photos —Page 200

Besides the ranch house, there were four other cow camps that we used. After Lee had been on the ranch a few years, the Huntin' Camp allotment was added to the ranch giving us the fourth cow camp.

With the range being so divided by deep canyons and thick timbered areas, to get to a place a couple of miles away, "as the crow flies," you might have to drive ten or twelve. To drive to the top from the ranch house, we had to go back up Joseph Creek nine miles then take the Red Hill Road to Coyote Camp Ground, which was another twelve miles. The lower end of the summer range, whether on Table Mountain or Tamarack, was about another five or six miles. Those roads were rough and crooked, and had to be traveled very slowly, especially if you were pulling a trailer load of cattle or horses.

The Red Hill Road was in better condition but on the grade, because of the steepness, it was slow going up or down. Out on top this road was crooked with timber coming right to the edge of the road. There could be livestock on the road around any bend so it couldn't be traveled at a very fast speed either.

To have any efficiency in managing the summer range, it was necessary to stay on top at the cow camps. At the beginning of the summer when the cattle were in the lower part of Tamarack, we stayed at Hunting Camp, at the head of East Tamarack. It was a favorite, nestled in amongst the pines. The original log buildings were completely dilapidated. Years ago Veryle Huffman, when he ran cattle on this permit in the '40s, built another log cabin up the draw a little ways from the original buildings. Bud Birkmaier tells of helping Huffman build the cabin. Bud helped mix the mud and chink the cracks.

Lee and I cleaned the cabin, then built a fence to make a horse pasture between the new cabin and the old buildings. It was a perfect horse pasture with lots of timber and brush for shade in the heat of the summer, but also had some openings with good grass. There also was a watering trough at the lower end of the pasture.

Lee and I had learned early on that it was much easier to have horses come in to grain than to try to run them down to catch them.

We would just step out of the cabin, whistle and holler, and pretty soon you could hear the horses coming up through the timber.

The Huntin' Camp Cabin had one room on the bottom level with a sleeping loft upstairs. There was a small propane cook stove with oven, a wood heater stove, a sink, but no running water, cupboards, a large table with benches on both sides, and a bed on the main floor. Because of Lee's bad knees, it was decided he would use the downstairs and I would bunk upstairs. There was an open stairway to the upstairs where there were five or six cots. On each end of the upstairs was a small window, which allowed a very welcomed breeze on hot summer nights. I positioned my cot under the window on the north end so usually enjoyed a breeze! Downstairs there were screened windows on the north end and east side, so we were able to keep it quite comfortable down there too, even when we were cooking.

Along the west side of the cabin was a covered porch with an enclosed feed room at one end. We built saddle racks on the back wall of the porch. The cabin was built on a slight slope so the porch side was about four feet off the ground. We put tie rings along the edge of the porch so we could tie the horses and saddle them right there.

With the porch and the front part of the cabin being up off the ground it made a perfect place for the dogs to sleep. The only problem was that you definitely wanted to be up wind from them when they crawled out from under the cabin and shook!

We had a fire pit and a picnic table out in front of the cabin where we could enjoy a campfire, if it wasn't too dry!

There also was a very typical outhouse! The first time I entered that contraption, I thought I was going to fall through the floor. Upon inspection it was discovered that the floor had one brace underneath, right in the middle. If you stepped too far to the left, the floor would list in that direction; if you stepped too far to the right, the same thing to the right! And as most unkept outhouses, it was home to every variety of spiders known. Then there were flies, hundreds of flies! The thing, though, that made it impossible for me to tolerate the place was the bees! When a bee moved in, I moved out! You could truly say this was the outhouse from_____! I guess it was destined thus to be, because just outside the outhouse was a huge yellow pine which had a double fork in the top. From a distance, it looked like a three tined devil's pitchfork with the handle stuck in the ground, the tines pointing heavenward!

As the summer progressed and we moved the cattle to the higher country, we moved camp to the Dog Fight Pond Camp. I had a 16x32 foot army tent that was big enough to have the cooking/eating area on one end, the sleeping cots in the middle, and our tack and woodpile at the far end. We cooked on a propane camp stove and heated the place with a wood stove, which I had had, at one time, in my house. It would hold fire all night and would keep the place pretty well heated except in the late fall when it started getting really cold. We had chunks of old carpet thrown down to help keep down the dust. Our supplies were in rubber tubs so they wouldn't get dusty and so the mice, chipmunks, and squirrels couldn't help themselves!

Outside, we had a fire pit and another picnic table. Funny how those Forest Service tables just showed up at each of our camps!

The army tent was made of heavy, dark green canvas so even in the bright of day it was dark inside. In fact, it was easy to oversleep if one didn't have a good alarm—the brightness of morning certainly wouldn't wake you!

We would leave the tent up through fall gathering and while we were doing clean-up riding. A couple of falls the snow got quite heavy before we broke camp. It piled up against the walls as it slid off, or we beat it off the tent. At times it piled up to about four feet deep against the tent walls. This made the tent warmer than ever!

Another cow camp was at the Kirkland Cabin. It was just a couple of miles from Dog Fight. We used it when we didn't put up the tent at Dog Fight. When we moved in, it had been deserted for years and years and had been taken over by mice and rats, so it was filthy! When cleaned up, though, it was quite comfortable, though very small. It was one small room with bunks at one end and cupboards, table and cooking/eating area at the other

There were shutters on the outside of the windows so we could close it up quite securely when we were not there. Early one morning we were preparing to leave and had already shut the shutters of the windows on the backside of the cabin. I was quite close to one window, busily packing things when I heard what sounded like fingernails on a blackboard. When looking at the window I saw a large bat crawling in between the window and the closed shutter, for his daily sleep. I am not necessarily afraid of bats but I must admit it gave me quite a start seeing his belly side smashed against the glass and his claws extended!

We had stashed extra salt out by some brush near the cabin. On numerous occasions, if we looked out at daybreak, there would be a couple of little bucks licking salt. They were always very alert as if knowing there was some danger nearby, though they weren't sure what or where.

This cabin was on a high knob so it caught the early rays of morning light and the last rays of sunshine of an evening, thus we had the pleasure of viewing many a beautiful sunrise and sunset from this cow camp!

Of course we had a fire pit and another of those great picnic tables! There also was an outhouse—one with a floor that did not teeter-totter. We trimmed the lower limbs from a nearby thicket of trees and chained the dogs there. It was a cool place in the heat of the summer days, but also provided warm, sheltered beds when the weather wasn't quite so good.

The Kirkland Cabin was special to me because of my family's history with it. When my Uncle Don was a young man, he worked for the Forest Service between the years of 1930 and 1938. One of his duties was being the fire lookout man at Kirkland. The Kirkland Knob was the highest point in that area. It was located on the north edge of the Cougar Creek Basin. When they first started using this location as a lookout point there was no lookout tower so Uncle Don climbed a large tree, cut the top out, then built a small platform on which to sit and watch for fires. There was no cabin at that time, so Uncle Don and Aunt Mary lived in a tent. Later the cabin was built and they stayed in it. Uncle Don built a wardrobe which was still in the cabin when we were there.

Later the Forest Service built a lookout tower and kept it manned for years. From this tower you could see to the south the Cougar Creek Basin; you could look up Joseph Creek and along Red Hill. In the far distance were the Wallowa Mountains. To the west you could see Miller Ridge and the Joseph Canyon; to the northwest, Baker Knob and Table Mountain. To the north was Horse Pasture Ridge, the lower

Kirkland Lookout Tower

Looking down from top of tower— Dog and saddle horses below, with our camping gear. Taken one March while on Spring Break from college.

Joseph Creek country, the Tamarack country, and in the far distance were the Blue Mountains across the Grande Ronde River in Washington. To the east-southeast in the distance were the Seven Devils Mountains across the Snake River in Idaho. Later this tower was torn down, leaving the little cabin to stand alone, as it still stood when we were on the ranch!

The Vawter Cabin, down in the bottom of the Joseph Creek Canyon, was used in the spring when we put cattle down the canyon for early grass, and again when we gathered them on Memorial Day Weekend to bring them out of the canyon and put them on top for the summer. We also used it in the fall when we were riding the canyon, pushing cattle back up the draws to get them to work the breaks rather than bunch up on the bottom. It was used also while we did the late fall gather to bring the cattle in to the feed lots.

This cabin was one room with a full upstairs loft that had been completely taken over by pack rats. It was heated by a wood stove, and had a set of bunk beds. It had some wooden cupboards that were impossible to keep the mice out of.

When staying at the Vawter Cabin we used a couple of little propane, one-burner cook stoves. Each stay we packed in the food we would need. We kept the cook stoves and a couple of gas lanterns at the cabin, tying them to the rafters when we left. We also stood the table on end so mice wouldn't nest and mess on it!

Vawter Place at the mouth of Swamp Creek—looking down from Vawter Bench

We kept a few pots and pans hanging from the ceiling poles. We got clean water from the spring along the creek bank, then heated it and had a mug of hot tea or a Cup-of-Noodles in just a few minutes.

There was always enough canned food, which the mice couldn't get into, to keep a person from going to bed hungry if he had to unexpectedly spend the night!

The door was left unlocked so backpackers would occasionally use the cabin. They would often leave a note of appre- ciation scratched on a paper plate or anything else they could find to write on. Since it was a long, steep climb out, backpackers would also lighten their loads by leaving their extra provisions, so we often found surprises in the cupboard!

There had always been a problem of mice getting in the bedding, even if it was hanging from the ceiling poles. To remedy this, Lee packed a big (2x2x5 ft.) steel box in on Ol' Suzy. He did this by putting a light hay bale on each side of her then he set the box crosswise on top of the bales. It made a high pack but the box was quite light and Suzy was such a trooper, they made it just fine!

It gave us a feeling of security to know there was a place where we could get in out of the weather, build a fire, get warmed up and dried out. We always left the place with enough wood split and stacked in the cabin, to start a fire the next time we were there.

One time when we were to stay at the cabin for several nights, the pack rats kept us awake a good share of the first night. Lee said, "By golly I'm not going to put up with that another night!"

The next evening when we got in from riding, we decided to go after those rats! The upstairs was shut off by a trap door that was hinged on the side next to the wall. Lee and I climbed up the stairs and pushed open the trap door. I then used the flashlight to spot the rats while Lee shot them. One old mama rat ran along where the roof met the floor, and had just started down a hole to escape when Lee shot her. When we looked closer, it seemed that she was still moving though she wasn't going anywhere. We went over and pulled her up out of the hole she had started down and there, still clinging to her body were five tiny baby rats. Of course we killed them too. That was how Lee was able to brag that he killed six rats with one shot! We then knew there had to be a nest there somewhere. Sure enough! It was within two feet of my head as I had stood there on the stairway flashing the light around looking for rats!

Each of those cow camps had its own unique history and a set of memories for us by the time we left the ranch!

Fall Gather

Lee on Jake with Mert (dog) bringing cattle into Dog Fight corral to wean calves

Fun around the campfire—Guatemalan, Dub, Pat Shelton and Lee

*Bob Shelton—
it had been a long day!*

*Lee, James Yost, Gavin Ehringer (from Western Horseman)
and Dave Yost swapping lies*

Fall Gather

*Pushing cattle toward Vawter Ridge—
Swamp Creek Canyon beyond Baker Knob in the background*

Scattering salt as we push cattle out onto the Breaks

Pushing cattle toward Rim Creek—Vawter Ridge in the distance with Table Mountain on the skyline

Lee seeking shelter from the wind

The canyon walls under the breaks were rugged

The draws and canyons were filled with color

We stopped for a quick lunch and built a fire at the mouth of Nell's Canyon—Lee and Tom Birkmaier

Tom's horses weren't sharp shod so he rode Joker and Lee was on Jack

Clean-up riding was generally a cold experience—Note Lee on edge of cliff, and frozen river in upper right corner

Frequently Joseph Creek would freeze over even before the snow came—often cattle crossed to the other side before it froze then occasionally Lee would have to rope them and drag them back across the ice— Joker was the only horse that would cross on the ice

Lee in the kitchen at the Home Place—Townley Place before remodel

*The Townley Place house after being remodelled—
the wall between the kitchen and living room was knocked out,
knotty pine was put on, and the ceiling was raised*

*The hunting camp cabin at the head of East Tamarack, built by
Verle Huffman with Bud Birkmaier's help
in the 1940s*

Katrina with her mare, Missy, on the porch of Hunting Camp Cabin

The hitching rail was near the camp tent at Dog Fight Cow Camp

*Dog Fight Cow Camp at Fall Gather—
the army tent was used for Cow Camp all summer.
The tent at the back and the blue tarp
were the cook shack and eating area.
Ocassionally the crew consisted of
8 to 10 riders.*

*Sometimes the snow came before we broke camp so-o-o...
snow would build up to several feet along the walls of the tent
as can be seen below after the tent was taken down*

The Kirkland Cabin that we used as Cow Camp when we were on top during the summer

Lee ready to pack supplies into the Vawter Cow Camp—Packing the stainless steel storage box on top of 2 bales of hay on Suzy was a challenge

Inside the Vawter Cabin—notice the bench is set on its end to keep the mice off

Looking at the Vawter Place from a point on the west side of Joseph Creek

Jerry Bjorgo and his wife Madge with pack animals leaving the Vawter Place—they had been helping us with the Spring Gather down Joseph Creek

Lee following with the rest of the pack animals

*Leaving the Vawter Place Cow Camp
after another
"MEMORY-MAKING EXPERIENCE"*

Hunters—Hunting & Wildlife

Color photos—page 225

When I was a child, most of the meat we ate was wild meat—deer and elk. Dad never did any trophy hunting. He very rarely killed a buck. He simply hunted to put meat on the table.

I started following him when I was little—long before I was old enough to carry a gun. I developed a love for the adventure and stealth of the whole experience. When I was old enough I started hunting, but I always had to borrow a gun so never got to really know a gun—how it would shoot.

When I was graduating from high school, the folks asked me what I wanted for a graduation gift. All of my girl friends were getting nice tailored suits to wear to formal functions when we got to college. I insisted that I wanted a rifle!

We had an elderly gentleman friend who used to come to Joseph Creek and stay with us each hunting season. He had gotten too old to hunt any more and was going to sell his rifle, so the folks bought it for me. It was a 300 Savage with a three powered scope.

I later put a 3x9 variable Leupold scope on it. I know that the ballistics aren't that good on that make of rifle, but I had a lot of fun and a reasonable amount of success with it!

One fall my husband, my son, Kurt, and I all had buck tags. The opening day of the season we went to the ranch on Joseph Creek, where I had been raised, to hunt. I was fortunate enough to fill my tag that morning. We hunted the rest of the day but didn't see any more buck deer so came home. I put my gun away where I kept it in my bedroom, since my tag had been filled.

The next morning was cold and there was a very fine drizzle so the guys decided not to go hunting. We had a late breakfast and I was at the sink doing the dishes when I saw a buck on the backside of the field out in front of our house there in the valley. The grass in the field had grown up to about 12 to 14 inches high.

When I saw the buck I started screaming, "There's a buck, there's a buck!" I ran through the kitchen knocking people out of my way as I headed for the bedroom. I grabbed my rifle, loaded it, and stepped out on the porch. Amazingly that buck was still there! It seemed he was searching for a place to get through the fence.

Leaning against one of the porch pillars and using it as a rest for my gun, I put the cross-hair on the buck and pulled the trigger. It is amazing how fast the mind processes information! As my bullet sped across the field it left a trail of mist that was being knocked from the grass in the field, or so I thought at that time. I thought, "I can't believe I shot that low!" and in the next split second the buck dropped. (Later I was told that if conditions are just right, a bullet will leave a vapor trail as it passes through the air.) I figured he was just stunned and would get up and take off so I yelled for my husband to bring the pickup as I jumped over the fence and started running up through the field. I very shortly ran out of air and slowed to a walk, keeping an eye on the place where the buck had gone down. He never got up. When I got up there, I could see that he had been hit in the neck killing him instantly.

He was a very large-framed white tail buck but was very thin. One of his hind legs had been broken in the hock sometime in the past and had healed back solid. That was why he was so thin and why he stopped at the fence so long—he couldn't jump it. He had a very atypical set of antlers—I'm sure as the result of the trauma his system had experienced as a result of the wounded leg.

A good share of the guys I taught with were hunters and a few of them had a hard time with the fact that some of us gals also hunted. It seemed to bother some of them if we had success, especially if they happened to not be successful.

Shooting that buck from my front porch really was kind of a unique hunting story but I didn't say a thing about it when I went back to school that following Monday. My silence seemed to indicate my lack of success, I guess, so one of the guys felt it was safe to ask about my hunting. I then told the story. I had stepped it off, after we got the buck to the house, and found that it had been a 333 yard shot. When I told this part of the story the very next question was, "Where did you hit him, Jul?" This was when the "ornery" in me surfaced. I just couldn't help it! I kind of hung my head and acted completely disgusted with myself as I said, "Oh, I was shooting for the head but I pulled off and got him in the neck!" Of course I had been aiming for the rib cage and had pulled off and was just fortunate enough to hit him in the neck!

One time I was elk hunting with some gal friends in the Chesnimnus area. We camped at the mouth of Sumac Creek on our ranch on Joseph Creek. We hunted the opening day with no success. The second day I was helping my husband bring our cattle home from over in Peavine. We trucked to the top of Red Hill then rode down to the benches where our cattle were.

On our way to the pasture we saw sign, so we knew there were elk in the area. I had taken my rifle along just in case I came upon something, though I had no intention of doing any riding just for the sake of hunting. Our main job of the day was to get the cattle home to Joseph Creek.

We often found elk right with our cattle—note the cow at left in the shade

We gathered our pasture and started for home. I was trailing the cattle up a draw while my husband swung out onto a ridge to check out some cattle we had seen. The road I was on was an old, rarely used logging road. There was dense timber and brush on both sides. I was riding my big black gelding, Sparky. The cattle knew they were going home and they knew the way so I simply had to follow along, encouraging the tail end to keep up.

I was daydreaming when all of a sudden my horse shied and looked at some brush in a shallow ditch along the road. With the whole herd of cattle going in front of me, I didn't expect to see any wildlife, much less an elk, but there in the brush not thirty feet away lay a spike, not moving a muscle!

This took me so much by surprise that I became somewhat rattled. I did have the presence of mind to just keep riding up the road past the elk. I then got off and tied Sparky to a tree. I slipped my rifle out of the scabbard, all the while expecting that elk to jump up and take off. I guess he thought that he was really hidden, with all of the cattle, and then me, going by without disturbing him.

I usually had to shoot pretty long distances across canyons so I had my scope set on 9x. When I pulled up on that elk, I was so close to him that all I could see was "fuzzy brown" with a black shiny spot in the middle. I figured the black spot had to be his eye so I fired. Absolutely nothing happened! The elk still lay there just like a statue! I couldn't believe it—couldn't believe I had missed and couldn't believe he was still lying there! The elk must have been sure that I was shooting at something else because NO ONE could miss at that short range! By that time I really was not thinking straight! It never crossed my mind to turn down the power of my scope, so I started backing up the road to where my scope cleared enough to see the elk clearly. The next time he never knew what hit him.

I gutted him then started on up the canyon, picking up the stragglers and pushing them on up with the rest of the cattle which had stopped to graze.

I met my husband up on top by the rig. After the cattle were pushed over the top and down through our gate, I got the meat sacks out of the pickup and headed back down to the elk to start skinning and quartering it. My husband drove back to the ranch to get another horse to pack the meat out of the canyon.

I got the elk skinned before darkness set in but had to do the quartering in the dark. I had him in the meat sacks by the time my husband was back with the packhorse. We loaded up and made it out without incident.

I continued to hunt with my gal friends for a few years but then after my husband's and my separation I gave it up for lack of time and money. When Lee and I went to the Monument Ranch and were going to be out there riding for cattle anyway, I started applying for tags again.

Our hunting experiences those falls were tempered by the necessary ranch work. We got buck tags many of the falls but got bull elk tags less often because of not being successful in the draws.

I would be gone to the valley during the week, teaching school, then I would go out to cow camp for the weekend. Usually Lee met some more hunters during the week and would be all excited to tell me about them, and would be anxious to have me meet them. We met a lot of wonderful people, some who became life-long friends!

We were able to get to know those hunters because we were on top doing clean-up riding. Hunting camps seemed to be bunched around sources of water or at the ends of the open roads. Many miles of roads were closed to any form of motor vehicles during elk season.

Down around Huffman Springs was the camp of the Willis family. That hunting party consisted of Grandpa and Grandma Willis, their sons, daughters-in-law, and grandchildren. One of the sons and his wife had gotten married just before elk season some years ago. They spent their honeymoon in elk camp and had been back every year thereafter.

The Willis family always brought the fixin's for an early Thanksgiving dinner, of which we were guests more than once. Grandma Willis was a painter so she spent much time at carefully selected spots where she could capture the beauty on canvas. She also took many pictures, which she would use as guides for her winter painting back home.

Where you turned off the Table Mountain Road to go into the Dog Fight Cow Camp, was a popular camping spot. Among one group who occasionally camped there, were Big Kid, Danny Worlick whose uncle had previously owned the Monument Ranch and Gordon Powelson.

They had tents, campers, and even a fancy motor home. That was Gordon's idea of roughing it! Gordon was a fellow who had done quite well for himself and was a warm, generous guy. One evening Lee dropped into camp to swap tales. Gordon almost immediately started in about how awful Lee's coat was. Throughout the evening Gordon just wouldn't let up, which surprised Lee because Gordon was not a man inclined to throwing out insults or rudeness. Later Lee admitted that it was starting to get to him, though he didn't let on. As Lee was preparing to leave their camp and go home, Gordon slipped away then returned with a Trail Blazers' coat—he had been setting Lee up for his presentation of the coat!

Another group of guys we met at hunting camp was Ted Sahlfeld, his family and friends. They also became special, life long friends! Lee met them during the week while I was gone teaching. When I went to cow camp that weekend, his first greeting was, "I met the nicest bunch of guys this week! I told them that I would bring you over to meet them."

Lee and I were hunting that year too, so the next morning we saddled up and started riding the breaks, checking cattle but also carrying our guns just in case...! We went around the breaks of Table Mountain then down the point to Haystack Rock.

I had never climbed Haystack Rock so I decided that was the day— I would never be any younger! I really wasn't dressed to be climbing as I had on bulky wool pants and big clumsy boots with a couple of pairs of socks. At the foot of the Rock were the remains of an old pole ladder, completely unusable. I left the camera with Lee and instructed him to take a picture of me when I reached the top. There was a crevice up one end of the Rock so I braced my back against one side and my feet against the other side of it and started wriggling my way up!

When I was almost to the top, I had to crawl out on a little ledge, then up and around to the top. I was feeling pretty smug about making it to the top! I put my name next to previous climbers, in a can which had been put there for that purpose. Lee hollered up to ask if I had put his name in the can, to which I, being a smart mouth, yelled back down, "Are you up here?"

I enjoyed the spectacular view in all directions—watched an eagle soaring in the updrafts—for a little longer. Lee took a couple of pictures of me, then I decided it was time to start down! I had forgotten one very important fact—it was much easier to climb a rock than it was to get back down! I tried several times, unsuccessfully, to back around the ledge, but I simply couldn't do it!

Often, as we rode the trails, we spotted eagles

I was beginning to panic, so I asked Lee to throw up his rope. He asked what I planned to do with it. I explained that there was a big outcropping of rock on top that I could put a loop around, then I could hang onto the rope to get around the ledge. I thought I had him convinced when he asked how I planned to get the rope down once I was down. I had to admit that I didn't know, to which he responded, "I'm not leaving my rope here!" (You know the two most important things to a cowboy are his rope and his hat!) At this point I was starting to wish I had not been such a smart mouth about putting his name in the can!

Now I really was panicking when Lee looked down the ridge and saw two riders coming up it. He said, "I think that's Ted and Jim!" They were the hunters he wanted me to meet. Well, sure enough it was Ted and Jim. Lee explained to them that I was stuck on top; couldn't get down! Ted was carrying a rope, so it was decided that if the two ropes were tied together, they would be long enough to go up and around that outcropping and then back down. I would hold onto both ends of the rope, let myself down, then we simply could pull the rope down and Lee wouldn't have to leave his rope!

Talk about a lesson in humility! I don't know when I have been so embarrassed! I hope I did have enough presence of mind to say thank you to Ted and Jim when I reached the ground, but I'm not sure I did! I know I was not friendly or probably even courteous! All I could think about was getting out of there and away from those guys, who more than likely were thinking that I was a real idiot!

To this day, Ted loves to get me in a crowd and ask them, "Have I told you about the first time I ever saw Julie?" He's gotten a lot of miles out of that one! I must admit, it seems funny even to me, now!

The Sahlfeld bunch always set up a state of the art camp! They had a sleeping tent, which had a plywood boarder all around the bottom of the walls to keep out any drafts. It had a heater stove in it and a table for playing cards. Attached to the front of this was another tent, which was the cook shack. It was here that they had storage bins, coolers, and propane cooking stoves. They also had a large restaurant grill on which they cooked steaks, stir fry, and many other wonderful foods!

In front of the cook tent was a lean-to where they kept wood and whatever didn't have to be in a tent. To keep down the dust and to make it warmer, they had carpet throughout. In fact the carpet extended beyond the lean-to, out toward the bonfire.

The tents and the area around the camp were lit with electric lights powered by a portable generator. They put the generator in a hole, out a ways from the camp. You could hardly hear it. They ran a cord back to the camp and out to where they saddled the horses.

One year they went all out and brought a watering trough to use as a hot tub. This hot tub was in its own tent and was heated by an immersible, gas burning heater. They said it worked great and felt wonderful to sore muscles after chasing the elusive elk all day! They told Lee to tell me to bring my bathing suit—I was welcome to use the hot tub. I said, "Thanks, but no thanks!"

When we went to the Monument Ranch there was a herd of mountain sheep, which hung out in the rims at The Bunnie Place, but in time they moved farther on down Joseph Creek. Somehow one ram got left behind or chose to be a loner. Occasionally we would see him around the Home Place. Eventually he moved down country too, but not as far as the others. He seemed to prefer the breaks around Cliff Creek, Rim Creek, and Table Mountain.

Once when we were riding under some rims, we looked up and saw this ram on top of a rim, looking down at us. I wanted to see if I could get closer, to get some pictures. It was decided that Lee and the dogs would try to keep him distracted while I rode on by, then came up on him from the back. It worked like a charm. Whenever the ram seemed to be getting nervous about my approach, Lee would tell Mert to move up.

She would crawl in a sneaking fashion, up the hill toward the ram until Lee would say, "Down." By repeating this procedure, Lee and Mert kept him distracted until I got some good pictures.

Jim Birkmaier, Bud and Zuah's son, had a trap line down Joseph Creek for several winters. He told us where the traps were located so we could keep the dogs out of them. He used rancid bait, so of course the dogs could smell it and they always wanted to check it out. Sometimes it took some pretty severe scolding to make them stay with us.

One evening we were heading home along the Joseph Creek Trail when we came upon Jim. He had a big, beautiful bobcat. It was pretty heavy so Lee said he would haul it out for Jim. Jim had a backpack type bag in which they stuffed the cat then hung it over the saddle horn of Lee's saddle.

Horses of course don't like the smell of cat and to have one hanging against his shoulder and neck was a lot to ask of Ol' Jack, but he did it!

One year Lee decided he wanted me to get a big buck. He was so sure we would be successful that he took the pack mule along.

We headed down Joseph Creek just before daybreak. Lee was in the lead with the pack mule. The plan was that when we spotted a buck, I would slip off behind a rock and he would go on with the horses. This, hopefully, would create a diversion and the buck wouldn't know I was even there—wouldn't get nervous.

We hadn't gone more than two or three miles when we spotted a big buck standing in the rims above us. I slipped off my horse and Lee went on with the horses, as planned. I was behind a rim with an outcropping that worked perfectly for a gun rest. As long as I had hunted and as many critters as I had killed, I never had much trouble with buck fever. I don't know what happened to me that day! Maybe I felt the pressure of Lee wanting so badly for me to get a big one! Anyway, when I tried to rest my gun on the rock, it was actually bouncing! I moved my hand under the gun to protect it from getting scratched up on the rock.

The buck was so high above me I wasn't sure how high to hold above him. Whether it was the shaking or just miscalculation, I missed on the first shot. The buck jumped and started around the rim. At this, I really panicked—I just couldn't let him get away. I quickly got off another shot and he went down. When the buck had been standing in the rims, I could see his antlers were really high—he looked to be a big four point. Well, it was so steep that when I hit him, he came tumbling down, end over end over end. I just stood there watching, thinking, "Oh, don't break those antlers, please don't break those antlers!" After having rolled about fifty yards, the buck hung up in some rocks.

Since it was a cold morning, I had on lots of clothes. I knew I could never climb up there with all of those clothes on so I started peeling them off layer by layer. I was intent on this process when I heard rocks rolling and looked up to see that buck rolling down the hillside again! I guess his death twitching had jerked him loose from whatever he was caught on. At first I thought this was great! I wasn't going to have to climb up there after all. But then I noticed that the farther he came, the faster he was going—he would never stop on the trail but would go right on down, and end up in Joseph Creek, some two hundred feet below. I calculated where I thought he would cross the trail, ran up there, and waited. It seemed all I could see was legs and horns, legs and horns, as he came a rollin'! I braced my feet and as he rolled over the trail, I grabbed one hind leg.

Now Lee had gone on around the point to find a place to turn around and wait. When the shooting had stopped, he started back. The first thing he saw was me hanging onto the leg of that buck and screaming, "Hurry, Lee, hurry!"

We drug him back up onto the trail, laid him on his back and gutted him. We then got him above the trail thinking that by us being above the trail, it would give us enough height advantage to be able to get him on Ol' Suzy, the mule. She was a sweetheart and stood perfectly still, but we could not get the buck up on her—he simple was too big and heavy!

We were trying everything we knew, when we looked up and saw a guy hiking up the trail. It was Bud Birkmaier's son-in-law, Byron Cheney. He was hunting too, and had dropped down from the top and was hiking back up the Joseph Creek Trail to the road where someone would pick him up. Byron was young and stout, so with his help we were able to get that buck loaded! The buck turned out to be an old guy who had reverted back to being just a forked horn, but his horns were really high!

One day Lee and I were down the canyon looking for stragglers after the fall gather. It was late fall/early winter and pretty cold, with snow on the ground. We went into the Vawter Cabin to warm up and eat lunch, as was our custom. We were in the middle of eating lunch when the dogs started barking. We assumed they were probably just barking at a deer that had come down for a drink. We hollered at the dogs but they just wouldn't quit. We finally went out to see what was going on. The dogs quieted down when we went outside but they still seemed agitated and were pacing around. We looked around, and not seeing anything, we went back in to finish our lunch.

After lunch we rode around to the mouth of Swamp Creek to check that gate and look for signs of cattle passing through. Well, we saw sign all right, but not of cattle. There were big cougar tracks where one had come down out of the north behind the cabin to get a drink in Swamp Creek. The tracks then went back up into the north.

We finished our riding, found a few strays, and trailed them home. We had to go to town that night, for some reason, so we stopped at Tom Birkmaier's and told him about the cougar. We knew he was trying to help Dean Garrett fill his cougar tag.

The rest of this story is as Dean related it to me.

Tom went to town for some reason that night too, and started trying to call Dean, but it wasn't until late that he finally got a hold of him. Dean was already in bed and fast asleep. When the phone rang, Dean jumped out of bed and on his way to the phone he stubbed his toe and broke it. Nevertheless, Dean was so excited that he got his stuff together and Tom, Dean, and some other guy headed for Tom's at about 3:00 A.M.

They then drove the ten miles on down Joseph Creek to the ranch. They hiked, in the dark, the five miles on down to the Vawter Place. The only boot Dean was able to get on over that broken toe was a big old "pack boot," which was not very good for hiking.

It was just getting light when they reached the cabin and Dean was hurting badly! They were all hungry so it was decided that Dean would stay at the cabin, build a fire, and heat up some of the canned food that was in the cupboard.

Tom and the other guy were able to find the tracks and started following them. They found the old cat, treed, but she had a kitten with her. Being the sportsmen they were, they walked off and left her!

Dean had eaten while waiting for the other guys, so knowing it would take him longer than it would the two "young bucks" to hike back to the ranch, he started up the trail. Tom and his friend ate the food Dean had heated up, then after giving Dean a head start of 30 to 40 minutes they started back up the trail too. They caught up with Dean, passed him, and beat him back to the rig by more than an hour! All that walking with a broken toe and still an unfilled tag!

There was a large herd of elk that stayed around Dog Fight. They seemed to make a circle, which took in the heads of Rim Creek, Cliff Creek, and Bull Canyon. They would go on around onto the Cougar Benches, then work their way up and around through the Sleepy Bill area and back into the Dog Fight Pasture. Sometimes they would complete that circle by going in the opposite direction. Because we knew their general travel pattern we could generally always find elk to show people, if they wanted to see them.

At times the elk seemed almost complacent with our presence. We often drove or rode up on the herd while they were napping.

Elk trailing around hillside in Sleepy Bill

One June day we were driving the loop around the Dog Fight Pasture with the pickup and trailer, when we came upon the herd of elk. Being June, there were some calves in the bunch. The elk took off over the hill, to drop down into the head of Thorn Hollow. I unloaded my horse, took my camera, and rode over the hill to see where the elk had gone. Well, they hadn't gone far! There were some elk calves that couldn't get through the fence. The elk moved off a ways, but then the mothers of the calves turned and came back toward the fence and their babies. They were close to a fence corner which had a gate in it. After watching for a while and taking some pictures, I went up and opened the gate then went back around the elk calves and drove them up through the gate!

Once when we were moving cattle out of the Dog Fight Pasture, Lee could hear something moving around in a really thick timbered area. He sent the dogs in to flush out the cattle, but instead, over one hundred head of elk came out!

Another time we drove up on a bunch of bull elk. There were over thirty of them just hanging out around Milk Pond on Table Mountain. There were five branch antler bulls and the rest were spikes.

One June day we were riding, checking the cattle on Cougar Bench and scattering some more salt. We had noticed a lone doe standing up on an open point above the benches. Even with our presence over a period of time, she didn't move off to the shelter of a timbered draw but just kept intently watching us and the dogs. She was near a pond so we decided to go up by that pond and check it out, but also to see why that deer chose not to leave. As we started up the ridge toward the point, she became more nervous, then moved off into the timbered draw. I was riding Katrina's mare, Missy. When we were in the general area of where the doe had been, I just happened to look down as Missy stepped over a "rock" that wasn't a rock at all. It was a newborn fawn that was just a few hours old. We were amazed that the doe had given birth right there on the hillside—there was no flat land for quite some distance! Newborn fawns have no scent so even though our dogs walked within feet of the fawn hidden amongst the rocks, they were never aware of its presence. It was so small that I laid my hat beside it, for a size comparison, and took a picture.

Early one morning we were headed up the Joseph Creek Road when, as we rounded a sharp curve in the road, there was a tiny fawn that could hardly run, it was such a "newborn!" Its little legs would almost collapse with each bound so we stopped the pickup to give it a chance to get off the road. The doe had jumped off the road down into a grassy bottom which also had some brush.

At this very place the road bank was quite high. It was high enough that my Uncle Don had built a chute type contraption which he used to load rock into a dump truck. With his Cat he would dig rock out of the bank above the road, push it across the road then down the chute into the truck. Some of the log framework still remained, so the fawn jumped down onto it and laid down, all in the same motion. It was so sure that it was hidden that it stayed there while I took pictures, and the doe looked on!

We didn't do a lot of fishing but occasionally if we got in early enough we would do a little fishing there close to the house. There was one hole in particular that always seemed to have some suckers in it. The suckers seemed to follow the spawning trout, to eat the eggs, so we figured we were doing a service to the trout population by ridding the river of the suckers. Some of them were quite big and were fun to catch!

Beaver can be a real nuisance if they build their dams at a location that will cause the river to be diverted and thus wash out a field, road, etc. Most of the canyon down river from the ranch house was so narrow and rimmed in that there was nothing to be washed out so the beaver really never posed a problem. Consequently we left them alone and let them build their dams wherever they wanted.

I always felt bad for them, though, because if there was no place for the water to be diverted to, it was a sure guarantee that the dam would be washed out the first time there was high water! They were such ambitious, ingenious little creatures that I could not help but admire them and their works of art!

Every year there would be several new dams. Sometimes they would rebuild at a location of a previously washed out dam; other times they would relocate.

It was amazing the things we found when riding through the brush, chasing cattle. Most hunters did a pretty good job of cleaning up when they broke camp, but then there were the others! Probably the most disgusting finds were the piles of cans and the discarded black plastic.

Lee fishing in Joseph Creek in the "sucker hole" near the house

Once someone went off and left almost an entire camp outfit on Table Mountain. The tarps were still stretched as a lean-to. After a couple of months had passed and winter set in, we decided whoever it was, wasn't coming back, so we cleaned it up, salvaging some useful items and packing the rest to the dump. We always wondered what the circumstances were—if there had been an emergency, causing the hunters to leave in a hurry!

One item we found back in the brush at another camp was a fiberglass, portable outhouse. We were able to hook onto it with our lariats and drag it out with the horses, to where we could tip it onto the

Beaver dam near the ranch house

back of the pickup and haul it to our Dog Fight camp. It was a bright turquoise so I spot sprayed it with various colors to create a camouflage effect. We placed it in the brush amongst the trees—you couldn't tell it was there if you didn't already know it!

    Bud Birkmaier told of his grandma, Gertie McFetridge, taking Bud and his brother Mack to a snake pit. She had an old broken off hoe handle with a hook in the end of it. It was the spring of the year and the snakes were coming out of the pit to sun themselves on the rocks nearby. It was early enough in the spring that the snakes weren't going far from the pit so they could go back into it when it cooled off at night.

Beaver dam down Joseph Creek from the ranch house—dam at bottom of picture and fallen tree above it

When Gertie and the boys got to the pit there were some snakes near the opening into the pit. Gertie hooked them and kind of slung them over her shoulder and down the hill to where the boys were. Their job was to kill the snakes before they could bite someone or get back to the pit!

I asked Bud why his grandmother had done this. He paused for a moment then said, "I guess to scare the H___ out of us!" I then asked if it had worked. Bud gave that "Bud Birkmaier" chuckle and said, "Yep!"

Lee and I had asked Bud several times where the pit was. He tried to tell us but we never could find it. I finally asked Bud if he would take me in to the pit and he consented! One day, in late fall, we went in. Because it was late fall there were no snakes around the opening—they had already gone to bed for the winter.

The day we went, Tom Birkmaier, Mack's son, said he wanted to go with us, so Bud and I rode our horses and Tom walked.

The pit was just as I had expected it to be. The opening was not very large. It went back into the rim a ways then dropped straight down. There was no way of knowing how big or deep the hole was, but for sure

Bud Birkmaier and nephew, Tom Birkmaier, at snake pit—looking down on Joseph Creek

it would have been deep enough to get below the frost line so the snakes would not freeze!

We made many memories and friendships during those falls and hunting seasons! Just as we had many fond memories, so had others previous to us! Out on Horse Pasture Ridge, in a saddle, hung a sign put there in memory of a man who had sat in the saddle for many years while elk hunting. He had passed away and his family and friends had returned and put up a sign, naming it "Les Morris Saddle." Maybe someday, somewhere, someone will put up a sign in memory of the great times Lee and I had while on the ranch!

Haystack Rock

Me on top of Haystack Rock—feeling real cocky that I made it to the top—before I realized I couldn't get down! I put my name in the can on top with names of previous climbers.

Making my way down the crevice, using Ted's and Lee's ropes

Me, on the Cliff Creek Breaks glassing for cattle and game

Luke Hamerl, Me and Frank Huston in the Sahlfeld Camp

Ram in the rims of Cliff Creek Breaks above Joseph Creek. He was being held at bay by Mert, Lee's dog, until I could circle around to take this picture.

Rocky Mountain Sheep on cliffs above the High Road going into the Monument Ranch

Same sheep taken through binoculars

Lee packed bobcat out—
note bobcat's feet sticking out of sack

Jimmy Birkmaier with a
bobcat he trapped down
Joseph Creek

Me with buck I killed in
Joseph Canyon—Lee and
Suzy looking on.

Byron Cheney helped load
the heavy buck on Suzy.

Elk heading down into the head of Thorn Hollow from the Dog Fight pasture

When some of the calves couldn't get through the fence, the cows came back for them

*I put my hat beside the fawn to show how small it was—
on ridge above Cougar Bench*

*The doe looked on with concern as her fawn hid in the old rock chute.
—note fawn in the lower left corner*

The little fawn looked at me with its big brown eyes

Tom Birkmaier and his Uncle Bud Birkmaier at the snake den

Note horses on top of cliff in upper right corner—Bud and Tom

Bud at the snake pit

My son Kurt capturing the fun on film

Julie and my granddaughter, Jessica, playing in Joseph Creek

Kurt gave Jessica and her friend, Josh Cook, rides on the 4-wheeler

Ted Sahlfeld, Paul Soward with me on Jack sorting calves to brand

Jessica and me on Doc with my dog Doll at Coyote Campground

Laurie, Lee's daughter, playing a game of cards at Dog Fight Cow Camp

*Melanie, Lee's daughter, on Katrina's mare Missy and
Mike Whalen, Mel's fiancee, on Suzy—
Table Mountain cliffs in the background*

Bob Shelton helping Lee push cattle into Bull Canyon. Photo by Pat Shelton

Jessica and Julie on Doc, Kurt on Joker and my dog Doll begging for a ride

Wayne and Ival Clark often helped us by bringing salt and lunch when we moved cattle—their dog Boots looking on—at Allen Springs

Cattle on the back of Table Mountain—Lee with Wayne and Ival who again brought salt—the cattle were salt hungry

Marilynn Davis with my mare, Candy, in the background. Marilynn helped us move cattle.

Fred Webb, Bud Zollman, Sherry VanLeuven, Shirley Botham, Sharon Gibson, Me and Duane 'Obie' O'Brien on Horse Pasture Ridge

Casey, Beckijo, Teresa and Patrick Smergut, on Table Mountain

My daughter Katrina on Doc, and my granddaughter Jessica on Suzy at Frog Ponds in Dog Fight Pasture

Dave Caudle on his gelding, Freddie, at the Dog Fight Corrals

Volunteers and Visitors

Lyle Harrison on his horse Bug, Me on Jack and Dave Caudle on his horse Freddie —on the back of Table Mountain

Dave Caudle and Ted Sahlfeld helping me salt the Corral Springs Pasture while Lee and others looked for horses that had strayed during the night

Ted Sahlfeld cooking on the porch of the Hunting Camp cabin

Ted getting ready to move cattle—at the Townley Place

Volunteer Help & Visitors

The life style of "Canyon Cowboying" can't be matched! It offers experiences that can't be found anywhere else. There were lots of long hours in all kinds of weather, to a point of exhaustion. But there also was the rewarding feeling of a job well done in the midst of God's wondrous creation.

Color photos—page 232

Lee's girls and my kids came occasionally. If we were riding, the kids would ride with us; if we were moving camp, they would drive rigs or ride horses. One time my son, Kurt and his wife and baby, Jessica, were down in the heat of the summer. We decided to go over to the river and play in the water and do a little fishing. I had gotten the kids a camcorder so Kurt was taking pictures of Jessica playing in the creek. I looked up at the river bank just in time to see one of the dogs jump straight in the air. I yelled, "Snake" then kept my eye on the place where I had seen the dog jump. I directed Lee to the place and sure enough there was a rattler. It wasn't a very big one and there were lots of rocks and limbs nearby so there was no problem in killing it. Kurt kept wondering where its brothers, sisters, aunts, and uncles were!

Once the boss's brother and some friends from Alabama came to visit. Dub had Lee and me pack them into the Vawter Place for a few days of fishing.

There were no words to describe the feeling you experienced when you had pushed a bunch of cows out on a point, then you sat for a while, watching them

Dub's brother Wally and his friends on Joseph Creek Trail

Tom Birkmaier with his dog, King—Mert's pup

Troy Brown, Tom's hired man having just helped to move cattle to Horse Pasture Ridge

as they mothered up. A hawk or eagle soared overhead, crows cawed in the distance, and occasionally a bear was working a log for grubs—those were the things we saw and heard on a regular basis!

Apparently Lee and I were not the only ones who felt this way because we had a lot of friends who wanted to come and help us. They were willing to do the hard jobs as well as the pleasurable ones.

The top of Table Mountain was a maze of gently rolling timbered hills interspersed with clearings, draws, and water holes. As the cattle became more acquainted with the lay of the land, they also became cleverer in circling back around through the brush and ending up where you started. With several good heading dogs and a knowledge of the terrain, Lee and I were able to usually get a pretty clean ride, especially if we were pushing the cattle from the back toward the front of the mountain. It was a little more difficult when we were pushing them toward the back.

When friends were willing and anxious to help us, we were receptive to the idea! When we had extra riders, we would spread out across the top, putting riders on the main trails and in the main draws. As some of

Lee, Dwayne VanLeuven, Sherry VanLeuven, Joey VanLeuven, Randy Warner, Tony Daggett, Mara Warner, Sharon Gibson holding Joey's child, ?. On the 4-wheelers: Gabby Gibson and Robin Warner. Not-shown: Darla VanLeuven

Lynn Mitchell and Marilynn Davis helping move cattle to Horse Pasture Ridge

the more cantankerous old lead cows would start their "circle back" trick, they would become quite surprised when coming face to face with another rider.

On one such drive we had the Gibson bunch and the Warner bunch helping us. A couple of people who preferred not to ride horses took the 4-wheelers with lunch, went around logging roads, and met us at lunchtime.

Branding time was a popular event, especially if we were going to

Russell Hanson on my horse, Dundee. Paul Soward, Lee, and Robin Warner as ground crew

Steve Rother on Randy Warner's horse. Paul Soward on ground.

Lee, Robin and Randy Warner

Pat Shelton on her horse, Copper

Bob Shelton and Lee working on trail

rope and stretch. There were guys who would jump at a chance to polish up their roping skills. We roped and stretched if the weather permitted. If it was rainy, we would sort the calves off from the cows, and put them in pens in the barn to dry. We would then go to the house, fix breakfast, and play a game or two of cards.

When the calves were dry we would put them through a calf table that was under a lean-to. With this set up we could set a date for branding, knowing rain or shine we wouldn't have to cancel!

Wayne and Ival Clark, who had previously owned the ranch, never got the ranch out of their blood! Often when we were moving cattle from pasture to pasture, they would come along with their pickup and bring the lunch and sometimes some salt for the cattle, if we needed it.

My daughter, Katrina, helped us move cattle on various occasions. My granddaughter Jessica started going with us when she was four or five and loved staying in the cow camps on top.

There were various other people who helped us install water troughs, move cattle, clean trails, or feed cattle. It seemed no matter what the task at hand, some people were always waiting to be invited to join us.

Bob Shelton was a friend of Dub's and later became a friend of Lee's. He and his wife Pat, came to help on the ranch quite often. They helped trail cattle, work on water holes, and do whatever else was needed. They were helping Lee move cattle down the creek one spring when he had a near fatal horse wreck; that story is in the chapter, "Wrecks."

After having met Ted Sahlfeld and his bunch in hunting camp, Ted came and helped Lee on many, many occasions. He apparently developed a real love for the canyon cowboy life style because he was always willing to do anything asked of him!

In the years that followed, Ted and various members of his party came back many times to help with the ranch work. Ted came to relax and get away from the pressure of living and working in the Portland Metro area, since he lived in Hillsboro.

Many times as soon as Ted got off work, he would jump into his rig that was all packed, then would drive all night, and arrive at the ranch in the wee hours of the morning. The next morning Lee would threaten all the "kids" with their lives if they woke Ted up before he was rested and woke up on his own. The whole bunch would then help with any work that had to be done, day after day. They played cards every night, worked all day, then claimed they were going home refreshed!

One time we sat on the breaks eating our lunches in the breeze created by the convection currents coming up out of the canyon. We watched the currents carry a hawk higher and higher until he was no longer visible. A crow or two flew over giving that "oh so familiar" caw of warning to the other wildlife, "We have been invaded by humans," followed by complete silence, except for the rustle of the grass as a breeze caused it to do a graceful dance there on the hillside. Lee and I looked at each other and asked, "I wonder what the poor folks are doing today?" That became the often stated summary of Lee's and my feelings of our life in the canyon!

Not only did we have people willing to help with the spring brandings, putting cattle out on spring pasture, moving the cattle from one pasture to another during the course of the summer, and doing the fall gathering, but there were people who enjoyed riding with us and helping us with whatever needed done throughout the entire course of the year!

There were two pretty bad spots in the Joseph Creek Trail and one in the Bull Canyon Trail. With heavy use those places just seemed to get worse. Lee repeatedly asked the Forest Service to come down and blast out a couple of the worst spots but they never seemed to have time to do it.

Finally we decided that the only thing to do, on the Joseph Creek Trail, was to just find a way around those bad spots, which we did. By taking a pack string around this new trail a few times, we were starting to get it pretty well beaten out.

Lee was in the Forest Service Office sometime after this, talking over pasture rotation plans for the season, when he happened to remember the trail issue so he said to them, "Oh, by the way, don't worry about those bad spots in the trail, I have found a pretty good way around them!" Man, they were down there the very next week working on the trail! They never wanted anyone making new trails that they hadn't mapped out and approved!

There was still the bad spot on the Bull Canyon Trail. We had a friend whose brother was pretty good with "powder". He came down with all the necessary supplies. A bunch of us rode around into Bull Canyon to witness the "blowing of the trail". It was pretty spectacular! Not only did a cloud of dust and smoke fill the canyon, but the echo of the blast bounced back and forth across the canyon time after time. We, the spectators, had situated ourselves back a couple hundred of feet from the blasting and we still were peppered with fine gravel.

I was only sorry that I hadn't taken a "before" picture of the ledge he blasted in Bull Canyon. It was so narrow that when we took a mule loaded with salt around it, the block of salt would bump the rim and almost knock the mule off the trail. We were always amazed that we hadn't lost a mule there!

One summer we had friends from Canada, Dave and Janine Caudle, Lyle and Lisa Harrison, and Bill Rouw, come down to join us for a trip into the Wallowa Mountains. Before we could go, there was a certain amount of ranch work that had to be finished.

Lee, Dub (the boss) and Bob Shelton at the Dog Fight Cow Camp

There was hay to haul, cattle to move, and salt to scatter. The Canadians were more than eager to help us with the ranch work, and they were good help. Dave was an experienced canyon cowboy as he had run a ranch on Imnaha, at Fence Creek, before he and Janine moved to Canada, and Lyle had worked on a large cattle ranch in Canada.

They brought their own horses so as to have them for going into the mountains, thus they were all set to help with the ranch work too. We hauled their horses to the hills and turned them out in the Dog Fight Pasture with our horses the night before we were going to do the riding. The next morning we went to Dog Fight to catch the horses only to discover that a couple of the Canadian horses were gone. We found tracks where they had jumped the cattle guard out into the Kirkland pasture, but could find no more sign. We searched this pasture for hours but with no luck. Time was running out and the salting was not getting done.

Ted Sahlfeld was up to help us too, and was camped down by the Hunting Camp Cabin. Ted, as usual, was willing to do whatever it took to help us get things

Ted Sahlfeld and Luke Hamerl

done so we could go to the mountains. After pondering the situation for some time, it was decided that Dave and Ted would go with me to scatter the salt while Lee and Lyle kept looking for the horses.

Lee never did find the horses that day so the next day we expanded our search area to include the Baldwin Pasture, which was the pasture that surrounded the Coyote Camp Ground.

Late that second day I had taken the pickup and trailer past the Coyote Camp Ground to the east fence of the Baldwin pasture, while some of the guys were riding through, hoping to cut the tracks of the horses. It was a hot day, so I was out of the rig lying in the shade of some trees when I thought I heard something coming through the timber. Sure enough, it was the missing horses! They were following along the fence line and if I hadn't been there, they probably would have jumped another cattle guard and ended up, who knows where! When I saw them, my heart began to race like I had a bad case of buck fever! If I couldn't get them caught and they disappeared into the timber, who knows how long it would be before we found them again! But, do you know, they acted almost as happy to see me as I was to see them. They were lost, lonesome, and seemed somewhat confused!

They had jumped two cattle guards without any major injuries. Dave's big gelding had apparently been the leader of the pack and Janine's little mare had wanted to not be left behind. She had followed him across the cattle guards but apparently had not been able to jump clear because she had a little scrape on one hind foot and was missing a shoe. She had probably jerked it off in a cattle guard.

There was celebrating in camp that night! With the cattle moved, salt scattered, and horses recovered, we were ready to start packing for the mountains!

The Mountain Trip

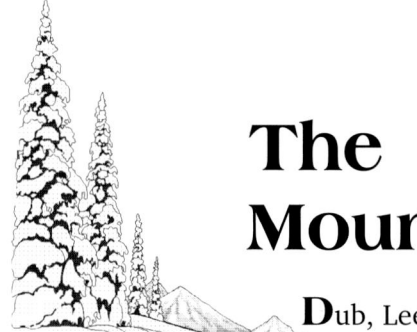

Color photos—page 273

Dub, Lee's boss, had agreed to let Lee go into the mountains for the first part of the trip. Lee would then have to come out and haul more hay. Having never been in the Wallowa Mountains, Lee was excited to get to go for even a few days, and it proved to be a trip none of us will ever forget!

We used my place in the valley as headquarters. I had corrals and pasture space for the horses and mules. There were the Canadian horses, my horses, ranch horses, and pack mules. We also borrowed a couple of mules, Buck and Sis, from Larry and Juanita Waters.

We headed up the Lostine River Canyon with pickups and trailers loaded with camp equipment, food, horses, and mules. Lee was driving the ranch pickup and trailer. The pickup overheated so we stopped to let it cool off. Lee raised the hood and to my horror there were flames dancing around on the motor. I panicked but Lee just ran to the road bank, scooped up a big double handful of dirt and threw it on the flames, putting them out. The pickup cooled off, we added water, and on we went without further incident!

We packed up and headed into John Henry Lake by way of the Bowman Trail. The weather was cooperative and the scenery was beautiful! That first night we set up a "rough camp" because we were tired and the weather seemed to be fine. I threw my sleeping bag down on a tarp

Bill Rouw, Me leading pack horses, Lee with more pack horses, Janine Caudle, and Dave Caudle also with pack horses.
—Resting animals at Wilson Pass.

not far from where Lee had put his. The rest of the people went ahead and put up tents.

The next morning, just at daybreak, I was awakened by Lee trying to use a voice somewhere between a whisper and a yell. As I started rousing from a deep sleep and realized it was Lee who was waking me, I was not too happy with him! This was unusual for me because I really do wake up happy most of the time, but I was tired and there was simply no reason for us to be getting up early. Then, when I realized what it was that Lee was saying, I woke up in a hurry! There right in the middle of our camp was a cow elk. She was not thirty feet from us. I had left my camera with my other gear, which wasn't near my sleeping bag, so I got no pictures of her.

We just watched her, then told the rest of our group when they got up. The next morning she was in camp again! This time we could see that she was eating something. We came to realize that it was a bar of hand soap. We had a basin of water wedged between two trees and the soap had been lying right by it. She had that bar of soap in her mouth, chewing vigorously! After a short time she immersed her entire mouth and muzzle into the wash water, blew bubbles and shook her head from side to side, as though she was trying to wash the soap from her mouth.

Never dreaming she would come back a second morning, I again had not put my camera near my bedroll. The third night I remembered

Bill, Janine, Me (in front of Janine), Dave, Lise and Lee—having lunch at Hobo Lake

Dave, Janine, Lise, Lee in camp at John Henry Lake

On Bowman Trail where we could look into North Minam Meadow—Lee, Lise, Janine and Dave

North Minam Meadow from the Bowman Trail.

the camera and was ready for her but do you know, we never saw her again! We figured she probably had a bad case of diarrhea from all of that soap!

While camping at John Henry Lake those few days, we took several day rides. I wanted to show the rest of them some of my favorite places. One day we backtracked on the Bowman Trail and then took the trail into Laverty Lakes, Chimney Lake, and Hobo Lake. We looked down on Wood Lake but didn't ride down to it.

Another day we rode on down the Bowman Trail toward North Minam Meadows, then took the trail into Bear Lake. Each of these days we would pack some snacks for lunch, some fishing gear, and make a day of it.

On the days that we stayed in camp at John Henry, we fished in the lake and explored the old mine there by the lake.

After we enjoyed a few days at John Henry we packed up and headed for North Minam Meadows. When we got there it seemed the only adequate campsites for a group of our size, were already taken. We rode the full length of the meadow with no success. Frustration was mounting as we didn't want to camp next to existing camps; we wanted solitude and privacy! Lee was quick to recognize the brewing of trouble, so to diffuse the situation he turned his hat sidewise and announced, "Me heap big scout! Me find you good campsite!" With that, he and Dave took off out through the meadow leaving the rest of us. It had been an

Lise "trying out" makeshift "Dunny"

Along the banks of the North Minam River

exceptionally dry year so meadows that usually were one big marsh were all dried up. The little ditches that wound their way through the marshes were dried up. The only water was the North Minam River zigzagging it's way through the meadow. We were able to ride out through the meadow to a clump of trees; a place you never could have gotten to nineteen out of twenty years! We had a fresh, clean campsite right on the banks of the river. There was horse feed up to the horses' knees. What a find!

The water was crystal clear, causing the depth to be very deceptive. The riverbed was covered with very small, round gravel. There was a large sand bar between camp and the river. Some distance from the river, a large spruce tree had fallen, ripping its roots from the ground, leaving a large hole where they had been. We stretched a piece of black plastic over this, tacked our toilet ring to a couple of remaining roots, thus making a pretty fancy outhouse, for out in the "boonies."

Lee "hamming it up"—getting ready to leave us.

Leaving North Minam Meadow—headed for the next camp. Dave and Lyle leading pack animals.

Lee was able to stay with us at this camp for a couple of days, then he had to ride out and go back to work. The rest of

Climbing from North Minam Meadow to Steamboat Lake—mountain is so steep I'm looking up at the bellies of the animals on these switchbacks

On the trail from Steamboat Lake to Swamp Lake

Bill and I held pack animals while Dave was looking for an unnamed "hidden" Lake

us stayed around camp, then one day rode up to Green Lake and went fishing.

    Dave had been in the mountains quite a lot as a teenager because he had a brother-in-law, Dale Lamm, who worked for the Forest Service. Dale worked trails and packed into the mountains, taking Dave with him. Dave remembered a little remote lake out on some benches on the breaks of the Minam Canyon. We decided that our next camp would be there. Dave thought it would be fun to go back to a place where he had camped as a kid. I thought it would be great to go to a place I had not been before!

We packed up and headed up toward Steamboat Lake, leaving the North Minam Meadow behind. We stopped at Steamboat for lunch then climbed up to Swamp Lake, then on even higher to the top that looks back down on Swamp Lake to the north, the head of the Minam to the south, the Blue Mountains beyond the Grande Ronde Valley to the west, and more of the Wallowa Mountain peaks to the east.

There was a grassy slope just as Dave had remembered it, so he left us with the pack animals while he went on to scout out the easiest route to the "hidden lake." As he searched for the lake, memories became fuzzy. It had been almost thirty years since he had been there and things didn't seem to quite fit together. Passing years have a way of changing distances and landmarks. Dave searched and searched but never could find the lake. Later he learned that it was just around the slope a little farther than he had gone. He simply hadn't gone quite far enough when looking for it.

As time was running out, we knew we had to set up camp somewhere. There was no horse feed and no water where we were on top. Knowing that there was water and horse feed back down at Swamp Lake I felt we should drop back down there. After some discussion that was what we decided to do.

We were packing a young mule of Lee's and she was getting tired and not leading very well so she was turned loose to follow. Little did we know that this would set in motion a chain of events which none of us will ever forget! This was the only time I can ever remember of turning a pack animal loose and I can guarantee you it will be the last! She didn't follow along on the trail but went off the trail this way and that, every chance she got. I finally got off my horse and hiked out along the mountainside to drive her back onto the trail.

When I went after the mule, I had one of the other gals, Lise, lead my horse, which was a young, inexperienced horse. She was one of those kind, gentle people who probably thought twice before swatting a fly. I had just gotten the mule back on the trail and we were part way back down the mountainside toward Swamp Lake when my horse, that Lise was leading, crowded up along the inside of the trail by her horse. That occurred at a place where there was a large slick rock on the lower side of the trail. Lise's horse's hind end was pushed over the edge of the trail with his hind feet on this rock. He was scrambling, trying to pull himself back onto the trail with his front feet. I could see that he was not going

The Mountain Trip

to make it so I screamed for Lise to jump. She half jumped, half rolled off onto the trail just as her horse gave one last thrust with his hind feet. Instead of this pushing him back up on to the trail, he actually did what looked like a backwards dive off a diving board! We were on switchbacks in the trail and Lise's husband, Lyle, was directly below her. Lise's horse knocked Lyle and his horse off the trail in a cloud of dust. For a little while you honestly couldn't see anything but dust, then out of the cloud of dust came the two saddle horses, actually running around the mountainside. When I saw the two horses I started screaming, "Where is Lyle, where is Lyle?" As the dust settled, we found Lyle sitting on a rock down under the trail. His eyes were open and he was talking, but he was completely "out of it."

Some of us gathered up the saddle horses and pack animals and made our way down to a little bench just above Swamp Lake. We quickly set up a makeshift camp. We built a fire, put some water on to heat, and made a bed to put Lyle on when we got him off the mountain.

After what seemed like forever, Dave and Bill came walking Lyle into camp, one on either side of him. Of the options, walking seemed the safest. It had become apparent that Lyle had a broken arm so Dave and Bill had put it in a sling before walking him down. All evening Lyle kept making comments which indicated that he still wasn't rational.

After several alternatives were discussed and dismissed, it was decided that Dave and I would ride out for help at the crack of dawn. Dave would ride his gelding, Freddie, who was a fast walker and I would ride the big gray warmblood gelding, Jack, who was one of the ranch horses we were using as a pack animal. He could really burn up the trail too!

Lise threw her bedroll next to Lyle. The rest of us threw out a large tarp and threw our bedrolls on it. We didn't bother with tents and didn't expect to sleep, but just wished to lie down and rest for a few hours before daylight started breaking. It was a bright night with the moonlight creating shadows almost as vivid as those formed by sunlight. It was because of this shadowing that Dave and I had decided to wait for daybreak, to ride out. Freddie and Jack were horses that were prone to "shying." We knew that they would both be eyeing each dark spot in the trail, looking for the "boogie man." If we would wait for daybreak they would relax and really move out, making much better time.

We didn't fix breakfast but Dave and I just grabbed some fruit and a sweet roll. Dawn found us once more climbing the trail to the top. At the forks we took the Coppercreek Trail and headed for Two Pan, the trailhead where we had one of our rigs waiting for us.

We had transferred it there because Two Pan was where we had originally planned to come out anyway.

We were in hopes of being able to call for help from the Forest Service guard station on down the Lostine Canyon a ways, but there was no one there. We ended up driving clear into Enterprise. We went straight to the Sheriff's office. Roger Decker was sheriff at that time. We related the whole story to him, asking if the Search and Rescue could go in and bring Lyle out. After much thought and consideration Roger said the rescue unit would not want the liability of moving Lyle where there had obviously been a head injury, and we didn't know to what extent. It was decided to call for the "Life Flight" helicopter out of Spokane, Washington.

We were able to tell Roger exactly where Lyle was located. Using maps and instruments, Roger took a bearing and gave it to the pilot. Later the pilot said he had never been given a more accurate reading!

When Dave and I had ridden out that morning, we had told those staying in the mountains that we would be sending in the Search and Rescue. We had left all of the animals tied very close to camp. Dave and I were concerned as to what the horses would do when the helicopter landed practically right on top of them. There was no way of getting word back into our people that a helicopter would be coming.

The helicopter flew straight to our camp, but our people were not expecting it to be for Lyle, so they did not run out and wave their arms as most people do when needing help. The rescue team on the helicopter thought it must be the wrong camp so they flew off. They looked around the basin and seeing no other camp decided that must be the one, so they went back and landed!

They picked Lyle up and flew him to Walla Walla, Washington, but because of the limited space, Lise was not allowed to go with him. Our group later told us that the horses all behaved beautifully when the chopper sat down, in spite of the wind it created—a wind so strong it blew one tent, that was rolled up and just laying on the ground, over the crest of the bench we were camped on.

While we were in the Sheriff's office, he was able to stay in contact with the helicopter pilot until he got into the mountains. The pilot had said he would take Lyle to Walla Walla so Dave made arrangements for his mom, Ida Caudle, to drive to Walla Walla and get Lyle when they had him all fixed up.

Having all the arrangements taken care of, Dave went to his mom's to grab a bite to eat and get a shower. I went home and did the same. I also called Dub, Lee's boss, and told him what had happened. In our county, news travels fast and I knew that Dub would hear that there had been an accident in the mountains, so I wanted him to hear the straight of it!

Dave and I then drove back up to Two Pan, grabbed our horses, which we had left resting and eating, and started back into camp. We didn't go back in as fast as we had come out but we didn't waste any time either! We got back to camp just at dark. It had been a long day for everyone!

After the day's events were shared—Dave and I telling our end of the story and those left in camp telling theirs—the pieces of the puzzle of events were all put together.

With Lyle gone we were going to have to rearrange our pack strings and we weren't exactly sure of the best way to put them together, but we would deal with that in the morning. We again fell into bed exhausted, but with a degree of relief.

We got up quite early the next morning, though not at daybreak! We didn't even build a fire as we just wanted to get packed up and on our way as soon as possible. We were in the process of gulping down some fruit and sweet rolls when we heard something on the trail above us. Looking up we saw a lone rider; a man on a big dark horse. At the pace he was coming, it was obvious that he was "a man on a mission!" My first thought was that it must be Randy Warner. Randy rode a big dark horse and was active in the Search and Rescue. Randy, being the thoughtful, caring man that he was, would have come in to help us had he heard about it, even if they hadn't officially sent in a rescue unit. As the rider came on down the mountain past where we had had our "wreck," it just didn't look like Randy or his horse. I was still puzzling over who it might be when the rider's booming voice rang out through the still mountain air, "Hurry up you _ _ _." Instantly I knew it was Lee!

When Lee had come into the valley ranch where Dub lives, for another load of hay, Dub had told him of our accident. Even though there was hay to haul, Dub told Lee to take his (Dub's) horse and go in and help us! I had told Dub where we were camped but Lee had never been there so he went to Ken Witty and had Ken show him on the map how to get there. Lee had always amazed me how he could find trails or figure out the best way to get into a place even if there were no trails. Ken must have given excellent directions and Lee must have listened well! Lee got up at 2:00 A.M. and drove to the trailhead. He then headed up the trail in the dark. Ken had given him very detailed information of what to look for to recognize where the trail forked. Lee was past the major forks in the trail when dawn started breaking. He continued to recognize landmarks Ken had told him about so he knew he had done it right!

*Coming out on the Copper Creek Trail into a basin above Swamp Lake
—we were so thankful to have Lee with us again!*

    As he rode into camp, his first words were, "Where's breakfast?" The poor guy had been dreaming of bacon and eggs all the way in! It is an understatement to say he was disappointed!

    In my ten years of friendship with Lee there were many, many times I was very glad to see him, but I can guarantee you, this one was at the top of the list! Lee was such an accomplished horseman and packer; he had such a way of saying, "It can be done, we just have to figure out how," that I felt secure when he was there. I knew he could take care of whatever the problem might be. On this occasion he was more "manpower" for getting the animals packed; he was another leader for the pack strings; but most of all he was happy, jolly Lee!

    We had an uneventful trip out. We did pack Lee's mule very light but before we got to the trailhead she was tired and kicking up about every fifth step. But let me tell you, we didn't even consider turning her loose! We were a tired, dirty lot who arrived at the trailhead. We unpacked the animals, ate a bite of lunch, then loaded up and started the drive to Enterprise. When we got there, Ida and Lyle were already back from Walla Walla and we had a grand reunion! It was such a relief to see Lyle doing just fine! Thus ended "The Mountain Trip!"

The Next Summer

Color photos—page 281

After the horrendous mountain trip, you might think our Canadian friends would never embark on another adventure with us. Not so!

The very next summer Lyle, Lise, and Dave came to spend a week with us at the ranch. Janine stayed in Canada to take care of business and Bill couldn't get away from his job.

The ranch had plenty of horses so the Canadians didn't go through the hassle of bringing their horses across the border.

We camped in the Hunting Camp Cabin for a few days. We gathered cattle and pushed them down Tamarack; we fixed fence and worked on water holes. We repaired the water trough in The Gap. Since this water hole was three fourths of the way to the top, we decided to go in from the top. The trough was already there so we just had to redo the intake and reset the trough.

After finishing the work on top, we moved down to the ranch house on Joseph Creek. Lee and Lyle took the horses off the top by "head-to-tailing" them. Dave, Lise, and I drove rigs to the bottom. Lee and Lyle beat us to the bottom. When we got there, Lyle was "decked out" in a long black wig. It seems my young horse, Dundee, had pulled back so hard he had jerked the switch out of the lead horse's tail! Lyle saved it and draped it over his head then put his hat back on. He looked like a long lost Indian when we got there!

In the distant past there had been a drift fence across the trail and creek between the Vawter Place and Slide Creek. Lee could see the benefit of rebuilding it. All that was left of the original fence was evidence of a jack here and there, so this wasn't just a repair job but a "build it from scratch" deal! Lee and I had scouted out where we thought would be the best place to put the new fence and had estimated how much material would be needed. All of this would be taken in on pack animals.

The ranch had "racks," to put on the packsaddles, that were designed to carry the fence staves. There were rolls of barbed wire, staples, spikes, and of course all the tools, to be packed. There were five of us to pack food for and we took in the Canadians' bedrolls. Lee and I would sleep in bedrolls that were already in the Vawter Cabin.

Everything took longer that day than it should have! The animals were hard to gather; having never used the racks before, we had to make some adjustments on them. When we were about half way through the packing we could see we were going to be getting a late start. We debated whether to go on with it, or unpack the animals and start over in the morning. We finally decided to go on that evening.

It was late afternoon when we finally got started down the canyon. It turned into a beautiful evening. A slight breeze came up the canyon and there was a red glow in the sky, hanging over the canyon rims to the west. The rims on the east side of the canyon reflected back a variation of golds, pinks, and purples into the canyon below.

We had gone only a couple of miles when Dave, who was in the lead with a string of mules, announced that there was a rattlesnake in the trail ahead of him. It was coming down the trail right toward him. He stopped, waiting to see what would happen. The snake came closer, then about ten feet out in front of Dave it slithered down a hole. Apparently all it wanted to do was to go home!

None of us had stopped to calculate what phase of the moon we were in. As it turned out, it was the dark of the moon! As we continued on down the canyon, darkness settled in. It got darker and darker, until it turned into one of those nights when you literally couldn't see your hand in front of your face! We were glad everyone was riding ranch horses that had been on that trail many times before, because there were several places that some have referred to as "pucker places!"

Dave in the lead, then Lee, Lyle and Lise on the Joseph Creek Trail—it started getting dark before we even got to Cliff Creek

When we first started down the canyon, we were visiting, joking, and laughing. As the canyon got darker and darker, we all became quieter and quieter. I am sure the Canadians thought we would never get there. Having never been down the canyon before, they had no way of knowing how much farther we had to go!

We proceeded without incident until we got to the place where we were going to drop the fence material. Dave and Lee were in the lead with the animals carrying the fencing material. The trail was a narrow, single file trail around a steep hillside so there was no place for the animals to go while they were being unpacked. Dave and Lee stepped off on the uphill side and started feeling their way around to drop the staves. Dave was working at undoing the very first mule's pack when something spooked him or gouged him. He started bucking "in-place." I was at the very back of the entire bunch so all I could hear was fence material rattling. When the bucking stopped, all was quiet then Lee hollered, "Dave are you all right?" My heart stopped when there was no reply. Lee asked again. Still no reply! It seemed an eternity before I heard Dave's voice.

The guys quickly finished dropping the materials and we headed on down the canyon to the cabin. We all worked feverishly, unloading our supplies and taking care of the animals.

We lit a lamp, then ate a snack as we discussed the trip. We never did figure out what set the mule off but when he started bucking, he had hit Dave in the head with the load of staves. It had knocked Dave back up on the hillside and sent his glasses flying. Dave was quite woosey so it had taken a little while before he could respond to Lee. Dave really needed his glasses, but knew they would be searching in vain to try to find them in the dark. The glasses had more than likely been trampled by the animals anyway. We fell into bed exhausted, but thankful that Dave was not seriously hurt!

Deep in the canyon bottom the sun doesn't rise early, even in the summer, so we were able to sleep in a little that next morning. We had a good breakfast, then planned out the day's events. Dave and Lyle would take the mules, go back to the ranch and bring in another load of fence material. Lee and I would start on the fencing project, and Lise would stay in camp—be the "camp cooky!"

Dave always carried a spare pair of glasses in his pickup so he would pick those up at the ranch. When Dave and Lyle got back up to where we had had the wreck the night before, Dave decided to look a little

While I was working on the fence, my horse, Dundee, went across the creek to graze so Dave brought him back

Lyle feeding grain to Dubee by the Vawter "horse barn"

Dave putting fly spray on the mules

for his glasses, just for curiosity's sake. Do you know, he found those glasses lying up on the hillside above the trail, completely unscathed!

Dave and Lyle went on to the ranch, got the materials, and came back to where Lee and I were building fence. We unloaded the materials, then went to the cabin. Lise had a cool drink mixed for us and supper cooking!

The next day the guys and I went back up the canyon to work on the fence, Lise again stayed in camp.

Where we built the gate across the trail was right under a rim. Someone had driven pegs into cracks in the rim so the gate pole/jack could be "tied off" to the rim. This would keep the jack and gate from sliding down the hill. On the lower side of the trail, we built another jack which also was made with a high gatepost. We connected the tops of the two gateposts with strands of wire which we twisted to pull it taut. To reach this wire, Lyle stood up on the packsaddle of the big warmblood gelding, Jack. It was such a spectacular sight that Lee took a picture of Lyle standing on the packsaddle of the horse, with the rim and hills in the background. He then was afraid that he might not have gotten it right, because he didn't take many pictures, so he hollered down to where I was working and asked me to come up and take a picture. Someone else must have thought it was spectacular too because when I sent them off to be developed, the picture I took came up missing. The picture right before it and the one right after it were there! I always hoped I would see that picture in some "spectacular pictures" contest or on some calendar! We did get back the one Lee had taken but he had held the camera so high he cut off the bottom part of the horse and was not at an angle to get a good background. I was thankful to have it though, with the other one "disappearing!"

When we went back to the cabin that night, Lise had scrubbed the cabin and everything in it. She had gotten water from the creek, heated it, and scrubbed dishes, tables, and cupboards until the water was dirty, then she used it to scrub the floor. She repeated this procedure until the entire place simply shone! I am sure it was the cleanest that cabin had ever been or ever will be!

Lise again had a cool drink for us and supper on the way. As we were sitting around the fire resting for a little while, Lise started to go into the cabin for something. She got to the doorway then made an about-face and marched straight to Lee. She had a startled look on her face as she calmly, but quickly said, "Lee there is a snake curled up on the cabin step. I think you should come and see what it is! Sure enough it was a rattler! Lee had his pistol with snake shot in it so he eliminated the snake in a hurry. Lise was glad the snake hadn't shown up earlier in the day when she was there alone!

The outhouse was all but fallen down so we tore it down, salvaging all materials that might be reuseable. We cut and drug in some poles for the frame, and the guys constructed a pretty good "Dunny!"

Shorty—the mule that kicked Katrina's mare, Missy

Lyle, when we were ready to head back up the canyon to the Home Place

The following day we again worked on the fence. The staves were not on it yet, but the Canadians were due back in the valley so we packed up and rode back to the ranch house. It had been a good trip in spite of a rocky start!

WRECKS

As previously stated, "Canyon Cowboying" is a way of life that can be matched by no other. It offers rewards and contentment that can only be fully appreciated by those who have "been there, done that!" But there is coupled with this, the ever present potential of danger of a "wreck!"

I guess when comparing the number of wrecks to the hours, days, weeks, months, and years we spent in the canyon, the ratio wasn't too bad! There were so many incidents that were "near misses" that we were continuously thankful for God's protective hand and guardian angels!

When we first went to the ranch, there were several horses which had come with the ranch. One was a big bay mare, True Bay, who had been brought to the ranch when Wayne Clark owned it. She had then been "passed on" from owner to owner. She was one of those horses that you could never completely trust!

Lee and I had just ridden to the top by way of the Shitter (sorry) Ridge Trail. Lee was remounting, after getting off to open a gate. It was late fall and there was a little snow and the rocks had a glaze of ice on them.

Lee on True Bay with his white mule who had kicked him in the knee twice, busting his knee each time.

Lee was riding a saddle with oxbow stirrups. He stepped up on a rock to give himself a little advantage for mounting. He had just thrust his left foot into the stirrup when his right foot slipped from the rock and he went over backwards.

Bronc riders like oxbow stirrups because they were designed so you don't lose your stirrup. In other words, your foot is pretty well stuck once it is in! I expected True Bay to blow up and run, but miraculously she stood right there. Lee twisted his leg and his foot slipped out of his boot. Lee and I always wore slip-on boots when we were riding, and this was just one of the times we were thankful that we did!

Maybe women are just a little more cautious, I guess because of a natural "protective instinct," but it seems I was always cautioning Lee. One thing I often got after him for was tying hard and fast when he was leading a pack string. We would head down the trail and he would put me out in front, I think so I couldn't check on him so easily. He would start out holding the lead rope, but after we had gone a ways and he figured I was through turning around to see how he was doing, he would slip a couple of half hitches over the horn.

On one such occasion we had gotten as far as the Cliff Creek Flat when we stopped just long enough to glance over the packs. It seemed that if a wreck were brewing, it would come to a full boil when you stopped.

Because there were some tough spots on the trail, Lee had strung the pack animals out with long enough lead ropes that each could see the

Mert, Lee's dog (center), watching the cows on Cliff Creek Flat, where Lee had a wreck with the pack string

trail and pick his footing. This worked great as long as we were in motion, but when we stopped, some of the critters immediately dropped their heads to grab a mouthful of grass. The lead pack animal was still tied to Lee's saddle horn, off the right side. The second horse stepped over his lead rope and pulled the lead rope up under his belly, which caused him to buck into the lead horse. This startled the lead horse and he jumped forward to the left of Lee. Well, with the lead rope tied hard and fast to the horn on Lee's right and the horse going off to the left, he didn't have a chance! With the lead rope pulling on the horn, and Lee being pulled off to the left, the saddle turned and Lee hit the ground amongst tromping feet! His foot was again hung up in the stirrup, even though he was no longer riding oxbows. Thankfully his foot slipped out of his boot and he was free, and luckily unhurt, that is except for his pride. When it was clear that he was unhurt, I am sure I gave him one of my "I told you so looks." We gathered up, untangled the horses, reset his saddle, then went on down the canyon.

On another salt scattering trip down the canyon, we again had several pack animals. I brought up the rear so I could watch the salt and watch that Lee didn't tie off hard and fast. We never had saltboxes or saltracks so we tied each block on with ropes. One of the pack string was a horse the ranch had bought recently. I had ridden him down the canyon the day before. I told Lee that the horse wasn't very smart—you had to watch him all the time or he would just step off the trail.

Well, on that particular trip, that horse was next to last in the pack string, with my colt, Dundee, at the end. We always used break-away ropes so if one animal went off, it wouldn't take the whole string. Sure enough, this dumb horse stepped off the trail and started rolling. Fortunately he came to his feet on a flat place, which was about two feet wide and right at the crest of a rim. If he had gone over, it would have been straight down for fifty feet into a brushy draw bottom.

When he went off the trail, my colt set his feet, pulled back, and broke the break-away rope. After the rolled horse got to his feet, he stood there dazed, then started picking his way around and up to the trail which came out on the other side of the draw.

The craziest thing, though, was that Dundee watched that horse roll and watched him get up. Then when the packhorse started picking his way on around the draw, Dundee stepped off the trail and slid on his haunches down to the packhorse and followed him on around and back up onto the trail. It was as though Dundee thought because he had been following all morning, he was supposed to go wherever that horse went!

I ended up having to get rid of Dundee because he just wasn't safe in the steep country! If he got onto a really steep place he would just let his knees buckle and would act like he was trying to lie down. On several occasions I had to quickly jerk his head downhill and whip him to make him stand back up and not go into a roll!

Not all wrecks ended with the absence of harm to horse or rider! One spring Bob and Pat Shelton had come down to spend some time with Lee and help push pairs down the canyon. It had been a very wet spring and the trail was soft in some places. They had gone down the canyon several of miles, when the trail gave way under the hind feet of Lee's horse. This threw Lee back, causing him to jerk on the reins, which in turn caused the horse to go over backwards. Lee was thrown off to one side so he wasn't crushed by the horse, but it dazed him to the point of not knowing what he was doing. Lee stood and started walking toward the edge of a cliff. Bob, who also was a big man, grabbed him, pulling him to the ground. Bob didn't let Lee up until he became rational.

Dundee, with Mert in foreground and her pup, Tub

The horse rolled end over end to the bottom of the canyon, which was about seventy-five yards below, then all was quiet. Because there was no noise from the brush, they knew the horse was dead.

The main concern anyway, was in getting Lee out of the canyon and to medical attention! Lee's philosophy had always been, "A poor ride beats a good walk, any day!" so he never walked anywhere, but that day he was so unstable that he figured he would get dizzy and fall off if he tried to ride. He had cuts and scrapes but no broken bones so he walked out. Bob and Pat then drove him out to Enterprise to the hospital.

Lee was concerned about his saddle and bridle so Tom Birkmaier and Bob went back down the canyon the next day to retrieve them. When they got to the horse, there he stood, looking like he had been run through a meat grinder! He had many scrapes but the worst was an injury to his right hip. He had a hole in his hip about the size of a large grapefruit. The guys knew he would need medical attention so they took lots of time and walked him out of the canyon.

With lots of care, his wounds healed and the hole in his hip filled back in to where there was just a scar to witness that a wound had ever existed! Lee's saddle had scars on it but the tree and horn had not been busted!
    Lee tagged the calves' ears soon after they were born, for identification purposes. With that many cows, you were bound to get a cranky one occasionally. One day Lee was tagging calves when one old cow got on the fight. Because a friend was staying and helping him, Lee wasn't using the "one man system" he had fixed up in the barn.
    It was late spring so the calving lots would thaw during the day and freeze at night. This caused the low places to fill with water, then freeze, becoming little skating rinks! The cow poop would become a runny mess during the day, covering the ice, and making it even slicker!
    That was the condition in which they were working that particular day. Lee was toward the front of the pickup when the cow charged him. Lee, being a large man, who had knees that had been busted up in previous wrecks, couldn't move very fast! He tried to skirt around the front of the pickup but slipped and fell. As he slipped he tried to save his fall by grabbing the front bumper. The cow never stopped her charge and hit his hand, mashing it between her head and the bumper. Lee didn't have on gloves, so as he fell onto the ground, he plunged his injured hand into the "liquid poop."
    The base of his thumb and the palm of his hand were literally mashed open, making about a three inch jagged wound, which was full of manure! He was taken out to the doctor who cleaned it and sewed it up!
    I used to tease Lee that he was "a wreck looking for a place to happen!" It seemed he could get into trouble in about any situation.
    Once he was chopping kindling wood for the kitchen cook stove. He was splitting with a splitting maul rather than an ax. It was cold and the wood was frozen. I don't know if it was because the wood was frozen or if he hit a knot, but something went wrong. He was holding the block of wood with his left hand, as we all do, and splitting with his right. On one particular blow the maul bounced up, over, and down onto his left hand so fast he didn't know what had happened. Luckily he had on heavy leather gloves or it might have taken his finger clean off! As it was, it just broke his middle finger, which then stuck up at a crazy angle.
    He knew it was bad so he jumped in the pickup and headed up the canyon. When he got to Tom Birkmaier's, about ten miles up the canyon, he was hurting pretty bad. He still was afraid to take his glove off, for fear of doing more damage and being afraid of what he might see.
    When Tom saw the gloved finger jutting out at a strange angle,

he thought that the finger was just dislocated at the knuckle joint so he offered to straighten it for Lee. Lee told him, in so many words, "Over my dead body!"

The doctors in Enterprise looked at it then sent him on to La Grande where they pieced the shattered bone back together with pins and screws.

One warm September morning Lee was at the Dog Fight Cow Camp. He wanted to get an early start—beat the heat of the day. He had a lot of miles to cover that day so he chose Jake, a long legged thoroughbred type horse, to ride. The rest of the horses were left in the corral for the day, probably so they wouldn't be in the way if he needed to bring some critters in, or he may have just wanted to leave the gates open going out of the Dog Fight pasture.

He followed the same procedure we had used for years—catch the horses in the corral, lead them over to the hitching rail by the tent, feed them some grain while we curried and brushed them, then saddle, and lastly, bridle.

Lee, being a big man, would lead his horse to a nearby log, stump or rock, to give him a little advantage when mounting. This not only made it easier for Lee, but also, it was easier on the horse's back.

Lee, on Jake, the horse that eventually "did him in."

Jake was notorious for getting his tongue over the bit. Maybe because Lee was in a hurry, he got the bit under Jake's tongue and didn't notice it, or maybe Jake flipped his tongue over the bit as Lee led him over to the log. In "hind sight," he figured this was the only thing that could have happened.

As Lee mounted, he apparently gave a tug on the reins, because Jake immediately went straight into the air. He then went over backwards. Lee, seeing the saddle horn coming at him, pushed off to the side just far enough to keep his chest from being crushed. His collarbone and shoulder took the brunt of the fall. Everything went black!

The next thing he realized was the sun was high in the sky, it was awfully hot, and he was perspiring profusely—so much so that his shirt was completely wet! He crawled over to the shade of a tree where he remained for an undetermined length of time. He was beginning to realize that he was seriously hurt! When his head was clear enough to start forming a plan, he felt he must first take care of his horse. With the rest of the horses being in the corral, Jake had gone over to be close to them. Lee, one-handedly, unsaddled him then threw the corral gate open so the rest of the horses could get out.

Lee got into the pickup, thinking he would drive until he ran into someone who could take him to the hospital. There was no one at Coyote Camp Ground. He started along the Red Hill Ridge road praying he would find someone before he got to the steep Red Hill Grade, as his vision was at times blurry. He drove the full length of the ridge, at probably the slowest speed he had ever driven it. Still nobody! He felt he had no choice, so he started off the grade, repeating to himself, "I just have to make it to Tom's, I just have to make it to Tom's." Tom was gone!

With panic welling up within him, he drew upon his last bit of strength and once again started up the road telling himself that he would find someone soon. But he didn't!

He drove to the valley ranch thinking that someone would be at the shop and they could do the driving, now that it would be on the highway and through town. Again he struck out! At this point his only strength came from knowing he was only a few miles from the hospital. By now he had already driven over fifty miles of country roads and he kept telling himself, "I can make it a little farther!"

The local doctor examined Lee and realized the severity of the injury. He also knew of Lee's heart, respiratory, and blood pressure problems. Lee was sent to La Grande, to a doctor who specialized in injuries involving bones.

A piece had broken out of his collarbone and had dropped down onto his lung. The surgeon knew he was racing against the clock during surgery. The piece of bone had to be lifted off the lung before the lung collapsed; Lee's heart could not withstand being under the anesthetic for a very long period, and there was the fear of his blood pressure going crazy.

The doctors worked rapidly. It was decided to suture the piece of bone back in place rather than install a rod or pins. This proved to be very unsatisfactory. With the movement caused by his breathing, the sharp jagged ends of the bone cut the suture in just a few days. One end of the piece of bone dropped slightly, but the doctor decided to leave it rather than put him through the stress of another surgery. He was expected to just "live with it!"

Again I told him that he could stay at my place until he healed up and could go back to work, which never happened!

—*You know, cowboys invented tailgate parties!!*—
*Jessica, Kurt, his wife Julie, and Lee having lunch
on the tailgate of my pickup at the Dog Fight Corral*

Katrina and Jessica eating lunch while sitting on the tool box on the back of the pickup

Bill Rouw with his horse, Toma, at Bowman Trail head

Lise and Lyle Harrison with their horses Willie and Bug

About ready to head up the Bowman Trail—me at far right

Bowman Trail above Brownie Basin, headed toward Wilson Pass. Lyle and Lise Harrison and me leading pack animals

*Camp at John Henry Lake
Lee, Lise Harrison, Dave and Janine Caudle,
Bill Rouw and Lyle Harrison*

At mine by John Henry Lake
Janine Caudle, Bill Rouw, Dave Caudle and Lyle Harrison

From inside the mine—
Lee on horse, Bill Rouw and Janine Caudle

Laverty Lake—Elevation 7,000—Depth 12 feet

Chimney Lake—Elevation 7,604—Depth 59 feet

Mountain Trip

Hobo Lake—Elevation 8,369—Depth 34 feet

*Wood Lake—Elevation 7,338—barely seen in middle of photo—
Depth 24 feet*

We took a day-ride into Bear Lake —Elevation 7,905— Depth 20 feet— and did some fishing

Campsite in North Minam Meadows— Elevation 4,300 on the west end to 5,000 on the east end— Me, Lee, Lyle Harrison and Dave Caudle

Mountain Trip

Me—fishing in Green Lake

Green Lake—Elevation 6,699—Depth 28 feet

Steamboat Lake—Elevation 7,363—Depth 101 feet

Looking down on Swamp Lake —Elevation 7,837— Depth 23 feet— from Copper Creek Trail

Me and Lee leading packstrings—coming out on the Copper Creek Trail

What a grubby bunch by the time we got back to the trailhead.
Back—Me, Lee, Bill   Front—Lise, Janine and Dave

Dave Caudle, Lyle Harrison, Lee, and Lise Harrison at Hunting Camp Cabin.

On the breaks above The Gap—ready to head down through The Gap to fix a waterhole. Looking south up Swamp Creek—Wallowa mountains in the far distance.

The horses waited patiently while we worked on the waterhole in The Gap

Dave Caudle on Katrina's mare, Missy, under the rim in The Gap

The Next Summer

Climbing up through The Gap. Dave in lead with pack mules, Lise, Me on Dundee, Lee on Jack and Lyle was taking the photo.

Lee on ridge

Pushing cattle down Hunting Camp Ridge. Dave, Lise and Lyle.

*Taking a breather after pushing cattle into East Tamarack pasture.
Lise, Lyle on Dubee and Dave on Missy*

*Dave and Lyle pushing cattle off Horse Pasture Ridge—
headed for the Corral Springs Pasture via the saddle in the upper left corner of photo.*

The Next Summer

Lee and Lyle leaving Dog Fight Cow Camp headed for the Home Place on Joseph Creek, while the rest of us drove rigs—they beat us there.

Lyle with "horsetail wig" made from the hair pulled from the horse's tail

Lee, Dave, Lise and Lyle taking the short way home— cross-country!

*Dave, Lee, Lyle and Lise headed to the Vawter Place
with fence material and camp gear.*

*Dave and Lyle leaving the Vawter Place,
headed back to the Home Place for another load of fence material.
The Home Place was 5 miles by trail up Joseph Creek.*

The Next Summer

Lyle, standing on pack saddle on Jack, tightening guy-wire on a gate we had just built across the Joseph Creek Trail.

Lyle "trying-out" new "Dunny" we built at the Vawter Place. Lee surveying their handiwork. (Dunny is the Australian term for outhouse.)

Relaxing at the Vawter Place after building fence all day.

Me swimming by the Vawter cabin

Packing out of the Vawter Place after days of work and fun—it was time for the Canadians to go home.

Lyle soaking his feet after a hot day's work

The Last Round-Up and Goodbyes

Of course Lee was not able to ride in the roundup that fall but he did have Joe Spence fly him over all of that country spotting strays. There was enough room in the plane for me too, so I went and took video pictures with my camcorder. Lee had a 2-way radio with him, and Dub had one with him at the Dog Fight Cow Camp.

It was a clear, crisp morning and the sun had not yet peeked up over the Seven Devils when the plane lifted off from the airport in Enterprise. It took only about 15 to 20 minutes to reach the Table Mountain area. The sunlight had just started to crawl down the west sides of the draws, but the east sides were still shadowed completely.

Joe dipped low over Cougar Bench then swung over Table Mountain, The Gap, and Horse Pasture Ridge. Next we doubled back to the lower end of the Tamarack pasture, then followed Hunting Camp Ridge south, passing over the Hunting Camp Cabin.

Lee and I had been taking note of the cattle we saw—two or three on one point, five or six on another; two or three pairs in one opening, a bull or two in another. When we got over the Dog Fight Cow Camp, Joe dropped down and we buzzed the camp. Cowboys came pouring out of tents like bees out of a struck hornets' nest! We circled until Lee was able to explain where the cattle were, how to find them, and the best way to bring them in.

Flying back to town we passed over the ranch on Joseph Creek where I was raised. It was the first time I had seen it from the air. I couldn't believe how it seemed so flattened!

Joe pointed out landmarks and places I knew, all the way back to Enterprise. Lee and I both enjoyed the ride and marveled at the beauty of it all!

Neither of us had any way of knowing that that day would be the last in which we would have any part in gathering on the Monument Ranch.

As previously mentioned, I had told Lee he could stay at my place until he healed up from that last wreck. Weeks turned into months, months grew into years. Lee's shoulder failed to heal properly. He had very limited rotation of the shoulder and couldn't raise his arm above his shoulder. While his shoulder failed to heal, his congestive heart condition worsened! His heart deteriorated to the point that it was pumping out only one-third as much blood as it should have with each beat.

With a lack of blood feeding his body, he tired very quickly and was extremely short of breath. He got to where he could do nothing that required any physical effort, but he never gave up trying to be helpful. He spent hours folding clothes, chopping salads, or anything else he could do while sitting and using a minimum of energy! He did a lot of cooking by taking it slow and setting on a stool, which he slid around the kitchen.

When I was working outside, Lee would drive the 4-wheeler around or would sit on a block of wood. If I was repairing hog pens, he would cut pieces of wire as I needed them, or he would hand me tools. While I was at school he would do various little repair jobs. He could work at anything as long as it didn't require physical exertion. He also could tell me the easiest and best way to complete many projects. He loved to just lean on the fence and watch the baby pigs run, play, and root!

Christopher Ryckman, Lee's grandson, Lee and Clancy Johnston, my grandson.

SAIF paid for medical expenses and loss of income for a while but then stopped payments. No one in all the medical contacts Lee had, had told him about the "Oregon Plus" medical insurance plan, for low income people. We did not even know that it existed! Finally, one of Lee's friends told him about it, so he checked it out. By this time, his medical expenses had eaten up all of his assets.

Those years were not all gloom and doom though. Lee and I both enjoyed the "little" things in life—a litter of newborn pigs, a beautiful sunrise or sunset, a game of cards, or a drive around the back roads!

We took a lot of road trips, most of which were here in the county. We did take a few trips out of the county though, some that took a long day's drive to reach our destination. I guess the longest was to Canada to see our friends, Dave and Janine Caudle, Lyle and Lise Harrison, and Bill Rouw.

A couple of times a year I would take Mom to Prineville to see my brother. Mom had a friend, Alice Haggerty, who had a sister-in-law in Prineville, so we would take Alice along too.

The four of us, Lee, Mom, Alice and I had some great times together! Often we would pack a picnic lunch, big enough for supper too, and just start driving with no destination in mind. Alice would treat us with her wonderful homemade gingersnap cookies! The first of our "foursome" to leave us was Alice. She passed away in August of 1998.

My Mom, Maxene Davis, Lee and Alice Haggerty

Then came the fall and Lee's condition worsened drastically! I rushed him to the hospital on numerous occasions when he could barely get enough breath to remain conscious. During the next few months he spent as much time in the hospitals as out—hospitals in Enterprise, La Grande, and Portland.

Lee was in the hospital over Christmas that year. My son Kurt, had come home, but my daughter Katrina and her family weren't coming because she was expecting to deliver their second child any day.

I had called Mom and asked her to go with me to the Christmas Eve service at the church, but when I stopped to pick her up she had decided not to go. She had been out and about that day, going to the bank and running various errands. When she got home and settled in for the evening she just didn't care to go out again. I went on to the service then stopped by again on my way home and we visited for quite a while. As I left, I asked her if she wanted me to lock the door, to which she responded, "No, honey, because I want to latch the screen door from the inside and I'll have to do that after you leave."

My brother's three girls were all traveling that evening to his and Marlene's place in Prineville, for Christmas. Mom was worried about them being on the roads, so she had told Ron to call her, no matter how late, when all of the girls had arrived safely.

After I had gone on home that evening, Ron called Mom at about ten o'clock and Mom talked to him and each of the girls.

Whenever my kids were home, I always had Mom out for meals, so I had asked her to come out for breakfast the next morning, Christmas morning.

When breakfast was almost ready, and Mom hadn't arrived, I called just to make sure she hadn't overslept. She didn't answer so I figured she was in the bathroom or taking a shower. I went on with preparing breakfast then called again, and again she didn't answer.

I hadn't checked the clock so really didn't know how much time had elapsed between the calls. I then did check the time, waited another twenty minutes, then called again. Still no answer! In the past, I had gone to her place many times, when not being able to reach her, and had found her just fine.

I put breakfast "on hold" and told Kurt that I had better go check on Mom. On the way in, my anxiety level kept rising but I kept calm by reminding myself how many times I had done this in the past and how everything had always been just fine.

My first surprise was finding the screen door unlatched. Next I found the door unlocked. When I opened the door, there sat Mom in a stuffed chair, not four feet from the door. She was in her nightclothes. She must have remembered that she hadn't locked the doors so had started toward them when she apparently didn't feel well so sat down in the closest chair. The chair she was in was one she never sat in—it was for company.

Many times she had told me that each night she prayed, "God when it is my time to go, just let me go to sleep." Her prayers were answered!

Before I had gone in to Mom's that morning, my son-in-law, Gary, had called to tell us that he and Katrina were at the hospital—she was ready to deliver! When he called back to tell us that we had a baby boy, Caleb, I told him to turn his back to Katrina so she couldn't see his face and read his expression. He was to make some excuse for leaving the room, go to another phone and call me back.

With Lee having been so ill, of course he thought we had lost Lee. It was a great shock to him when I told him that we had lost Mom. With Katrina having just delivered, we discussed when would be the best time to tell her about Mom, and it was decided to let her get a good night's rest first.

That day I was blessed with another grandson, but lost my Mom, only four months after losing Alice. Now I had lost two of my traveling buddies. The "foursome" was down to two—Lee and me!

During the next few months, Lee was still in the hospital a major part of the time. Larry Miller, a man I had taught with for years, before he retired, a man who had befriended Lee, became nothing short of a "God-Send!" He took Lee to La Grande, to Portland, or wherever Lee needed to go.

On one occasion when they were on their way home from Portland, they stopped in La Grande for dinner. Just as they finished, Lee collapsed. The EMTs rushed in and revived him, then transported him to the Grande Ronde Hospital there in La Grande. A medical team worked feverishly until 3:00 A.M. just to keep him alive. By 5:00 A.M. it was felt that he was stable enough to transport, by air, back to OHSU in Portland.

At OHSU an internal defibulator was installed, the purpose being to cause the heart to beat as strongly as possible rather than just flutter. He then came back "home" but continued to be in and out of the hospital.

Lee had made a personal commitment to God a few months after we had met, but he had never been baptized. He decided that he wanted to be baptized. I was concerned that he wasn't strong enough and he might collapse in the baptistery. He insisted on being baptized so it was planned that he would be, on Easter Sunday. When Easter Sunday came, Lee was too ill. The following Sunday was Lee's birthday, April 11. Again it was planned to have a baptismal. Lee's girls and their families came. One of the nurses at the hospital volunteered to accompany Lee to the church, to be there during the service, and stay with him until he was safely back in the hospital. Janice Garrett, a friend and the wife of Dean, the guy who had rescued the ranch pickup that fateful day in Cougar Creek, brought her mini van to the hospital and hauled Lee to and from the hospital.

The service went off without a hitch. Lee even had the strength to accompany us to the cafeteria in the hospital, where we had lunch before he went back to his room to rest, and his kids went home.

Lee continued to get stronger and was released from the hospital. Things got back pretty much to "normal." We took up our usual daily routine.

One of the young men, Troy Rohweder, who had been on Joseph Creek with the grouse study, and had since moved to Alaska, was back in the county and came by to see Lee on a Thursday. Later Troy told me that one of the things that Lee told him that day was that he just hoped he was doing something he liked when he died.

The next day was Friday. As usual, I was home from school shortly after noon. It was a beautiful day—blue skies framing the snowcapped mountains. I needed to do some repairs on pig pens and Lee wanted to be out, so I took a resin lawn chair along. He sat in it and cut wire, handed me tools, and enjoyed the splendor of the day. After some time I suggested that he go in and rest, but as he gazed at the mountains he said, "No, I am fine. It is so beautiful I don't want to miss any of it."

By late afternoon Lee was tired enough that he agreed to go to the house. I had a lot to do so I kept working until about eight o'clock, at which time I went in. I was quite tired so said I didn't care for much to eat. I cleaned up, put on my nightgown and robe, lay on the couch, and read the Chieftain, our local weekly paper. Lee asked me to read the paper to him, as he often did. He lay on the floor next to the stove, propped up on some huge lounge pillows.

The time passed quickly, and suddenly I realized it was after ten o'clock. I had a couple of pens of tiny bummer pigs in the barn, under the heat lamps. To feed them I would mix the powdered milk/feed on the back porch and carry it out in mason jars. The bummers were due to be fed at ten so I jumped up, but Lee said he would do it. I felt he may have already overdone it for the day, and again said that I would feed the bummers. Being persistent as he was, Lee insisted he would enjoy a walk in the fresh air and said he was fine!

As Lee headed for the back porch, I headed for my room. I enjoyed reading a "devotional" and my Bible for a little while each night before I turned off my light. That night I was so tired that I went to sleep while reading, leaving my light on.

At about eleven o'clock I woke with a start, realizing I had not heard Lee come back in. I jumped out of bed, slipped into a robe and slippers. As I went down the hall I could see Lee's bedroom door was open and the light was on. He wasn't there and his bed hadn't even been turned back. With my heart racing, I dashed to the back porch. The light was on. Lee wasn't there, nor were the milk bottles. In the garage the light was still on. I slipped a chore coat on over my robe and ran toward the barn.

I could see the lights were on. The main alley was empty so I went on to the side alley where the bummer pens were. In that alley that afternoon I had scattered a fresh bed of about a foot of straw. That was where I found him. The milk had been poured in for the pigs, the jars had been set on the shelf above, but the tops of the pens had not been put down.

Lee had apparently been watching the cute little bummers "making pigs" of themselves when his heart simply stopped. He was doing something he loved—watching the baby pigs! His last resting place was a bed of straw, just as he would have wanted it!

I lost the third member of my "traveling pardners!" Lee had been a great friend and companion!

Conclusion

In looking back over the years, I have many memories—there were those times riding down a wind swept ridge in a snow storm, when it seemed we would be blown off our horses; when we were almost too cold to care. There were those days when we would once again say, "This has to be the most beautiful day I have ever seen." There were the struggles of assisting in the birth of, or bringing in a chilled-down calf; of trying to push cattle when they refused to move; the lazy lunches by a cool stream as the horses grazed in grass up to their knees; the ecstasy of glassing the breaks and spotting that herd of elk bedded down on a south bench, or an eagle lazily soaring in the updrafts silhouetted against the royal blue sky.

Having spent those years on the Monument Ranch, I again developed a real attachment to the ranch and the canyon! Through riding for cattle I came to know every canyon, ridge, and draw as well as I knew the "back of my hand!"

Did the good balance the bad! NO!!! It far outweighed it! We were rich beyond anything that money could buy. No wonder we frequently found ourselves saying, "I wonder what the POOR folks are doing?"

You see, working the Monument Ranch was not a job—it was a way of life! The Monument Ranch was what Wallowa County used to be!!!!!

Melvin U. Davis

Julie Davis Kooch

Maxene J. Mink

Genealogy

About The Author

Julie Davis Kooch was born and raised in Wallowa County, Oregon. She attended a one-room country school for all of her elementary grades.

She was a tomboy and always preferred the outside ranch work to the dullness of domestic "woman's work!"

Julie is a third generation elementary school teacher—her mother and grandmother both having taught in one-room country schools in Wallowa County.

Julie has lived the majority of her life on cattle ranches in the canyon country. She finds riding the steep, rough, canyon country, adventuresome, exhilarating, and fulfilling!

On her father's side, her great-uncle, Marshall Davis, homesteaded on upper Prairie Creek and had a mill at the base of the mountain over next to the moraine. He came west in a covered wagon in 1879. He had just taken Susan Miller as his wife so she crossed the plains as a new bride! He kept a diary of the trip and it seems to have been quite an ordeal!

His brother, Jessie Washington Davis, Julie's great-grandfather, homesteaded in a canyon just north of Wallowa. The canyon still is called Davis Gulch. Jessie was born in Indiana in 1822 and he died in Wallowa in 1898.

Henry Davis's homestead house in the Zumalt area

Julie's grandfather, Henry Davis, Jessie's son, homesteaded in the head of a draw that drains into Lightning Creek (the Lightning Creek that runs into Little Sheep Creek.) This is just past the head of OK Gulch, east of Enterprise, as you head into the Zumwalt country.

Her grandmother, Katie McCrae Davis, Henry's wife, had a reputation among her relatives of being quite a horseman and a good farmer. She preferred the outdoors work to the inside housework. She

Barn on Henry Davis's homestead

Gramdma Katie and Grandpa Henry Davis's wedding picture—1897

was a good cook though not fancy! The story is told that when Kate was a young girl, Henry came to Kate's dad's place to buy a horse. The horse of his choice was a favorite of Kate's. Kate's dad jokingly said, "If you take that horse you'll have to take the girl!" Years later he did "take the girl!"

Kate's father, Roderick McCrae, was born in Nova Scotia in 1850. In 1867 his family moved to Kansas. He became a U.S. citizen in 1871, then married Ellen Ward Allen in 1872. In 1888 Roderick, Ellen, and their four children (Kate being eight years old), moved by train to Oregon. They were met in La Grande by Ellen's

About the Author

Grandma Berthe's dad, John Womack

Gradma Berthe was a real horseman and an accomplished rancher, who prefered working outdoors— but also she was a lady and looked pretty in her fine clothes

brothers, who had already moved to Wallowa County. They were brought to the lower valley by horse and wagon. Roderick homesteaded about nine miles north of Wallowa in the Dry Creek area.

On Julie's mother's side, her great grandfather, John Womack, homesteaded on upper Diamond Prairie just east of the mouth of Bear Creek, which is west of Wallowa. This area is now called Womack Basin.

Julie's grandmother, Bertha, (she went by Berthe), Womack Mink was one of John's children. Bertha was born in her folk's log cabin. Bertha became an accomplished horseman and

Grandpa Max with one of his favorite cats

Grandma Berthe and Grandpa Max at a picnic at the head of Wallowa Lake

farmer. As a young, single woman Bertha homesteaded on Marr Flat, which is a ridge east of Joseph, between the Imnaha River and Big Sheep Creek.

Julie's grandfather, Max Mink, also homesteaded on Marr Flat.

"The fruit doesn't fall far from the tree" is possibly the most accurate explanation of Julie's love of "pioneer ways!" She comes from a long line of Wallowa County homesteaders and pioneers!